Modern Challenges to Past Philosophy

Modern Challenges to Past Philosophy

Arguments and Responses

Thomas D. Sullivan and Russell Pannier

B L O O M S B U R Y

NEW YORK · LONDON · NEW DELHI · SYDNEY

Bloomsbury Academic

An imprint of Bloomsbury Publishing Inc

1385 Broadway
New York
NY 10018
USA

50 Bedford Square
London
WC1B 3DP
UK

www.bloomsbury.com

Bloomsbury is a registered trade mark of Bloomsbury Publishing Plc

First published 2014

Library of Congress Cataloging-in-Publication Data
Sullivan, Thomas D.
Modern challenges to past philosophy : arguments and responses /
Thomas D. Sullivan and Russell Pannier.
pages cm
Includes bibliographical references and index.
ISBN 978-1-4411-4166-8 (hardback : alk. paper) – ISBN 978-1-4411-7063-7
(pbk. : alk. paper) 1. Philosophy. I. Title.
BD41.S85 2014
190 – dc23
2013045226

ISBN: HB: 978-1-4411-4166-8
PB: 978-1-4411-7063-7
ePDF: 978-1-4411-4602-1
ePub: 978-1-4411-4496-6

Typeset by Integra Software Services Pvt. Ltd.
Printed and bound in the United States of America

We dedicate this book to our loving and supportive wives, Ann and Ginny

Contents

Acknowledgments

A number of people deserve our gratitude for assisting in some way with the writing and production of this book: Thomas Sullivan Jr., Seanne Harris, Julie Brooks, Michael Sullivan, Patrick Sullivan, Kerry LeClair, James Greene, Richard Kaplan, Thomas Nobrega, Marco Fioretti, Dwight Nelson, Kenneth Kemp, Michael Winter, Greg Coulter, Sandra Menssen, John Kronen, Pavel Gravilyuk, Jeremiah Reedy, and Michael Weiss.

The superb copyediting of Ann M. Hale was indispensable and accomplished with extraordinary good cheer.

Our editor, Haaris Naqvi, could not have been more supportive or patient about delays in delivering the goods to him.

We are also very grateful to project manager Avinash Singh for his smooth guidance of the manuscript to the end. Thanks also are due the production team at Bloomsbury for their excellent work.

We wish to thank The University of St. Thomas for research funds granted over the years.

Russell Pannier thanks his wife Ann for a lifetime of love, inspiration, and helping him keep the cats off the computer keyboard.

Tom Sullivan thanks his wife Ginny and his family for loving, unflagging support.

1

Problems and Perspectives

Problems and purposes

Overview

The irreplaceable gifts that have come down to us over the centuries from philosophers of genius are no mere souvenirs from a bygone era. The content of historical philosophers' thought bears on our own questions. Through diligent study, we can appropriate some of their wisdom to our considerable advantage.

But is it really worth the effort to make cognitive contact with dead thinkers from remote times and places? Why struggle with their demanding and often cryptic thought? Is any philosophy worth much if it is devoid of modern science? And has not the philosophical community pushed forward in ways that render earlier philosophy irrelevant to modern problems?

Here, in brief, is our answer to these and related questions, an answer that sketches the trajectory of this entire book.

We all philosophize

Out of wonder or need, we all philosophize. We ask: What does it all mean? Is life worth living? Not just my life, but anyone's? Can we really know anything? Can we always be just? What would a just world look like? Do irredeemable evil and suffering ultimately triumph? Is there a providential Mind? Is there a living Being of infinite power, goodness, and wisdom? Is it at all plausible that such a Being has spoken to us "at sundry times and in diverse manners"?[1] Or are we on our own in a frigid and uncaring universe?

The choices

Such philosophical questions include myriad others, less urgent but nonetheless intriguing: What is a proof? What is a number? Space? Time? Space-time? Chance? A poem? Beauty? A self? How can we move our bodies

---

[1] Heb. 1:1.

by willing it? How do we manage to think and speak and feel? How does consciousness arise out of neuronal structures? Such questions, we know, may only whisper to us along the margins of consciousness. Or they may work their way into its very center, where they clamor for attention. However philosophical questions speak to us, we can respond in one of two ways: reflect on possible answers or not.

Reflecting means more than just taking a position. Nothing prevents us from taking a position without reflecting at all. We can simply adopt whatever answer comes to mind, unthinkingly, as we respond to so much in our environment. What if the clamorous resident of our consciousness demands: "What is a number?" Well, maybe it is an abstract entity. Maybe it is a neuronal product. Maybe it is just a piece in a game like chess. Maybe … The nonreflecting individual thinks, "Let's forget this. I pick door two and hope for a prize, and that is that." By contrast, a reflective answer takes alternatives seriously, comparing the advantages of each while attending to their meaning.

While we must be unreflective about most of the questions that make a conscious appearance quietly or insistently, if we socialize at all, it is almost impossible to be absolutely unthinking about all philosophical matters. Even small, homogeneous groups exhibit at least *some* differences in outlook; and, when those differences become apparent, they generate emotional and cognitive reactions. We can hardly help, then, finding ourselves thinking more deeply about some philosophical questions. We may have little interest in numbers, but can we really be as unresponsive as a stone when it comes to issues of race, gender, equality, rights, claims about God, or revelation?

Circumstances may dictate that we sustain attention to only a few questions. But if the opportunity arises, then we again have two choices: proceed to investigate the issues alone or in the company of others. Should we decide, as seems sensible, that we are more likely to do better if we take advantage of what others have thought about a philosophical question, rather than closeting ourselves in the prison of our comfortable solitary epistemic quarters, then we have three choices: join the company of only the living, only the dead, or both.

Practically speaking, however, the options reduce to two. For, if we are at all alert, we can scarcely avoid encountering *current* philosophy. Of course, we need not subscribe to philosophical journals or read books on metaphysics, epistemology, or political and moral philosophy. Since philosophy pervades our culture, we take in a good deal with the air we breathe. Much philosophy comes by way of unexamined assumptions, but it is nonetheless all about us, and it influences our thought. The practical choices, then, come to either attending only to current philosophy or attending to both current and past philosophy.

Thesis T

In this book we argue for Thesis T: investigating past sources of philosophical inquiry is an excellent means of promoting one's own first-order philosophical inquiries.

Thesis T needs refining

Do we mean to be altogether indiscriminate about past philosophy? Would we recommend *all* of it? No. Leibniz supposedly said he never read a book that was so bad he did not get something from it. Despite that fact, Leibniz was not induced to read bad books in preference to good books. In turning to the past, as in attending to the present, we reasonably prefer some works to others. Yet, since no philosopher or school has a monopoly on wisdom, Thesis T applies to the entire history of philosophy and to writings composed on every continent and sub-continent. Of course, no one can come close to mastering more than a minute portion of the whole. Still, our thesis pertains to all philosophy that has fortunately come down to us.

Why should we be dealing with Thesis T at all?

Thesis T may strike some readers as so evident it hardly needs to be stated, let alone debated for more than two hundred pages. If we have time for investigating, how can we just ignore what the best minds have had to tell us about the most significant questions? Because they recognize the wisdom of consulting the works of those who have distinguished themselves over the centuries, don't nearly all university philosophy programs require majors in philosophy to know something about the body of work running from the pre-Socratics to the recent past? And don't professional philosophers continue to write books on both major and minor figures within both the major Western and Eastern traditions, with expansions in recent years into less well-known areas of thought?

Reasons to reject Thesis T

While true, these observations do not settle the matter. For one thing, the fabulous success of empirical science makes the continual wrangling in philosophy over millennia look like a disease. If we really want to get at the truth, shouldn't we forget about philosophy and turn instead to science? As distinguished chemist Peter Atkins put it recently, "Although some may snipe and others carp, there can be no denying the proposition that science is the best procedure yet discovered for exposing fundamental truths about the world."[2] Why in the world should anyone but a student of the history of ideas ever look back at theories postulating that everything is ultimately earth, water, fire, or air? Or at the speculations of medieval or early modern thinkers who were not much closer to the truth. If you want to know how the world is constituted, why not read Atkins or other prominent chemists and physicists? Even with respect to normative issues, do any of these look the same since Darwin?

Not unexpectedly, professional philosophers often reject unbounded scientism. But this does not automatically lead them to embrace Thesis T. They may think there is enough truth in scientism to justify confining philosophical studies to works and problems that presuppose a scientific point of departure. Thus, when writing about the philosophy of physics Tim Maudlin declares, "[W]hen choosing the fundamental posits of one's ontology, one must look to scientific practice rather than philosophical prejudice."[3]

By no means, however, is lack of interest in past philosophy always rooted in an awe of science. For other quite understandable reasons, analytic philosophy, which is dominant in Anglophone countries, tends to begin with the very latest thought. It is argued by some philosophical revolutionaries that only now (the *now* keeps moving) do we have the right method for doing philosophy. Others argue less grandly that, on the whole, our current instruments of analysis, for example, mathematical logic, are much sharper than those possessed by earlier thinkers. Still others argue that though philosophers in the past spoke meaningfully to their own problems, they could not envision ours. Then there are some who maintain that the problems are to some extent continuous, the options keep branching, so that no one in the past travelled down any one path as far as we—the fortunate denizens of the now. The conversation has moved on. Still others allow that earlier thinkers confronted problems that are still with us and expressed their ideas in profitable ways, but what is worth keeping has been absorbed, much in the way that modern physics absorbed Galileo and Newton, modern chemistry absorbed the solid bits in alchemy, and contemporary biology absorbed the discoveries of Darwin and Wallace.

It must also be acknowledged that philosophers linked to academic institutions are brought up in environments governed by certain expectations. Though we like to think of ourselves as independently minded, it is doubtful that a sociologist would have much trouble exploding that illusion. The sociologist might point to the fact that tenure requires publication. It is

---

[2]   Peter Atkins, "Science As Truth," *History of the Human Sciences* 8 (1995): 97.
[3]   Tim Maudlin, *The Metaphysics Within Physics* (Oxford: Oxford University Press, 2007), 1.

easiest to launch a career as a writer by taking up a narrow, well-defined contemporary problem, fixing on prominent positions, and working to say something new about the new, at least until one gains some freedom from institutional constraints.

Our interest in this book is not so much in sociological reasons for current philosophical practices as it is in the wisdom of embracing or rejecting Thesis T. Are the primary reasons for doubting the truth of Thesis T sound? These objections need to be confronted. However, before dealing with objections to Thesis T, we must first elucidate the thesis itself. What, after all, do we mean by "philosophy"? Does it have an essence? If so, what is it? Furthermore, we must make a positive case for it before we take up the objections. Only after doing these things can we indirectly strengthen the positive case by answering possible objections as well as we can.

For whom is this book written?

This book is for our philosophical colleagues as well as any thoughtful person with some philosophical experience and, above all, a willingness to consider elaborated arguments with an appropriate degree of patience. While we have attempted to make the book accessible to a general audience, there are patches in it that will tax less experienced readers of philosophy. Almost always, however, the main lines of the argument can be grasped without understanding all references to all of the philosophical and scientific literature.

Is it worth the effort? It is, for at least some, we hope, since what is at stake is more than just a better retention of our cultural heritage. What is in question is the quality of our thought about some of the most important matters ever treated by the only animal on the planet that can transcend its physical and temporal environment.

So much for an introduction to the introductory first chapter. We now get down to business.

Preliminary clarification of Thesis T

Thesis T is the proposition that investigating past philosophical sources is an excellent means of promoting one's own first-order philosophical inquiries. Before getting into the substance of our argument, we offer a few preliminary clarifications of the Thesis.

What do we mean by "philosophy"? Using the term raises a process–product ambiguity. On one hand, it can refer to the written output of philosophers. On the other, it can refer to the practice of engaging in philosophical inquiry, whether or not the results of that inquiry are ever written down. We will focus primarily upon the second sense because the activity of engaging in philosophical inquiry is fundamental for our purposes. "Philosophy" in the first sense is the product of "philosophy" in the second sense. It is only "philosophy" in the second sense that can be given a unified analysis of the kind we shall provide. "Philosophy" in the first sense is a disorderly thicket. Using "philosophy" in the first sense invokes the written production of everyone who has ever engaged in "philosophy" in the second sense. Although, of course, in proposing Thesis T we urge inquirers to investigate at least selected parts of "philosophy" in the first sense, we make no effort to provide a comprehensive account of the total extension of the term in that sense. In the unlikely event we could find a publisher for such a book, probably no one would bother reading it.

What do we mean by "first-order philosophical inquiry"? It is the pursuit of philosophical questions in order to assist one's own philosophical search for the truth about reality. In contrast, second-order philosophical inquiry is the pursuit of philosophical questions in order to achieve purposes other than assisting one's own search for the truth about reality. The primary case is the philosophical historian's objective of articulating and defending an interpretation of a past philosopher's analysis of philosophical issues. The historian's primary purpose is "getting the views of X straight." Although she might permit herself to evaluate the coherence and truth values of those views, she does so only as part of the larger purpose of "getting the history straight," as contrasted with the historian's investigation of past philosophy as a means of promoting her own first-order inquiries.

Thinking about the nature of philosophical inquiry is itself a first-order inquiry. As Timothy Williamson argues, investigating the nature of philosophy is itself an essential part of the philosophical quest.[4] Inquiries focusing upon the arguments and distinctions of past philosophers can turn out to be either first-order or second-order inquiries, depending on the motivation of the particular inquirer. If his primary motivation is making a historical inquiry in order to assist his own first-order inquiries, then the inquiry qualifies as first order. In contrast, if his primary motivation is to "get X straight," then his inquiry is second order.

Our first-order/second-order distinction must not be confused with other common usages. As already indicated, it cannot be identified with the

---

[4] "I also rejected the word 'metaphilosophy.' The philosophy of philosophy is automatically part of philosophy just as the philosophy of anything else is, whereas metaphilosophy sounds as though it might try to look down on philosophy from above, or beyond." Timothy Williamson, *The Philosophy of Philosophy* (Oxford: Blackwell, 2007), ix.

standard distinction between philosophy and metaphilosophy. In addition, it cannot be identified with mathematical logic's distinction between first-order and second-order formal systems, or with its distinction between object languages and metalanguages.

In distinguishing between first-order and second-order investigations of past philosophy, we do not intend to demean the latter in any way. Second-order inquiries into the philosophical past are important. There is an intrinsic intellectual value in understanding the philosophical past as best as we can, just as there is an intrinsic intellectual value in understanding the past of anything as best as we can. Further, there is an important instrumental value in understanding the philosophical past as best as we can in order to promote our own first-order inquiries. Exploring the philosophical past for one's own first-order purposes is greatly assisted by having at hand competent accounts of what that past was.

In this regard, we mention Jorge J.E. Gracia's masterful treatise on the second-order investigation of past philosophical sources: *Philosophy and Its History: Issues in Philosophical Historiography*.[5] The book is comprehensive, profound, thorough, clearly written, well-argued, and always challenging and illuminating.[6] We have learned much from it. Anyone thinking of pursuing second-order inquiries into philosophical history should read it. However, we also note that, at least as we interpret him, Gracia focuses upon what we are calling the second-order objective of getting the history straight, in contrast to the first-order objective of investigating philosophical history as a means of assisting one's own first-order inquiries. Of course, we do not intend to suggest that Gracia would object to the first-order motivation for looking back to the past. He has done it many times himself.[7]

Finally, we do not maintain that all contemporary analytic philosophers reject Thesis T. There are outstanding examples to the contrary.[8] However, we shall focus upon what we take to be the tendency of many contemporary analytic philosophers to ignore this way of using the philosophical past.

---

[5] Jorge J.E. Gracia, *Philosophy and Its History: Issues in Philosophical Historiography* (New York: State University of New York Press, 1992).

[6] One of the many illuminating sections of Gracia's book is the section entitled "Evaluation" (Gracia, *Philosophy and Its History*, 72–86), in which he argues for the controversial proposition that an essential part of second-order inquiry into past philosophical sources involves evaluating the truth-value of their assertions as well as the validity and soundness of their supporting arguments. It seems to us that Gracia's thesis brings his conception of the second-order investigation of past sources at least a step in the direction of the first-order investigation of such sources, although it is just one step.

[7] See, for example, Jorge J.E. Gracia, *Metaphysics and Its Tasks: The Search for the Categorial Foundation of Knowledge* (Albany, NY: State University of New York Press, 1999).

[8] See, for example, Tyler Burge, *Foundations of Mind: Philosophical Essays, Vol. 2* (Oxford: Clarendon, 2007); John McDowell, *Mind and World* (Cambridge, MA: Harvard

What is philosophical inquiry?

Why ask that?

Imagine listening to someone asserting that anyone engaged in some particular pattern of activity would be substantially helped by investigating at least some aspects of that practice's history. Presumably, you would promptly form several assumptions.

First, you would assume that the proponent had in mind some particular conception of the practice he was talking about. Your expectation would be based upon a simple semantical principle. A necessary condition for apprehending the meaning of phrases of the form "the history of practice P" is apprehending the meaning of phrases of the form "practice P." If the proponent had made his assertion without having any antecedent conception of the practice he was talking about, he would not have understood what he was asserting. Given that assumption, you would like to know the content of his conception. Of course, you might well have your own conception, but you would have enough life experience to realize that there are indefinitely many alternative conceptions of any given practice, and, consequently, it is quite possible that your conception and the proponent's differ.

You would assume that the proponent's conception of the practice could be used to both justify and explain why it would be useful for a practitioner to investigate at least some aspects of that practice's history. You would have this expectation because you could bring to mind an indefinite number of practices whose practitioners are able to succeed without knowing anything at all about the history of their practices. They wouldn't have to understand *how earlier practitioners had engaged in that practice.* Rather, all they would need to understand is *how present practitioners are now engaging in that practice.* Consider, for example, basketball, physics, mathematics, and cooking. Practitioners can begin by simply learning the presently taught skills of the practice and moving on from there. You would also naturally assume that anyone claiming that there is a certain practice whose practitioners would be helped by investigating that practice's history would have a heavy burden of proof. Such a practice would be a startling exception to the general rule.

University Press, 1994); E.J. Lowe, "Form Without Matter," in *Form and Matter: Themes in Contemporary Metaphysics*, ed. David S. Oderberg (Oxford: Blackwell, 1999); D.M. Armstrong, *A World of States of Affairs* (Cambridge: Cambridge University Press, 1997); Alvin Plantinga, *The Nature of Necessity* (Oxford: Clarendon, 1974); Roderick M. Chisholm, *On Metaphysics* (Minneapolis: University of Minnesota Press, 1989); Laurence Bonjour, *In Defense of Pure Reason* (Cambridge: Cambridge University Press, 1998).

Readers might protest by pointing out that, with respect to, for example, physics and mathematics, it is necessary for practitioners to learn the content of principles that were discovered by past practitioners—for example, Fermat's and Descartes's formulations and explanations of analytic geometry, Newton's formulations and explanations of the laws of motion, Newton's and Leibniz's formulations and explanations of the calculus, and Cauchy's and Weierstrass's formulations and explanations of limits. Of course, beginners must learn about these fundamental concepts and principles, but they can do so without having to delve back into the writings of Fermat, Descartes, Newton, Leibniz, Cauchy, or Weierstrass. They can focus instead upon rigorously cleaned-up and clarified textbook formulations and explanations of those concepts and principles. Trying to learn calculus by reading, say, Newton or Leibniz,[9] or trying to learn the foundations of analysis by reading, say, Cauchy,[10] would serve at best as a frustrating, and at worst a fatal, distraction to beginners. Once beginners learn the contemporary foundational formulations of their practices, they are off-and-running with no reason to look back. Anything worth preserving in the works of such historical practitioners has been absorbed, restated, clarified, explained, cleansed of errors, and made ever-more rigorous by every succeeding generation of practitioners, right up to the present. If you want to learn calculus or physics, you naturally turn to the latest respected calculus and physics textbooks.

The same holds even for non-academic practices, such as basketball. The jump shot was first developed decades ago. But contemporary players need not investigate precisely how the early jump shooters did it. All they need do is understand what their coaches teach them about jump shots and how contemporary basketball stars shoot theirs. Basketball practitioners don't need to look back.

You also would be surprised if the proponent asserted that any conception whatever of the practice he was talking about would support his claim that investigating the practice's history would help practitioners in their own first-order efforts. You would assume that some accounts of the practice would work better than others when it comes to arguing for his claim. Some

---

[9] "Even Newton and Leibniz did not complete the calculus. In fact, it may be a comfort to students just beginning to work in the calculus to know that Newton and Leibniz, two of the greatest mathematicians, did not fully understand what they themselves had produced." Morris Kline, *Calculus: An Intuitive and Physical Approach*, 2nd ed. (Mineola, NY: Dover, 1977), 5.

[10] "The formulations of Cauchy in the 1820s were still not definitive and remained flawed in a number of subtle logical points." Alexander J. Hahn, *Basic Calculus: From Archimedes to Newton to Its Role in Science* (New York: Springer-Verlag, 1998), 208.

accounts might exclude historical inquiries altogether. Even within the class of accounts that do not rule out the value of historical inquiry, some might provide stronger cases than others.

These assumptions suggest five questions one would have about any such proposal to investigate the history of a practice: (1) Are there multiple alternative descriptions of the given practice? (2) What is the proponent's presupposed conception of the practice in question? (3) Does the proponent have a heavy burden of proof in arguing that the practice in question is an exception to the general rule that practitioners of a practice need not concern themselves with the history of that practice? (4) How does the proponent show that his presupposed conception of the practice in question justifies and explains his thesis about the value of practitioners understanding their practice's history? (5) Does the proponent agree that some accounts of the practice in question are superior to others when it comes to supporting his claim?

What do these challenges imply for our project? We accept their relevance. In asserting Thesis T, we have committed ourselves to maintaining that philosophers engaged in first-order inquiry would be substantially helped by examining at least some aspects of past sources of philosophy. In so doing, we answer questions (1), (3), and (5) affirmatively, and respond to questions (2) and (4) by accepting the burden of explicating our presupposed conception of philosophical inquiry and showing that it supports our claim about the value of investigating the philosophical past.

How then should we proceed in proposing our account of philosophical inquiry?

We shall begin with a sketch of an argument that we will elaborate in following sections.

There are three ways in which we might proceed. First, we could offer a stipulative account. That is, we could just stipulatively define "philosophical inquiry" in a way that explicitly requires recourse to philosophical historical inquiry for one's own first-order purposes and then urge others to agree, as in the long-standing tradition of "persuasive definitions" and "expressiveness" accounts of normative discourse. Such an approach should not be satisfactory to anyone. Stipulative definitions are easy, but that easiness comes at the cost of reducing issues to triviality. Sure, we could stipulate an account of philosophical inquiry in a way that explicitly serves Thesis T, but no one should be persuaded by that maneuver, and rightly so. Even those, if any, who would be persuaded would be mistaken if they didn't first ask, "But what is it about the fact-of-the-matter that *justifies* my being persuaded?"

Second, we could offer a sociological account that describes the ways in which contemporary philosophers conceive of their practice. The problem with that is the lack of consensus among contemporary philosophers as to the nature of their practice. We would be stuck with choosing some proper subset of contemporary inquirers whose shared conception of philosophy happens to suit our purposes. But what would that accomplish? Suppose that this proper subset turns out to be less than a majority of all inquirers. Would that mean that Thesis T is false? It seems not. Why should the nature of philosophical inquiry be a matter of majority rule? Even if it should turn out that a statistical majority of present inquirers agrees with our conception, why should that be decisive? In order to even begin building a persuasive case for Thesis T, we need to formulate an account of philosophical inquiry that is the *normatively right* one, the account that *ought* to be accepted by *all* inquirers.

We are left with the project of making a normative case. How can that be done? We think that the only plausible way is arguing (1) that philosophical inquiry has an essence or nature[11] of its own, (2) that this essence provides the basis for building a normative case for Thesis T, and (3) that our depiction of philosophical inquiry adequately characterizes that essence. Arguing for those propositions is our overall project in Chapters 2 and 3. However, as just noted, this is only a brief sketch, which needs clarification and expansion to which we shall now proceed.

Does philosophical inquiry have an essence?

We shall argue that the practice of philosophy has an essence, but before presenting that argument we pause to respond to a preliminary challenge.

A preliminary challenge to our project: Don't bother to even start. It is hopeless

We anticipate essence skeptics would argue this: "Why think that philosophical inquiry has an essence? Why not simply concede that there are many conceptions of philosophy, none intrinsically better than the others, just as there are many conceptions of the best ice-cream flavor, none intrinsically better than the others?" Interview 100 philosophers about their conceptions of philosophical inquiry, and you will probably hear as many distinct conceptions. There is no such thing as the essence of philosophy, just as there is no such thing as the essence of the best ice-cream flavor. Why

---

[11] We use the terms "essence" and "nature" interchangeably.

not just stipulate whatever account of philosophy you think provides the strongest case for Thesis T and then try to persuade others to accept it, in the spirit of the noncognitive tradition of persuasive definitions. Don't even try looking for philosophy's essence. There's no such thing.

Accepting this advice would amount to reducing our thesis about the value of historical philosophical inquiry to a *purely hypothetical conditional* of the form: "If, for whatever reason, you happen to accept our account of the practice of philosophy, then you would have an excellent reason to investigate past sources of philosophical inquiry for your own first-order purposes."

That is an extremely modest claim—a purely hypothetical conditional. One can reject the antecedent (you happen to accept our account of the practice of philosophy) without encountering any normative issues, unlike conditionals whose antecedents purport to carry normative weight, as in, for example, "If our account of the practice of philosophy is the best account, in the sense of capturing the essence of philosophical inquiry, then you would have an excellent reason to investigate past sources of philosophical inquiry for your own first-order purposes." Freedom to reject the antecedent of the purely hypothetical conditional without having to confront normative issues means an extra layer of freedom from the logical force of a potential *modus-ponens* inference, an inference that commits one to accepting the conditional's consequent if one accepts its antecedent and the conditional itself. Of course, one can always also reject the antecedent of a conditional whose antecedent asserts normative weight, but with a purely hypothetical conditional one doesn't have to worry about working up the normative sweat typically involved in rejecting a normative antecedent.

Nevertheless, we won't ignore the purely hypothetical conditional. Indeed, we intend to use it for our own Thesis T purposes. Philosophers who do not believe that philosophical inquiry has an essence[12] can be sorted into two subclasses: those who happen to share our conception of philosophy and those who don't.

Those who happen to share our conception are free to accept the purely hypothetical conditional as giving them a reason to study past philosophical sources for their own first-order purposes. On the other hand, those who don't are free to accept the hypothetical conditional as offering them insight into the implications of an alien (from their perspective) conception regarding the first-order value of past philosophy.

---

[12] There are at least two possible motivations for a denial. On the one hand, those who deny the existence of essences would, *a fortiori*, deny that the practice of philosophical inquiry has an essence. On the other hand, those who believe that there are at least some essences might, for specific reasons, deny that philosophical inquiry has an essence.

Consider the second subclass and imagine that you belong to it. Imagine further that you reject the (possibly Wittgensteinian) account of philosophy as the sustained effort to permanently rid oneself of the desire to engage in philosophical inquiry itself.[13] Despite your rejection of such a radical account of philosophy, you might nonetheless reasonably believe that you would profit from reading a book that argues for that radical view and draws out its implications. Reading it would give you a better understanding of a position you already oppose. The additional illumination found in the book might either strengthen your antecedent opposition, or, on the other hand, motivate you to re-examine your antecedent opposition and perhaps even change your mind. Either way, reading the book could help you in your own first-order efforts. Analogously, we believe that our book can be useful even to those who antecedently reject the claim that philosophy has an essence.

Of course, these are not the only two alternatives for essence skeptics. They can always reject the purely hypothetical conditional itself. Part of our burden of persuasion in this book is making such an alternative difficult. At a bare minimum, we shall try to make a case for a conditional asserting that our conception of philosophical inquiry, if accepted, would provide an excellent reason for investigating past philosophical sources for one's own first-order purposes.

It might be thought that our adoption of the purely hypothetical conditional for our own Thesis T purposes constitutes a concession to essence skeptics. That would be a mistake. We challenge the underlying assumption of the skeptical objection that motivated us in taking up the purely hypothetical conditional in the first place, namely, the assertion that preferences for certain conceptions of philosophy over others are not essentially different from preferences for certain ice-cream flavors over others, and, consequently, that there is no fact-of-the-matter about the question of philosophy's essence. So, we do not concede that using the purely hypothetical conditional for our own purposes commits us to accepting the underlying assumption of essence skeptics.

Imagine asking a randomly selected set of people, "What is your favorite flavor of ice cream?" Presumably, there would be a wide variety of responses, including, "I don't like ice cream." It seems obvious that no such survey could identify the "objectively best" flavor. A prefers vanilla; B prefers strawberry; C prefers chocolate; D doesn't like ice cream at all, and so on. Once such differences are identified and statistically measured, there is nothing more that can be usefully said. No such survey would be relevant to the question, "What is the objectively best flavor of ice cream?"[14]

---

[13] Later we shall take up the question of two interpretations of Wittgenstein on this point.

[14] Of course, we assume that the answer is not exclusively determined by the answer to the statistical question about flavor preferences.

But we must qualify. There might be a reason to believe that anyone who likes chocolate ice cream would, say, also like vanilla-fudge ice cream. Then one could appropriately assert the hypothetical conditional, "If you like chocolate ice cream, then you would also like vanilla-fudge ice cream." As just argued in the context of alternative conceptions of philosophical inquiry, such a hypothetical conditional is of some interest in its own right.

There may be those who know that they like chocolate ice cream, but have never tried vanilla-fudge. Experimentally acting on the basis of this conditional, they might discover a liking for an ice-cream flavor they would otherwise never have discovered. Even those who don't like ice cream at all might find the hypothetical conditional of at least psychological or sociological interest.

So, hypothetical conditionals of that sort might be of some use. However, we would leave such conditionals in their purely hypothetical states. In particular, we would not strengthen the conditional just mentioned by building into its antecedent, say, the additional assertion that chocolate ice cream is the best ice cream, in some sense of "best" distinct from the statistical sense of degree of popularity. We would not do so because we think that ice cream preferences are reductively analyzable in terms of the traditional maxim, "Concerning matters of taste, there is no dispute."

Similarly, we would not strengthen the hypothetical conditional by building into its antecedent the assertion that chocolate is an "objectively better" flavor than certain other flavors, where such terms are construed in some sense distinct from the degree of statistical popularity. Even more broadly, we would not impose any ordering upon the class of ice-cream flavors in terms of some nonstatistical, two-place relation such as, "x is as objectively good an ice-cream flavor as y."

Thus, the case of conflicting ice-cream preferences is not relevantly comparable to the case of conflicting conceptions of philosophy. On the one hand, there is no such thing as the objectively best flavor of ice cream, nor, more generally, that it would be coherent to impose an ordering on the class of ice-cream flavors tied to degrees of the intrinsic merit of distinct flavors. On the other hand, it seems at least *prima facie* clear that some conceptions of philosophy are more adequate than others, in a sense of "more adequate" that provides the basis for an objective ordering of a kind that would not be conceptually appropriate for the set of ice-cream flavors. We think that most philosophers would defend their own conceptions of philosophy in terms that at least implicitly invoke the relation, *x is objectively more adequate than y*. Witness the mutual disdain "analytical" and "Continental" philosophers have for each other. In this long-standing conflict there is obviously more at stake than ice-cream preferences. The dispute is over how to pursue philosophy in the *right* way.

We conclude that there is at least a *prima facie* case for believing that the practice of philosophical inquiry has an essence. The *prima facie* difference between the project of objectively ranking ice-cream flavors and the project of objectively ranking alternative accounts of philosophical inquiry justifies pursuing the question of the essence of philosophy. We reject the essence skeptics' claim that our project is hopeless.

But what are essences?

Of course, the question whether philosophical inquiry has an essence presupposes an assignment of meaning to "essence." Following the Aristotelian tradition, we assume that an essence is *what-it-is-to-be-an-F*, where "F" stands in for a general term, for example, "horse," as in what-it-is-to-be-a-horse, or, "philosophical inquiry," as in what-it-is-to-be-a-case-of-philosophical-inquiry. Thus, an account of the essence of an F is an account of what-it-is-to-be-an-F.

An account of what-it-is-to-be-an-F is an appropriate answer to the question "What is it?" asked of an F. Suppose that someone points at a horse and asks you, "What is it?" You could appropriately respond by offering an account of what-it-is-to-be-a-horse. That would not be the only linguistically appropriate response. You might instead say, "That's my sister's favorite riding horse"; or, "That's the horse that won last year's Kentucky Derby." However, although the latter two responses would be linguistically appropriate, they would fail to specify essences in the Aristotelian sense. We shall use the phrase "what-it-is-to-be-an-F" to distinguish essences from the semantical correlates of other such answers to the question, "What is it?"[15]

It is not sufficient just to baptize essences with instantiations of the phrase "what-it-is-to-be-an-F." We must assign a meaning to that phrase that will serve as a criterion for filtering out such "non-essence" responses to the question, "What is it?" There are two filters that might be used, both from the Aristotelian tradition. On the one hand, one can define the essence of an F as the set of attributes that are (1) individually necessary for an F to be an F, and (2) jointly sufficient for an F to be an F. Call this the *inclusive* essence. On the other hand, one can more narrowly define the essence of an F as that set of attributes that are (1) a proper subset of the inclusive essence, and

---

[15] Other philosophical works that rely upon conceptions of essences and that we regard as analogous to ours in certain respects, are Tyler Burge, *Foundations of Mind*; David S. Oderberg, *Real Essentialism* (New York: Routledge, 2008); Michael J. Loux, *Primary Ousia* (Ithaca, NY: Cornell University Press, 1991); Rom Harré, *The Principles of Scientific Thinking* (Chicago: University of Chicago Press, 1970); William A. Wallace, *The Remodeling of Nature* (Washington, DC: Catholic University of America Press, 1996).

which (2) jointly causally explains an F's possession of the other attributes belonging to the inclusive essence. Call this the *primary* essence.[16] In our analysis of the essence of philosophical inquiry, we shall primarily focus upon the inclusive, rather than primary, essences. The distinction between primary and inclusive essences applies most appropriately to discussions of the essences of substances, in contrast to discussions of the essences of their powers and practices, which will be our main focus.

One can think about essences in at least two ways. On the one hand, they can be thought of *as types*. In this sense, one can appropriately say that any two particular humans share a single essence—*being a human*. *Qua* being humans, there is nothing to distinguish the two, except for their numerical distinctness. In such cases, we shall say that one is thinking about an essence as a *species essence*.

On the other hand, essences can also be thought of as *instantiated*. In this case it would be appropriate to distinguish A's humanity from B's. Thus, although one would presumably assume that part of what-it-is-to-be-a-human in the species-essence sense is possessing the power of thinking, one might also reasonably believe that A's power of thinking is greater than B's. If you doubt this, consider substituting the names "Gauss," "Newton," or "Einstein" for "A" and either of the names of the authors of this book for "B."

Acknowledging these two ways of thinking about essences enables one to characterize the metaphysical function of essences as providing the basis for *unity in difference*, to use a traditional phrase. Any two particular instantiations of a species essence are unified by the fact that both instantiate the same species essence, but are distinguishable by the differences between the modes of their respective instantiations of that species essence. We will elaborate on this distinction later.

What kinds of things have essences?

Some might ask, "What is the intended range of the variable 'F'? What sorts of things have essences in your sense?" We make no effort to define the boundaries of that range. The project is too extensive for the book's limitations and, in any case, is not necessary for our purposes. We shall focus upon essences instantiated in organic substances (e.g., humans, brown trout, and humming birds) and especially upon their fundamental powers and practices (e.g., the human power and practice of thinking and speaking, the

---

[16] This usage is closer to Aristotle's own. See, for example, *Topics* 102a. 18–30.

power and practice of brown trout rising to take floating insects, and the power and practice of humming birds flapping their wings at high rates of speed while feeding).[17]

The linking of *powers* with *practices* perhaps needs explaining. A power is an organism's capacity to act in certain ways. Powers, *qua* capacities, have the potentiality of expressing themselves in actions. Some of those capacity-expressing actions constitute *patterns of activity*, or as we shall often say, *practices*. Powers are the explanatory factor for practices. Given a particular practice of an organism, the explanation for why that practice is what it is invokes the power for engaging in that practice. In Aristotle's sense, the power causally explains the practice, not the other way around.

Some might grant our assumption that organic substances have essences, but draw the line at the claim that the fundamental powers and practices of organic substances also have essences. However, such a line cannot be drawn successfully. Any adequate account of the essences of organic substances must at least implicitly include an account of the essences of their basic powers and practices. For example, in proposing an account of the essence of a brown trout, it would not suffice simply to describe their physical structure. One must also offer an account of their basic powers and the patterns of activity in which those powers are actualized. At least part of what-it-is-to-be-a-brown-trout is exercising the power to eat underwater and surface insects. Given that brown trout share a single species essence, their basic powers and practices also have essences because the latter are constituents of that species essence.

However, that argument may invert the typical epistemic process for many, insofar as it assumes that people find it epistemically easier to begin the essence analysis of an organic substance by first trying to identify its essence, *qua* substance, rather than by first trying to identify the essences of its basic powers and practices. But that assumption may not hold for everyone. Perhaps the epistemic procedural truth of the matter, at least for many, is that the essences of an organism's basic powers and practices are more epistemically accessible than is its essence, *qua* substance. Setting aside the visual appearance of an organism, among the first things likely to strike observers are its basic powers and practices. Even supposing that those essences can eventually be ascertained, the organism's essence, *qua* substance,

---

[17] There is a long-standing controversy generated by the theory of evolution as to whether species essences mutate into other species essences, and, if so, how that happens. The controversy is not relevant to our invocation of species essences at any given time. Indeed, it seems that the hypothesis of species mutation itself presupposes that, at any given time in the immensely long process of species mutation, organisms have whatever essences they happen to have at that time.

which causally explains those powers and practices, might remain hidden for a longer time, perhaps even forever. Some might object to this assessment of relative difficulty by proposing that the nature of the underlying substance can be characterized as simply the entity that possesses and exercises those powers, but that would be mistaken. Of course, the underlying substance is the entity that possesses and exercises those powers, but that is a trivial observation. One should rather be looking for an adequate response to the question, "But what is it about the nature of the underlying substance that *causally explains* the fact that it possesses and exercises those particular powers and practices?" Helpful responses to that question are much harder to come by than are responses to the question, "What are the basic powers and practices of that organism?"

In any case, we shall offer an account of the essence of a particular human practice—philosophical inquiry—rather than an account of the human essence as such. Thus, we follow the epistemically easier route, although it is a route that raises difficulties enough of its own.

Perhaps it is worth noting that, in drawing this distinction between an organism's essence and the essences of its powers and practices, we are assuming that an organism's powers and practices could not exist on their own. They must be metaphysically rooted in something that is not itself a power or practice. The proposal that powers and practices can float by themselves in metaphysical space, untied to organic substances, seems plainly false, despite Russell's valiant claim that an act of walking could exist on its own, metaphysically untied to an entity that is doing the walking.[18]

A challenge: But whenever one focuses upon any particular human practice, such as the practice of philosophy, one sees only differences, never a unifying essence

We now take up an anti-essence objection that is similar, but not identical, to the objection discussed in the section titled "A preliminary challenge to our project: Don't bother to even start. It is hopeless." The difference is

---

[18] See Bertrand Russell, *The Analysis of Mind*, intro. Thomas Baldwin (London: Routledge, 1995), 194–95:

> There is a notion that an instance of walking, as compared with Jones, is unsubstantial, but this seems to be a mistake. We think that Jones walks, and that there could not be any walking unless there were somebody like Jones to perform the walking. But it is equally true that there could be no Jones unless there were something like walking for him to do. The notion that actions are performed by an agent is liable to the same kind of criticism as the notion that thinking needs a subject or ego, which we rejected in Lecture I. To say that it is Jones who is walking is merely to say that the walking in question is part of the whole series of occurrences which is Jones. There is no *logical* impossibility in walking occurring as an isolated phenomenon, not forming part of any such series as we call a "person."

that, whereas the earlier objection urged us to abandon our inquiry into philosophy's essence before we even began, this objection challenges the particular way in which we have chosen to begin—invoking an Aristotelian conception of essence as a way of giving an account of philosophical inquiry.

We've noted that there are indefinitely many differing conceptions of philosophy. Even a brief survey of philosophical publications should serve to convince doubters. This tangled jungle of conceptions results from the tangled jungle of different ways of engaging in philosophical inquiry. For example, consider the standard distinction between what are typically described as the "Analytic" and the "Continental" modes of inquiry. Stopping with that dichotomy would vastly oversimplify the actual complexity of philosophical practices. Not only can each class be indefinitely subdivided, but there are also fuzzy overlaps between the two. Should Rorty be considered a Continental or an Analytic philosopher? How about McDowell, or Habermas? In such cases neither label seems to fit perfectly.

The existence of an indefinitely large number of diverse patterns of philosophical inquiry is an indisputable fact. The interesting question is, "What can be inferred from it?" Those driven by a Wittgensteinian passion for differences ("I'll teach you differences.")[19] would conclude that philosophical inquiry has no nature. There is just a tangle of diverse practices and that's the end of the matter. Of course, following Wittgenstein himself, they might admit the existence of intertwined "family resemblances," but will insist that family resemblances don't justify a belief in essences.[20] Essences don't exist. Examine closely any purported human practice. Those with keen Wittgensteinian eyes will see only differences, never unifying essences underlying and unifying those differences.

Imagine a difference-hawk analyzing a situation in which 100 persons who just attended a performance of Mozart's Piano Concerto No. 27 are asked to describe their experiences while listening to the second (Larghetto) movement. The difference-hawk would predict that the accounts would differ dramatically. We concede that. Indeed, it is unfortunately possible that

---

[19] The relevant quotation is:

> Drury: What about Hegel? Wittgenstein: No, I don't think I would get on with Hegel. Hegel seems to me to be always wanting to say that things which look different are really the same. Whereas my interest is in showing that things which look the same are really different. I was thinking of using as a motto for my book a quotation from *King Lear*, "I'll teach you differences."

Recollections of Wittgenstein, ed. Rush Rhees (Oxford: Oxford University Press, 1984), 157.

[20] "I should reply: Now you are only playing with words. One might as well say: 'Something runs through the whole thread—namely the continuous overlapping of those fibres.'" Ludwig Wittgenstein, *Philosophical Investigations*, 3rd ed., trans. G.E.M. Anscombe (New York: Macmillan, 1958), para. 67.

some didn't even realize that they were listening to a Mozart composition, much less to the Larghetto movement of his Piano Concerto No. 27.

The difference-hawk would make three additional moves. First, he would infer from his prediction the conclusion that there is no essence of the practice of listening to the second (Larghetto) movement of Mozart's Piano Concerto No. 27. Second, he would generalize that conclusion to cover the entire practice of attending classical-music concerts. Third, he would argue by analogy from his second conclusion to the proposition that the practice of philosophy lacks an essence.

We reject the first and second moves. We reject the claim that there is no essence of the practice of attending a Mozart concerto, or of the practice of attending any classical-music concert. Of course, attendees will experience a wide variety of thoughts, sensations, and emotions, but it doesn't follow that the practice of attending concerts lacks an essence. Given any practice whatever, there are certain variations between instantiations of that practice. The appropriate question is not whether there are variations between instantiations, but, rather, whether those variations are so substantial as to exclude the possibility that the instantiations are nevertheless sufficiently unified so as to constitute a single practice. For example, there are many different things that can occur while riding a bicycle, such as chewing gum, wearing sunglasses, thinking about Church's solution of the decision problem for first-order predicate logic, or yelling at a careless auto driver. Sure, there is much diversity, but there is also the fundamental unity of riding a bicycle—sitting on a bicycle seat, pumping the pedals in a circular motion, maintaining an upright position, and many other things.

It is useful to think of the essences of human practices as *potentialities that may be actualized in greater or lesser degrees by the agents who own them.* Instead of referring to such essences as "essences," it is more illuminating to designate them as "essence potentialities." As just argued, essences can be thought of either as types or as instantiated types. On the type level, all humans share the same species essence, *qua* humans, and the same set of powers and practices, *qua* humans. On the instantiation level, they have distinguishable instantiations of that species essence and distinguishable instantiations of the type-level essences of the fundamental human powers and practices. The fact that there are distinguishable instantiations of the type-level essences of the human powers and practices is a function of two factors. First, distinct humans instantiate the generic human powers and practices in differing degrees of capacity. For example, some are born with instantiated physical or intellectual powers superior in degree to others.

Second, even as between humans who have instantiated the same degree of, say, physical or intellectual powers, they nevertheless may not actualize those potentialities to their fullest possible degree because of other factors, such as lack of opportunity, lack of effort, or disabilities. The instantiated powers and practices of individual humans inevitably differ in degree.

Given these observations, one can at least begin to describe the essence of the practice of attending a classical-music concert—focusing upon a variety of musical sounds and structures and allowing them to carry one down to a depth of thought and emotion attainable only by musical experience. Of course, such a description is inadequate. Even so, it supports our point about the value of thinking of essences as potentialities. Concertgoers intentionally put themselves in a position in which they can actualize the type-essence capacity for listening to music to one or another degree. Of course, they will inevitably actualize that type-essence potentiality in varying degrees for the reasons just mentioned, but the underlying unifying essence of the practice is always present, waiting to be actualized. Perhaps the complete actualization of the essence of any human power or practice is beyond human reach, but that doesn't mean that human powers and practices lack essences. It means only that their essences are ideal potentialities, whether for good, in the case of good potentialities, or for evil, in the case of evil potentialities, and, that the actualizations of those essences come in degrees.

The same analysis can be applied to the practice of philosophy. The sociological fact that there is a large variety of patterns of philosophical inquiry doesn't preclude the possibility of there being an underlying and unifying essence of that practice. On the contrary, conceiving of the practice of philosophy as an essence potentiality enables one to explain the variety of practice patterns as varying degrees of actualizing that underlying and unifying potentiality. Later we shall offer a more detailed account of that potentiality, but for the moment we offer this short-hand account: Philosophical inquiry is the effort to understand reality and one's place in it. It seems reasonable to understand any particular pattern of philosophical inquiry as an actualization to a greater or lesser degree of that unifying essence potentiality. However narrow and parochial the scope of some patterns of philosophical inquiry might be, they can be understood as constituents of broader inquiries aiming at providing a comprehensive account of reality and of one's place in it.

With respect to the essences of human practices, what difference-hawks fail to notice is the pervasive phenomenon of what we've called *unity in difference*. It's not possible that the world contain *only* differences. For, if we suppose that were true, then there would be at least one unity in the world—everything is different from everything else—contradiction.[21]

We mentioned that different conceptions of philosophical inquiry arise from differing patterns of practicing philosophy. Thus far, we've focused upon the differing patterns. We now turn to the fact that there are differing conceptions of philosophical practice in order to reinforce our point about practice patterns. As a matter of intuitive semantics, the phrase "conceptions of philosophical inquiry" presupposes a single intended object of focus of those conceptions. The phrase "conceptions of" requires a succeeding noun-phrase. This grammatical point is a function of the dialectical fact that a use of the phrase "conceptions of" opens the door to the question, "conceptions of *what?*" Any use of the phrase "conceptions of" raises a presumption that the speaker presupposes something that the conceptions are conceptions *of*. In speech contexts involving phrases of the form, "conceptions of ____," the presupposed objects of focus are often the essences of particular attributes and relations.[22] The attribute whose essence is the object of focus in this book is, *being the practice of philosophy*.

Compare the fact of there being differing conceptions of philosophical inquiry with the fact of there being differing conceptions of, say, stars. Asking 100 randomly selected people to articulate their conceptions of the nature of stars would probably result in 100 different accounts, but it wouldn't follow that stars lack an essence. Stars share the nature they have regardless of the differing conceptions of stars people have.

Thus, the existence of differing conceptions of something doesn't mean that one can just stop with the differing conceptions and conclude that there is nothing further to be said. The very fact of there being differing conceptions presupposes an attribute or relation that is focused upon, one whose nature those conceptions are used to illuminate to one degree or another.

In general, the essences of powers and practices tolerate both differing degrees of actualization and differing conceptions.

---

[21] In the famous passage about "family resemblances," Wittgenstein himself introduces a unifying essence, namely "family resemblances." *Philosophical Investigations*, para. 67. Indeed, the *Philosophical Investigations* are filled with invocations of essences, for example, "forms of life," "language game," "picture," "the grammar of," "a queer process," and "reminders for a particular purpose," indefinitely. Philosophers who try to do away with all unities, inevitably invoke unities in their very efforts to get rid of them.

[22] There are usages of "conceptions of ____" we set aside, for example, questions such as, "What is your conception of X?" where X is a person. Such questions do not ask, at least explicitly, for an explication of the essence of X, *qua* human being. If that were the speaker's intent, the question would be better expressed as, "What is the essence of the attribute, *being a human* being?" In that case, the reference to X would be purely incidental.

But giving adequate accounts of essences is not easy

These remarks about essences might suggest that we think it easy to explicate essences. Indeed, reading traditional accounts of essence analysis might suggest the same about their authors. For example, traditional accounts typically illustrate essence analysis by asserting that the essence, *being a human*, is analyzable in terms of the property, *being a rational animal*. Even conceding, as we do, that this is a useful way to begin an analysis of the essence, *what-it-is-to-be-a-human*, it's not adequate by itself. What is it to be an animal? What is it to be a power of rationality? How is it that some animals, but not others, have powers of rationality? How does it come about, if it does, that the power of rationality causally explains the presence in humans of other powers, such as intuition, emotion, and choice?

The ideal of any effort to explicate an essence is providing a *fully explicated analysis* of the essence expressed in terms whose meanings are transparent and whose epistemic status is *certainty*. The fact that this ideal can, at best, only be approximated does not render it irrelevant. The inevitability of approximation can be understood only in terms of the ideal that serves as its measure. The analysis of the human essence as *being a rational animal* constitutes just a step in the direction of the ideal analysis.[23, 24]

So, whatever naïve assumptions about essence analysis are made in some traditional expositions, we don't share them. The project of ascertaining

---

[23] This concession that the *rational-animal* analysis constitutes at least a step in the direction of an adequate analysis is itself immensely controversial, as even a cursory examination of the philosophical and scientific literature shows. Not only are there many conflicting accounts of human nature, but there are also many denials of the thesis that there is a nature to be analyzed. See, for example, Jean-Paul Sartre, *Being and Nothingness: An Essay on Phenomenological Ontology*, trans. Hazel E. Barnes (New York: Philosophical Library, 1956).

[24] Some might wonder why we haven't talked about defining the essences of mathematical entities, since one of the traditional ways of introducing the topic of essences is beginning with mathematical questions, such as, "What is the essence of a Euclidian triangle?" or "What is the essence of a Riemannian triangle?" We choose not to do so because the question whether mathematical objects have essences at all, and, if so, in what sense, raises difficulties beyond the scope of this book. For example, there is fundamental disagreement as to precisely what the objects of mathematical inquiry are. Are they mind-independent entities? Are they entities created by individual mental activities? Are they physical entities that are parts of the spatiotemporal universe? Are they fictional and therefore not really objects at all? The presence of such issues at the very entrance to the mathematical realm makes it difficult to ascertain what exactly is being argued about with respect to questions such as, "Do sets have an essence?" Our decision to limit our inquiry to the essences of natural-kind organisms and their basic powers and practices enables us to bypass these kinds of difficult issues. At least in cases such as the essence, *being a brown trout*, or the essence, *being a human*, there is no reasonable doubt about what the *objects* of the inquiry are. Whatever else it might be, a brown trout is not an

the essences of organisms and their powers and practices is difficult and inevitably controversial. Even Thomas Aquinas, a sophisticated practitioner of essence analysis, concedes:

> For even in the case of sensible things, the essential differences themselves are not known; whence they are signified through *accidental* differences which rise out of the essential ones, as a cause is signified through its effect; this is what is done when *biped*, for example, is given as the difference of man.[25]

The task of ascertaining the essences of organisms and their powers and practices is ideally a cooperative project involving the efforts of disciplines other than philosophy. For example, the projects of explicating the essences of human practices such as eating, sleeping, sexual activity, physical activity, meditation, music, mathematics, and philosophy can be assisted by disciplines such as neuroscience, physiology, anthropology, history, psychology, and sociology. We shall focus upon the nature of philosophical inquiry through the lens of philosophy. That lens incorporates both third-person and first-person accounts.

What do we mean by "first-person" and "third-person" accounts? The first-person case is the easiest. They are accounts of a human practice offered by those who have personally engaged in the practice themselves and who describe their experience.

What are third-person accounts? Starting with the standard grammatical distinctions between "I," "You," "She/He," we classify as paradigmatic cases those accounts offered by persons other than those whose practices are being examined. For example, imagine that A is engaged in meditation while a neuroscientist, B, watches an fMRI scan of A's brain and describes the scan results. What if A were to watch and describe an fMRI scan of her own brain

---

abstract entity, mental creation, or a fiction. Everyone knows what is being talked about. Contrast the challenge, "Show me an irrational number," with the challenge, "Show me a brown trout." In the first case, any attempt to "show" someone an irrational number is in itself a controversial maneuver, one likely destined to fail to convince anyone who does not already subscribe to the proponent's favorite theory of the ontological status of irrational numbers. Imagine a Platonically inclined mathematician trying to "show" Wittgenstein an irrational number. In contrast, in the case of a brown trout inquiry, all that could be reasonably required is plunking down a brown trout on the seminar table. Even Wittgenstein should deem that a "showing" of an instance of the kind of thing being discussed.

25 Joseph Bobik, *Aquinas on Being and Essence: A Translation and Interpretation*, (Notre Dame: University of Notre Dame Press, 1965), para. 94.

while she is meditating? If you doubt the psychological possibility of such a two-sided activity, imagine that A first meditates and then later looks at the brain scan. Would A's account of her own scan amount to a third-person account of meditation or a first-person account? Insofar as the account is offered by A, the meditator, it's a first-person account. On the other hand, insofar as the same account could have been offered by anyone other than A, so long as that person was watching the same fMRI scan of A's brain, it's a third-person account. Thus, the account A gives could *just as well* have been given by a "third person" in the literal sense. The so-called "first-person" account of the fMRI of A's own brain that A offers *does not add anything* to a "third-person" account of the scan. Thus, the neural brain activity of an individual is not directly accessible to that person's own conscious awareness. Of course, she can watch an fMRI scan of her own brain activity, but that constitutes only an indirect access, an access fully available to anyone else. On the basis of such considerations, we shall expand the extension of the property, *being a third-person account of a human practice*, beyond its standard grammatical confines to include cases in which anyone else could have offered the same account.

We can now elaborate the distinction between first-person and third-person accounts of human practices. Third-person accounts of a human practice are those that can be offered by anyone, whether or not the person offering the account has personally engaged in the practice. In contrast, first-person accounts of human practices are those that can be offered only by those who have personally engaged in that practice themselves. First-person accounts of human practices spring from the "inside" of conscious awareness. They arise from human agents' *own immediate consciousness of what it is to personally engage in those practices*.

Of course, both kinds of accounts are potentially helpful. However, at least with respect to human practices such as philosophical inquiry, first-person accounts are necessary for an adequate understanding of them. Some of the disciplines we've mentioned—neuroscience, physiology, and history—are restricted by their very nature to third-person accounts. Our use of the lens of philosophy to investigate the nature of philosophical inquiry allows us to invoke both first-person and third-person perspectives, where the latter focuses upon past sources of philosophical inquiry. Of course, as we've conceded, disciplines other than philosophy can also appropriately offer third-person accounts of the historical practice of philosophy. However, third-person accounts of historical practice offered by philosophers are likely to be more illuminating than third-person accounts offered by those practicing in disciplines distinct from philosophy. That's not surprising.

Third-person accounts of the history of any intellectual discipline are likely best provided by those who are actively engaged in the discipline. For example, who better than a mathematician can illuminate the profound significance of Euclid's proof of a denumerable infinity of prime numbers?[26]

---

[26] See, for example, John Stillwell, *Roads to Infinity: The Mathematics of Truth and Proof* (Natick, MA: A.K. Peters, 2012), 1–27.

2

The Essence of Philosophy

What is the nature of philosophical inquiry?

We now turn to our analysis of the essence of philosophical inquiry.

Philosophical inquiry essentially focuses upon a set of ultimate questions: There are two strategies for explicating the nature of ultimate questions—offering paradigmatic examples and offering a general characterization

Imagine someone who has never seriously engaged in philosophical inquiry asking you, a philosophical inquirer, "What is philosophical inquiry?" Imagine also that you respond by giving an account of the *kinds of questions* philosophers pursue. Your choice of approach in itself could lead to either of two procedures. You could give an account by offering *paradigmatic examples* of such questions. On the other hand, you could give an account by offering a *general characterization* of such questions. We shall discuss each procedure in turn.

Explaining the nature of a mode of inquiry by offering paradigmatic examples of the questions pursued

Imagine you are a mathematician explaining to a nonmathematician the nature of mathematical inquiry. You might proceed by offering paradigmatic examples of the kinds of questions mathematicians pursue. For example, you might offer representative questions pursued in number theory, abstract algebra, analysis, set theory, and geometry. You might follow up with the hand-waving remark, "Mathematics deals with questions like these. If you don't fully understand them now, you will eventually catch on if you pursue mathematical inquiry yourself." Your advice would conform to that given by Richard Courant and Herbert Robbins in their book *What Is Mathematics?* After making some generalizations about the nature of mathematical inquiry, they conclude, "Fortunately, creative minds forget dogmatic philosophical beliefs whenever adherence to them would impede constructive achievement. For scholars and layman alike it is not philosophy but active experience in mathematics itself that alone can answer the question: What is mathematics?"[1]

Courant and Robbins's advice implicitly contains two suggestions. First, at least for beginners, the nature of mathematical inquiry is best understood in terms of paradigmatic examples of mathematical questions. Second, the nature of such questions can be fully understood only by trying to resolve such questions oneself. In general, the method of conveying the nature of an intellectual practice by offering paradigmatic examples of the questions pursued in that mode should involve more than offering examples. That's just a start, although a good one. Providing someone who has not personally engaged in mathematical inquiry with just a list of paradigmatic questions might not help much. It might even confuse or intimidate. The mathematician should go on to recommend that the beginner try to resolve such questions for herself.

With respect to such recommendations, there is a significant contrast between human and nonhuman practices.

As to nonhuman cases, after offering paradigmatic examples of exercises of a basic power of an organism, there is no point in going on to encourage inquirers to exercise that power themselves in order to achieve a deeper understanding of that power. Humans don't have the cognitive means to grasp the "subjective inside" of such powers, other than by speculative fantasy.

Imagine being told that one of the basic powers of (most) birds is the power to fly on their own. That information would leave one, at best, with only a speculatively imaginative understanding of that practice. You might object, "But of course. Humans can't fly. That's why they can't exercise the power themselves and are left with just trying to imagine it." Your objection would miss the point. Even if humans could fly, they would still have no way of knowing whether they could understand *what-it-is-to-fly-as-a-bird-does*. Forget flying for a moment. Even with respect to powers of nonhuman organisms that humans share, in some *generic* sense, one cannot justifiably assume that humans could share the very same type of conscious experience in exercising human instances of those generic powers as nonhuman organisms do. Both leopards and humans can run. They share the generic power of running. However, it is not discoverable whether the conscious experiences leopards have while running is qualitatively the same as the conscious experiences humans have while running. Even if humans were somehow able to run as fast as leopards run, they could never know

[1]   Richard Courant and Herbert Robbins, *What Is Mathematics?*, 2nd ed., revised by Ian Stewart (Oxford: Oxford University Press, 1996), xix.

whether their experience was qualitatively the same as the leopard. At best, they could understand only what-it-is-to-be-a-human-running-as-fast-as-a-leopard, when what they would like to understand is what-it-is-to-be-a-leopard-running. Without being able to experience running from within the consciousness of a running leopard, there is a dimension of that practice humans cannot access.[2]

Human cases are different. In addition to offering paradigmatic examples of exercises of a basic power, one can appropriately invite others to exercise the power themselves and then reflect upon what they have done. One could do so with the reasonable expectation that he would thereby achieve a deeper understanding of the power, because he possesses it himself. *Qua* humans, they can understand the nature of the power "from the inside," experiencing what-it-is-to-exercise-that-power.

However, some might ask, "Why assume that offering paradigmatic examples of the exercise of a basic power of an organism is an adequate method of explicating the nature of that power?" We don't claim that offering examples is, by itself, fully adequate, but it is at least a useful means and, indeed, even a necessary one.

More generally, it is not possible for humans to cognitively grasp the nature of any property or relation, whether or not possessed by organisms, without first grasping at least some of their paradigmatic instances. This is a profound observation about the nature of the power of human cognition recognized by Aristotle in the *Posterior Analytics*:

> So out of sense-perception comes to be what we call memory, and out of frequently repeated memories of the same thing develops experience; for a number of memories constitute a single experience. From experience again—i.e., from the universal now stabilized in its entirety within the soul, the one beside the many which is a single identity within them all—originate the skill of the craftsman and the knowledge of the man of science, skill in the sphere of coming to be and science in the sphere of being.[3]

Applying the method of offering paradigmatic examples to philosophy

Philosophical inquiry can be characterized in terms of the kinds of questions it pursues—*ultimate* questions of a certain kind. But what are they? Here are

---

[2]   Directly relevant is Thomas Nagel's essay, "What is it like to be a bat?," in Nagel, *Mortal Questions* (Cambridge: Cambridge University Press, 1979).
[3]   Aristotle, *Posterior Analytics*, Bk. II, Ch.19, 100a, 4–8, in *The Basic Works of Aristotle*, ed. Richard McKeon, trans. G.R.G. Mure (New York: Random House, 1941).

some paradigmatic examples of such questions, expressed in the first person to highlight their inherently individualizing nature.

Questions about the ultimate nature of reality: Is mind or matter the ultimate reality? Is there a third alternative? Why should the answers matter to me as a human daily confronted with the question how to live, as opposed to mattering to me only as an academic? (We will repeat this last question in some of the following items, where it will be abbreviated as, "Why should I care about the answers?")

Questions about the nature of humans: What is my ultimate nature—mind, matter, or something else? Why should I care about the answers?

Questions about how to live: Are some life patterns normatively superior to others? Is there an ultimate metaphysical purpose for human life? If so, should I pursue it? If not, should I commit suicide and thereby avoid anxiety? Can I find a pattern of living that simultaneously yields the deepest-possible human fulfillment, while satisfying the constraints of unconditional duties? What patterns of mutual conduct among members of communities are normatively preferable? What obligation do I have to maintain them?

Questions about human freedom: What would it mean to have freedom of choice? Do I have such freedom? If so, what are its limits and what are the implications for my moral responsibility for my choices? If not, what are the implications for my moral responsibility for my choices?

Questions about the Ground of Being: Is there a Ground of Being? If there is, can any attributes, other than *being the Ground of Being*, be justifiably predicated of it? Is it conscious? Can it act? Why should I care about the answers?

Questions about universals: Are there universals (types)? Why should I care about the answers?

Questions about particulars: Are there particulars, that is, entities that are not types? If so, what is their nature? Why should I care about the answers?

Questions about time: What is time? Does it exist independently of the consciousness of time? Does the future already exist? Does the past still exist? Did time have a beginning? Is time space-like in the sense that it is possible to stand "outside" of it and "see it as a whole"? Can time exist independently of space? Why should I care about the answers?

Questions about space: What is space? Is it empty, apart from the things that are in it? Can space exist independently of time? Why should I care about the answers?

Questions about causation: What is it for something to be a cause? Can some things be uncaused? If there is causation, is it deterministic? Why should I care about the answers?

Questions about the nature of thinking: What is it to think? Could a purely physical entity think? Does thinking involve cognition of types? Is it possible to cognitively apprehend the nature of reality, or is my power of cognition limited to knowing a world of appearance that is only a mirror reflection of my own mind? What is reasoning? What are the standards for good reasoning? Why should I care about the answers?

Those are just a few of the paradigmatic questions pursued in philosophy. For anyone who has never engaged in sustained philosophical inquiry, the list may help to some extent, since everyone has thought about such questions, at least from time to time. Even so, as we have argued, one who has never engaged in sustained philosophical inquiry would achieve a deeper insight by more seriously pursuing such questions themselves.

Explaining the nature of a mode of inquiry by offering a general characterization of the questions it pursues

Instead of explaining the nature of a mode of inquiry by offering paradigmatic examples of the questions it pursues, one can offer a general characterization of such questions. Consider Bertrand Russell's characterization of the questions pursued in mathematics:

> Pure mathematics is the class of all propositions of the form "p implies q," where p and q are propositions containing one or more variables, the same in the two propositions, and neither p nor q contains any constants except logical constants.[4]

Applying this method to philosophy

We have offered examples of the ultimate questions pursued in philosophical inquiry. But is there an illuminating way of giving a general characterization of them?

What about a general characterization expressed in terms of the questions' degrees of generality?

Perhaps the kinds of ultimate questions pursued in philosophical inquiry can be usefully characterized as questions possessing a certain degree of

---

[4] Bertrand Russell, *Principles of Mathematics*, 2nd ed. (New York: W.W. Norton, 1938), 3.

generality. However, one difficulty with that suggestion is clarifying the relevant sense of "generality."

One's first thought might be that the relevant sense can be picked out by invoking the sense in which "general" questions are typically opposed to "particular" questions. For example, consider questions such as whether seven is a prime number, or whether seven is both the successor and the predecessor of an even number. It seems they can be appropriately characterized as "particular" questions, in contrast to "general" questions, such as, "What is it to be a prime number?"; or, "Are there an infinite number of prime numbers?"

Applying this distinction to the issue of the nature of ultimate philosophical questions would require classifying them as "general," as opposed to "particular," questions. But that wouldn't provide a *sufficient* condition for classifying them as philosophically ultimate. The question, "What is the healthiest diet for humans?" qualifies as a general question in terms of the "general" versus "particular" usage, but does not qualify as an ultimate question for philosophy.

On the other hand, one might think that generality in this standard sense qualifies as a *necessary* condition for a question to be a philosophically ultimate question. That doesn't seem to hold either. Consider the paradigmatic philosophical questions: "Is there a Ground of Being?"; and, "If so, what are its attributes?" By analogy with the examples of questions about the number seven, such questions are just as particular as the questions about seven. It would be a mistake to characterize ultimate philosophical questions as necessarily general in the standard "general" versus "particular" usage.[5]

However, perhaps there is an interpretation of "generality" that would classify questions about, say, the Ground of Being, as general, but not in the sense of the "general" versus "particular" usage. Perhaps, instead of categorically sorting questions into two classes—general versus particular—one could use a comparative quantitative approach. Order the class of all questions by increasing degrees of generality. Given any two questions, Q-1

---

[5]   Of course, questions about the particular, the Ground of Being, themselves eventually lead to more "general" questions in the standard sense. The same could be said about most questions about "particulars." For example, questions about the number seven might eventually lead to more "general" questions about, say, prime numbers, or rational numbers, or even numbers as such. Similarly, questions about some particular salt-water crocodile might eventually lead to more "general" questions about, say, reptiles in general, or even about all living organisms. That kind of analysis would presumably lead to classifying all questions as "general," which is not the kind of criterion for which we are looking.

and Q-2, there would be three possibilities: (1) Q-1 has a greater degree of generality than Q-2; (2) Q-2 has a greater degree of generality than Q-1; or (3) Q-1 and Q-2 have the same degree of generality. Given such an ordering, it might be possible to draw a principled boundary line separating the questions that are not philosophically ultimate from those that are. One proposal for drawing the dividing line would be to separate questions of the highest possible degree from the others. A more expansive proposal would be to divide questions of a certain minimum level of generality from the others, where the minimum level is specified quantitatively, for example, 50%.

Such proposals have problems of their own. First, it might turn out that the set of all questions cannot be ranked in a single spectrum, at least not in a way that is not *ad hoc* and effectively decidable. Not only would there be the problem of formulating an effectively decidable criterion for measuring the degree of generality of particular questions, there would also be the difficulty presented should it turn out that some questions are incommensurable with respect to degree of generality. For example, how should one decide whether, "Do humans have freedom of will?" and "Is the Ground of Being conscious?" have the same or different degrees of generality?

Second, even if such difficulties were surmounted, there would remain the problem of choosing how to characterize the dividing line. Should it divide questions of the greatest-possible degrees of generality from the others? Should it divide the questions of some particular minimum degree of generality from the others?

Even if the latter difficulties were resolved, there would remain another. Imagine a real-number spectrum along which all questions could be located in terms of degrees of generality. It might seem that it would not be possible for two questions to have the same degree of generality, but for one to qualify as a philosophically ultimate question, while the other does not. However, that possibility is easily illustrated. Consider the question, "What is the nature of a mayfly?" Compare it with the question, "What is the nature of a human being?" It seems that both questions have the same degree of generality, whatever that degree might be. It also seems that the first question, when pursued for its own sake, and not for some more general intellectual purpose, is not one of the ultimate questions pursued in philosophical inquiry, whereas the second question is clearly one of those ultimate questions. Hence, such a real-number spectrum by itself would not serve to pick out the relevant questions.

We conclude that explicating the nature of the ultimate questions pursued in philosophical inquiry by invoking "generality" is not likely to be fruitful. However, that conclusion suggests another proposal.

What about a general characterization of ultimate questions formulated in terms of the property, being a systematic worldview?

Consider characterizing ultimate philosophical questions as those that would be pursued by anyone seeking to formulate a systematic worldview. Such a proposal presupposes an account of the property, *being a systematic worldview*. What is that?

What is a systematic worldview? Initial difficulties with the concept. The need for a semantic filter

Standing alone, the phrase "systematic worldview" is not much help. Its semantic scope admits of interpretations that are not relevant for our purposes. For example, one might construe it as, "a set of beliefs about every possible question that could be asked about the world." Given that interpretation, a systematic worldview would presumably include answers to questions such as, "How many grains of sand are there on the Earth?" (Archimedes's question); "What physiological mechanism enables dogs to bark?"; or, "How many galaxies are there?" However, questions like these are not questions whose responses would make up a systematic worldview in the sense we have in mind. We need to impose some kind of a semantic filter on the overly generous range of interpretations that the phrase, "systematic worldview," generates.

The need for semantic filters is an inherent part of everyday conversation. Imagine you are a mathematician specializing in model theory, and a colleague introduced you as, "a pure mathematician working in model theory." If those to whom you have been introduced know nothing about the intended senses of "pure mathematics" or "model theory," you might well wish that your introducer had imposed semantic filters in order to exclude unintended interpretations (e.g., "pure," as in morally correct?; "model," as in fashion model?). Without filters, communication would be even more difficult than it is.

What about a semantic filter incorporating certain kinds of motivations for engaging in philosophical inquiry?

What kind of semantic filter should we use? We suggest focusing upon the motivations people might have for pursuing philosophy in the first place. Some subset of all such motivations could then be used to impose at least limits on the semantic range of the phrase "systematic worldview." Of course, there are many motivations people might have for engaging in philosophical inquiry. With respect to just the academic context, there is a spectrum of possible motivations, ranging from the embarrassing to the worthy.

Examples of the embarrassing are: discovering that you can earn superior grades in philosophy courses; being told by a philosophy teacher that you have genuine philosophical talent; turning to philosophy as a default option because you failed to earn top grades in physics; finding that you have emotional highs when defeating others in philosophical debate; rebelling against parental wishes that you attend law school. Of course, such motivations can overlap.

We concede that such motivations sometimes move individuals into philosophy. However, we exclude them from our focus because they fail to impose any principled limitation on the semantical scope of "systematic worldviews." Those engaging in philosophy on the basis of such motivations would not necessarily be inclined to pursue lines of inquiry aiming at systematic worldviews of the kind we have in mind. Rather, they would be inclined to pursue whatever types of inquiry that are presently favored in their own academic environments.

We turn to motivations of a deeper kind by focusing upon what we regard as the two most fundamental motivations: (1) *the desire to find answers to questions arising out of the human condition*, and (2) *the desire to find answers to questions arising out of Aristotelian wonder*. We shall refer to questions of the first kind as *human-condition questions* and questions of the second as *Aristotelian-wonder questions*. We shall argue that motivations of both kinds provide a natural and justifiable basis for pursuing a systematic worldview in our intended sense and that both can cohere in the minds of individual inquirers.

The motivation of pursuing human-condition questions.
Human-condition questions are those everyone asks, on some level of consciousness, simply in virtue of being human. They must be responded to, in some way, even if the response is an attempt to quarantine the questions.

We begin with what we shall call the *fundamental* human-condition question: How should I live? The question presupposes the possibility of alternative ways of living. By "alternative ways of living," we don't mean the kinds of alternatives presupposed by questions such as, "Should I attend the Beethoven concert tonight?"; or, "Should I major in electrical engineering or computer science?" Such questions are appropriate and often important, but we have in mind questions of a greater degree of generality,[6] such as,

---

[6]   However, notice the next footnote.

"Should I live a life of malice—feeling joy when others suffer and suffering when others are joyful?"; or, "Should I live on the assumption that I am the ultimate meaning of the universe?"[7]

Adequate responses to the fundamental human-condition question potentially involve responses to a host of related questions, which we shall call *derived* human-condition questions. Thus, responding to derived questions is a necessary condition for fully responding to the fundamental question itself.

Some derived human-condition questions are obvious. Do I have some degree of freedom of will? This question is clearly related to the fundamental human-condition question. Anyone who responds by denying freedom should respond to the fundamental human-condition question in words something like this: "I have no freedom to choose between any alternatives whatever, so I should stop fretting about the question."

The same obvious relationship to the fundamental human-condition question holds for many other questions. Is there something that ontologically grounds everything else, but does not itself ontologically depend upon anything else? Is there an ultimate purpose of human existence? Is there an objective distinction between good and evil? Am I wholly physical? Will I survive death? Am I essentially depraved, essentially good, or a mixture of both? What is the best achievable state of society? Can religion provide something that philosophy cannot? Can I know anything? Can experiences of music, poetry, literature, friendship, love, and the natural world provide illumination that philosophy cannot? How should I live with the awareness of my own inevitable death?

However, there are other questions that at first glance might be thought not to qualify, but may qualify given appropriate circumstances. For example, consider the traditional question about the ontological status of types (universals). One might suppose that it fails to qualify as a derived human-condition question, but that fails to consider its potential relation to other questions that do clearly qualify. For example, the question about types is relevant to the derived human-condition question of the power of human cognition. Does it include the capacity to apprehend types? If so, what is their ontological status and how do minds access them? The question is also relevant to the derived human-condition question about the nature of the Ground of Being, if there is one. If types have some kind of ontological status, is that status ontologically independent of the Ground of Being? If so, does it

---

[7]   Serious responses to these kinds of general human-condition questions will often have implications for the less-general kinds of choices that, as we just said, we do not "primarily" have in mind.

follow that the Ground of Being would not be the Ground of *all* Being? If not, how does the Ground of Being create types? Similar analyses can be made of other questions that might at first seem to not qualify as derived human-condition questions, such as questions about the nature of the principles of reasoning or the nature of concepts.

This analysis of questions that qualify as derived human-condition questions because of their relationship to other human-condition questions focuses upon the abstract intrinsic relations between propositions, without regard to whether any particular inquirer is aware of those relations. The general form of the analysis has been: Question X is relevantly related to Question Y and, therefore, X qualifies as a derived human-condition question because Y qualifies. This level of abstraction is appropriate because it discloses the potential scope of the class of derived human-condition questions. The analysis may not generate a completely determinate boundary for the class, but it does identify a significant core.

However, introducing individual philosophical inquirers into the analysis seems to render the boundary even less determinate. Now, one can ask whether a particular question qualifies for derived human-condition status *in the mind of some particular philosophical inquirer*. It seems that whether it does is a function of the motivations of particular inquirers and their particular contexts. Consider again the question about types. If an inquirer pursues that question out of the motivation to respond to another derived human-condition question, then the question of types becomes a derived human-condition question, *for that inquirer*. In contrast, imagine a second inquirer pursuing the same question out of some motivation unrelated to any effort to pursue another human-condition question. Perhaps the second inquirer pursues the question because her thesis advisor so advised, or because types are a fashionable issue just now. In such a case the question would not qualify as a derived human-condition question, *for that inquirer*.

Thus, there is a sense in which the *psychological* boundary of the class of derived human-condition questions is a function of varying motivations of individual inquirers. On the other hand, there is also a sense in which the boundaries of the class are *normatively* fixed by the ideal standard of what questions an ideally competent philosophical inquirer would pursue, assuming that she begins with the fundamental human-condition question, "What should I do with my life?"[8]

---

[8] One way of expressing at least part of this point is by characterizing the nonideal philosophical inquirer as failing to recognize the transitivity of the relation *question b is a human-condition question derived from question a*, where *a* may be either the

However, some might persist by asking whether, given our admission of the potential flexibility of the psychological boundary of the class of human-condition questions, any limit at all can be imposed upon the class. Perhaps it is potentially limitless, containing all questions. However, the fact that a class has somewhat indeterminate boundaries does not seem to imply that the class contains everything. For example, the fact that the class of trophy-size brown trout has somewhat indeterminate boundaries does not mean that all brown trout are trophy-size. Similarly, the fact that the class of human-condition questions has somewhat indeterminate boundaries does not seem to imply that all questions are ultimate. *Prima facie*, there seem to be many questions that don't qualify as human-condition questions, at least when considered in abstraction from all particular contexts, for example, "Why use a #10 Royal Coachman for rainbows on overcast days?"

On the other hand, isn't it always possible to imagine possible situations in which even questions like these turn out to be human-condition questions, at least for some particular inquirers in some particular contexts? Consider the question, "Should I set my alarm for 6:00 or 6:30 tomorrow morning?" On its abstract, propositional face, it seems not to qualify for human-condition status. Imagine, however, that you have long been pursuing the human-condition question, "Is there a conscious Ground of Being?" You arranged to meet tomorrow morning with a philosopher who you believe has something crucial (yet unpublished) to say about your question. The only time you can meet is at an airport during a 45-minute interval between planes. It may be the last chance you will ever have to meet with him, since he is old and in poor health. If you get up at 6:00, you are confident that you will arrive in time. If you wait until 6:30, you might not. In this situation, it seems that the question—"Should I set my alarm for 6:00 or 6:30?"—would qualify as a derived human-condition question, at least for you as an individual inquirer in that particular context. Of course, with subsequent hindsight, it might turn out that your meeting was not crucial for your human-condition quest, after all. Perhaps you would be able to later telephone or write the professor. Perhaps his published writings already contain everything he might say to you. Nevertheless, potential hindsight is irrelevant at the moment. You must decide now. The crucial human-condition criterion for you is whether the resolution of the particular question-at-hand will have any effect upon your pursuit of your human-condition question.

---

fundamental human-condition question itself, or another derived human-condition question. Abbreviate that relation as *xDy*. Transitivity of that relation would require that if *xDy* and *yDr*, then *xDr*. A nonideal inquirer would fail to recognize at least some such entailments. An even more fundamental failure of a nonideal inquirer would be failing to pursue the fundamental human-condition question itself.

In general, once particular inquirers and their particular contexts are introduced—the *concrete* approach—the analysis of the class of human-condition questions becomes more complex than it is when conducted solely on the basis of abstractly considered questions—the *abstract* approach. When using the abstract approach it seems appropriate to classify many questions as not qualifying for human-condition status. In contrast, when using the concrete approach it seems possible to imagine, for any given question, some particular inquirer in some particular situation in which that question would turn out to be a human-condition question, for that inquirer in that situation. Indeed, this should not be surprising when one considers the continual existential necessity of translating the pursuit of any abstract question into terms of concrete specificity for one's own particular situation. Imagine, again, deciding to pursue the question of human freedom. There will inevitably arise on a day-to-day, moment-to-moment, basis an interminable and confusing sequence of specific contexts in which you will have to answer questions. Should I study Kierkegaard's *Concluding Unscientific Postscript* right now, rather than attending this afternoon's Beethoven concert? Should I draft an essay right now, rather than meeting a friend at the coffee shop?

In general, when considering abstract questions, without specific contexts, it seems that the class of human-condition questions is just a small proper subset of the class of all questions. For example, the question, "Do I have freedom of will?" qualifies. The question, "Should I set my alarm for 6:00?" does not. In contrast, when considering questions as embedded in specific situations for specific inquirers, the analysis differs dramatically. Here it seems that, given any question, it is possible to imagine some particular situation in which that question becomes a human-condition question for some particular inquirer. Recall the question about setting an alarm in the context discussed earlier. In contrast to the abstract analysis, the concrete analysis seems to generate a potentially limitless class of human-condition questions.

However, two qualifications are in order. First, given any abstract question, it is possible that it *could* become a human-condition question for *some* particular inquirer in *some* particular situation. It does not follow that, necessarily, *every* abstract question will become a human-condition question in *all* possible situations. On the contrary, there will be countless situations in which any given abstract question is *not* transformed into a human-condition question. Imagine, again, that you have chosen to spend the next three hours drafting your thoughts about human freedom. During your writing session you consider whether to drink a cup of tea while working. Assuming that neither alternative will make any difference to your efficiency or creativity, the question "Should I have a cup of tea?" is not a human-condition question in that context.

Second, in referring to potentially limitless classes, we are invoking the Aristotelian conception of potential infinity, in contrast to the Cantorian conception of actual infinity. Thus, when we say that the class of human-condition questions, concretely considered, is potentially limitless, we do not mean to say that it contains an actual infinity of members.

In summary, we propose that whatever else philosophical inquiry may essentially involve, at the very least it involves the systematic pursuit of human-condition questions. Philosophy is not the only practice to pursue such questions; religion and theology do so as well. As such, the pursuit of human-condition questions is not unique to philosophy, which raises an important, but difficult, issue. Assuming that philosophy is not identical with either religion or theology, what is the distinction between them? One might be inclined to say that, although all three practices pursue the same class of questions, they pursue them with different methods. That seems correct on some general level, but it is not easy to state precisely what those differences are. One might suggest that philosophy proceeds by argumentation, whereas religion and theology do not. However, that seems false, at least if it means that there is no argumentation in religion or theology. Regarding theology, read Aquinas, Luther, Calvin, or C.S Lewis. As to religion, read sermons in the Christian, Jewish, or Islamic traditions, or, for that matter, the *Bhagavad Gita*. One might think that religion and theology rely upon divine revelation, whereas philosophy does not. But that doesn't seem true either. Do the *Upanishads* rely upon divine revelation? Not at least in anything like the way in which Christianity does. Religion essentially involves communal rituals and practices. Philosophy does not, but then neither does theology. The demarcation problem is difficult. It may turn out that there is no simple way of drawing the boundaries. Perhaps the boundaries are not sharp after all, but rather indefinite gradations of shading in the manner of the color spectrum. In any case, we will not try to resolve the issue here, but will take it up later.

The motivation of Aristotelian wonder

Aristotle begins the *Metaphysics* with, "All men by nature desire to know."[9] He argues as follows:

> An indication of this is the delight we take in our senses; for even apart from their usefulness they are loved for themselves; and above all others the sense of sight. For not only with a view to action, but even when we are not going to do anything, we prefer seeing (one might say) to

---

[9]   Aristotle, *Metaphysics*, 980a, in Aristotle, *The Basic Works of Aristotle*.

everything else. The reason is that this, most of all the senses, makes us know and brings to light many differences between things.[10]

He points to a fundamental desire to seek knowledge for its own sake, as an intrinsically desirable end,[11] rather than for its instrumental value in pursuing another end. Everyone is so motivated, to one degree or another.[12] Knowledge of this sort is Wisdom—knowledge of the deepest explanations of facts, as contrasted with knowledge of just facts. Such deep explanations are ideally formulated in terms of the essences or natures of things. This account of Wisdom presupposes a distinction between *that questions* and *why questions*:

> Again, we do not regard any of the senses as Wisdom; yet surely these give the most authoritative knowledge of particulars. But they do not tell us the "why" of anything—e.g., why fire is hot; they only say *that* it is hot.[13]

Wisdom is knowledge of the "first causes and the principles of things."[14] It follows that knowing why a fact is the way it is presupposes knowing that fact itself. *Knowing why* rests upon an epistemic foundation of *knowing that*. Thus, although there is a sense in which Wisdom is distinguishable from knowledge of facts, there is also a sense in which Wisdom necessarily incorporates factual knowledge, in the sense of presupposing it.

What is the motivation for seeking Wisdom? According to Aristotle, the *passion for wonder*:

> That it is not a science of production is clear even from the history of the earliest philosophers. For it is owning to their wonder that men both now begin and at first began to philosophize; they wondered originally at the obvious difficulties, then advanced little by little and stated difficulties about the greater matters, e.g., about the phenomena of the moon and those of the sun and of the stars, and about the genesis of the universe. And a man who is puzzled and wonders thinks himself ignorant (whence even the lover of myth is in a sense a lover of Wisdom, for the myth is composed of wonders); therefore since they philosophized in order to escape from ignorance, evidently they were pursuing science in order

[10] Aristotle, *Metaphysics*, 23–980a, 28.
[11] Aristotle, *Metaphysics*, 981b, 19. Wisdom does not "aim at utility."
[12] As emphasized in Jonathan Lear, *Aristotle: The Desire to Understand* (Cambridge: Cambridge University Press, 1988), 1–14.
[13] Lear, *Aristotle*, 981b, 10–981b, 13.
[14] Lear, *Aristotle*, 981b, 27–981b, 28.

to know, and not for any utilitarian end. And this is confirmed by the facts; for it was when almost all the necessities of life and the things that make for comfort and recreation had been secured, that such knowledge began to be sought. Evidently then we do not seek it for the sake of any other advantage; but as the man is free, we say, who exists for his own sake and not for another's, so we pursue this as the only free science, for it alone exists for its own sake.[15]

What do we make of Aristotle's concept for our purposes?[16] He posits a fundamental human desire to understand reality, understanding not only *what* it is, but also *why* it is the way it is. The desire is pursued for its own sake, not for the sake of any other end. We adopt Aristotle's thesis. It provides us with a second fundamental motivation for engaging in philosophy— pursuing philosophical questions for the intrinsic fulfillment of deepening one's understanding of the nature of the world.

This requires two clarifications. We are not suggesting that Aristotle did not have a motivation to pursue human-condition questions. If nothing else, the *Nichomachean Ethics* expresses his focus upon them. In addition, although our account of Aristotelian wisdom is inspired by Aristotle, we make no pretense of presenting a scholarly exegesis of his many texts on the matter. In accordance with our approach to using historical philosophical sources for one's own first-order purposes, we use Aristotle's words for what they suggest to us. As far as we are concerned, whether Aristotle would agree with every detail of our use is not relevant.

When considered together, what do these fundamental motivations yield in terms of clarifying our intended meaning of "systematic worldview"? Is there an overarching theistic perspective that provides a basis for unifying them?

How have we arrived at these questions? Recall that we are searching for a way to characterize the class of philosophically ultimate questions. We proposed one in terms of the attribute, *being a systematic worldview*, the idea being that philosophically ultimate questions are those that would ideally be pursued in the course of formulating a systematic worldview. But what is a systematic worldview? Because the term is vague, we proposed using a semantic filter

---

[15] Lear, *Aristotle*, 982b, 11–982b, 27.

[16] We put aside aspects of Aristotle's account of the motivation of wonder that we deem unnecessary here. For example, although we regard his account of the four causes that are necessary to fully explain *why* something is the way it is—the *material*, *formal*, *efficient*, and *final* causes—as illuminating, we do not think it necessary to build that level of detail into our account.

as a way of isolating our intended sense. We chose a filter tied to the possible motivations for pursuing philosophy, the idea being that a proper subset of such motivations could be used to narrow the range of possible senses of "systematic worldview" by stipulating that systematic worldviews in our intended sense arise out of certain kinds of motivation. We selected two motivations we deem fundamental—pursuing human-condition questions and pursuing Aristotelian-wonder questions. Thus, our overall proposal at this point is characterizing the class of philosophically ultimate questions as those questions arising in any effort to construct a systematic-world view,[17] which is motivated by one or the other, or both, of the two fundamental motivations. How do those motivations fare in that regard?

Characterizing philosophy as the pursuit of human-condition questions provides at least some degree of specificity about philosophy's nature. We have acknowledged that the boundary of the class is not completely determinate, but argued that, nonetheless, it does not include all questions in all contexts.

If pursuing human-condition questions were the only fundamental motivation for pursuing philosophy, we could reasonably conclude that the essence of philosophy is completely determined by such questions. The motivation to pursue them would function as a semantic filter, straining out questions outside its scope. However, as we have argued, philosophy is not so easily analyzable. Aristotelian wonder is another fundamental motivation for philosophy, one that can potentially work independently of the human-condition motivation. What is the effect of incorporating both in our analysis?

We believe that Aristotelian wonder can motivate pursuing a potentially unbounded class of questions. However, some might have doubts. Consider the question, "How does a jet engine work?" Sure, the question is pursued by engineers because they want to design engines, by mechanics because they want to maintain them, and by sales agents because they want to sell them. All are instrumental motivations, grounded in ends distinct from the end of understanding jet engines for the intrinsic sake of understanding them. Since motivations of that kind are not genuine instances of Aristotelian wonder, neither are the questions they pursue genuine Aristotelian-wonder questions. Hence, it might seem that Aristotelian wonder does not motivate pursuing a potentially unbounded class of questions.

But instrumental motivations are not the only possible motivations for pursuing the jet-engine question. It can also be pursued out of Aristotelian wonder—seeking an understanding of jet engines for its own sake. The same can be said of other cases: "What's the best recipe for chocolate cake?";

---

[17] Notice that we have not said much about what it is for a worldview to be "systematic." We will say more shortly.

"What's the best way to tie a Royal Coachman dry fly?"; "How does a hydrogen bomb work?" Although questions like these are typically pursued out of instrumental motivations, they do not have to be. Aristotelian wonder can motivate the pursuit of any question. Why? The class of questions divides into "that questions" and "why questions." Aristotelian wonder incorporates both subclasses. Hence, both are within the scope of Aristotelian wonder.

If that is so, then it might seem that invoking Aristotelian wonder as a means of explicating the nature of philosophy is not helpful. Modes of inquiry distinct from philosophy also pursue questions out of Aristotelian wonder. Take physics. Although many of its applications are driven by instrumental motivations (building rockets, bombs, computers, electronic security systems, microchips), many are not. The long-sustained project of identifying the fundamental particles and forces of matter is motivated, at least in part, by Aristotelian wonder. So, one might think that, since modes of inquiry distinct from philosophy, such as science, are also sometimes motivated by Aristotelian wonder, it is pointless to characterize philosophy as pursuing questions out of that motivation. If part of the essence of philosophy were pursuing questions out of Aristotelian wonder, then philosophy would be identical with the set of sciences driven by the same motivation. But that's ridiculous. *Modus tollens.*

We agree that modes of inquiry distinct from philosophy pursue at least some questions out of Aristotelian wonder, but reject the inference that philosophy incorporates all such modes of inquiry, or, for that matter, that all the other modes incorporate philosophy. Although several modes of inquiry pursue questions out of Aristotelian wonder, they pursue them with different methods. For example, we can distinguish between *philosophically oriented* Aristotelian wonder and *physics-oriented* Aristotelian wonder. Here are just a few of the distinguishing methodological features. Physics can be appropriately characterized as: (1) using sophisticated mathematics to reach conclusions, (2) using a wide variety of sophisticated devices for measurement and other purposes, (3) using controlled-and-repeatable experimentation to confirm or disconfirm hypotheses, (4) focusing upon questions that can be both quantitatively formulated and quantitatively answered, and (5) appropriately ignoring questions that only philosophy can adequately deal with—a distinction closely related to (4). In contrast, the typical methods of philosophy do not include any of those characteristics. We shall take up these distinguishing factors in greater detail later.

Thus, we do not concede that philosophy can be identified with the physical sciences. But what about the fact that, whatever other questions philosophically oriented Aristotelian wonder draws within its scope, it draws in human-condition questions. Any human-condition question can be pursued out of

Aristotelian wonder as well as out of an individual's concern to decide how to live. Does this potential intersection of questions imply that we should not distinguish the two?

Despite this potential intersection, there is an important difference between the two motivations with respect to the differing ways in which they pursue such shared questions. Philosophers motivated by the human-condition concern pursue human-condition questions by beginning with the fundamental human-condition question, "What should I do with my life?" All other human-condition questions are pursued in order to answer that primary question. In contrast, questions pursued out of Aristotelian wonder are pursued with an *existentially detached* state-of-mind. Aristotelian wonder is driven by the desire to understand for its own intrinsic sake. It would not be Aristotelian wonder if it instrumentally pursued a question for the sake of some other objective, such as trying to decide how to live.

Consequently, although there is a sense in which an inquirer can pursue a human-condition question solely out of Aristotelian wonder, she cannot pursue it in the same way as an inquirer motivated by the human-condition concern. Consider the derived human-condition question, "Do *I* have some degree of libertarian freedom?" Here we use the first-person mode to indicate that the question is pursued with a focus upon the inquirer's own life. Human-condition questions are most appropriately expressed in the first person. Now consider the situation in which the same question is pursued out of Aristotelian wonder. Here the typical formulation of the question would substitute the third-person mode: "Do humans have some degree of libertarian freedom?"

We do not maintain that this grammatical distinction is decisive. It is possible for an inquirer motivated by the human-condition concern to use the third-person mode and for one motivated by Aristotelian wonder to use the first-person mode, although the latter is more difficult to imagine. Nevertheless, the grammatical distinction is illuminating because it exposes an important difference in the ways in which the two motivations work. Of course, human-condition inquirers may reflect upon the life situations of others in the course of their inquiries, but the ultimate purpose of such other-directed thoughts would be bringing them to bear upon the inquirers' own life situations. In contrast, Aristotelian wonder seeks to understand the world solely for the intrinsic value of achieving understanding. In situations in which Aristotelian wonder happens to focus upon human-condition questions, they are not pursued primarily in order to answer the inquirer's questions about her own life situation. That can be done only by choosing to be led by the human-condition motivation. In making this point, we don't intend to deny the possibility of an inquirer being motivated from time to time by both Aristotelian wonder and human-condition concern. We are just saying that, when an inquirer turns his primary focus to his own life, he must temporarily move Aristotelian wonder backstage.

What does all this suggest for our question about the effect of invoking both motivations? We already concluded that Aristotelian-wonder motivation cannot *subtract* any questions from the class generated by the human-condition motivation, although we have distinguished the ways in which the two pursue such questions. So, the remaining question is whether invoking the Aristotelian motivation *adds* questions to that class, where adding questions would mean that there are questions within the scope of Aristotelian wonder that are outside the scope of the human-condition concern. It seems that there are such questions, although it is difficult to find a completely convincing example. The reason is one we have already mentioned. Any particular question that might be proposed as an example can be embedded in a hypothetical situation in which it turns out that the question is transformed into a human-condition issue in that particular situation.

However, at least this much can be said: An inquirer motivated *solely* by Aristotelian wonder could easily encounter issues that have nothing to do with human-condition questions. That is, it is possible for certain questions to float in an inquirer's mind on the sole basis of Aristotelian wonder, without any conscious connection to human-condition concerns. Does that possibility really matter? Perhaps one should ask about a different possibility. Are there questions initially pursued out of Aristotelian wonder that could not possibly be pursued later out of a human-condition concern? It seems not. However, perhaps that possibility is not decisive.

Why not? It seems that at any given time in the historical development of philosophical inquiry, there could be questions pursued by some on the basis of Aristotelian wonder, but not pursued by anyone at that time on the basis of human-condition concerns. It seems possible that, at any given time, the class of actively pursued human-condition questions is a proper subset of the set of pursued Aristotelian-wonder questions. However, that possibility does not mean that such a state-of-affairs must persist forever. At all times, there would be at least some questions pursued solely out of Aristotelian wonder, but no such outlying questions can be guaranteed to remain forever outlying. There is always a possibility that any such question eventually will be brought within the scope of the human-condition concern by some inquirer motivated by human-condition concerns. In the ideal state of philosophical unity, there would be a perfect coincidence between the class of questions generated by Aristotelian wonder and the class generated by human-condition concerns.

For theists, this conception of a fluctuating, but ideally stable, state of inquiry should not be surprising. Presumably, theists believe that there is a personal Ground of Being who is causally responsible for all of reality distinct from Himself, and that understanding every aspect of creation is personally relevant for anyone's struggle to pursue the fundamental human-condition question, "How should I live?" Every aspect of creation potentially bears upon that question. The greater one's understanding of creation, the greater the strength of one's theistic motivation to unite one's own finite spirit with the Ground of Being. Hence, for theists the class of Aristotelian-wonder questions is ultimately identical to the class of human-condition questions, although, as we have argued, each of the two motivations pursues those questions in differing ways. Theism provides a basis for the unifying Aristotelian wonder with the human-condition concern.

But what does it mean to single out some worldviews as "systematic"?
We have made a preliminary attempt to characterize the class of questions essentially pursued by philosophical inquiry. In doing so, we argued that the class is generated by two mutually compatible motivations: pursuing human-condition questions and pursuing Aristotelian-wonder questions. However, we began with a proposal to characterize the class of questions essentially pursued by philosophical inquiry in terms of the property, *being a systematic worldview*. How does that property fit into our analysis?

What exactly is a systematic worldview? One question is whether the term "systematic worldview" is redundant. Isn't any worldview necessarily systematic? If so, then the term "systematic worldview" is redundant. But the result of adding "systematic" is not a redundancy. The reason is that there is a sense in which everyone has a worldview, in the sense of having a set of beliefs that guide their choices. As William Hocking observes:

> We are speaking of "beliefs" now in the wide sense in which belief includes all those views about the world by which a man actually guides his actions…We mean by a man's beliefs all those judgments, from certainties or convictions at one extreme to mere impressions at the other, upon which he customarily acts. Beliefs are the opinions a man lives by, as distinct from those he merely entertains: in this sense they constitute his philosophy. And in this sense we can understand Chesterton's remark that "the most practical and important thing about a man is his view of the universe,"—his philosophy.[18]

Everyone has a worldview in that sense, which we will refer to as *minimal* worldviews. Hocking goes on to argue that a proper subset of persons work

---

[18] William Ernest Hocking, *Types of Philosophy* (New York: Charles Scribner's Sons, 1929), 3–4.

toward a worldview in a stronger sense, inasmuch as they engage in an "*examination of belief*, thinking one's way to a well-grounded set of beliefs."[19] We adopt this distinction, but shall offer our own explication of it.[20] We will use the phrase "systematic worldview," for what Hocking called a "well-grounded set of beliefs" that are reached through an "examination of belief." Thus, the term "systematic worldview" is not a redundancy because not every minimal worldview qualifies as a *systematic* worldview.

Because systematic worldviews are a proper subset of minimal worldviews, understanding the former requires first understanding the latter. Minimal worldviews share at least four characteristics. First, they are typically internally inconsistent.[21] Imagine an inquirer who believes the widespread view that all human actions are completely determined by the past states of the universe. Yet that same inquirer will probably be quick to normatively condemn those whose choices conflict with his, presumably on his assumption that they could have chosen otherwise. Or, imagine an inquirer who maintains that there is no objective distinction between right and wrong. She will probably be quick to normatively condemn anyone who disagrees with her as acting immorally.

Second, a minimal worldview will typically not be a *reasoned* set of beliefs. That is, it will typically not be a set of beliefs, each of which has been subjected to a sustained search for epistemic grounds, a search focusing upon both arguments against and arguments for that belief. Imagine an inquirer whose minimal worldview includes the belief that humans have at least some degree of libertarian freedom. Typically, he will not have subjected his belief to a sustained search for epistemic grounds. Thus, even though his belief might be *justifiable*, in the sense that, all things considered, the case for his belief is stronger than the case against it, it is nevertheless not a reasoned belief.

Third, a minimal worldview will typically not be *comprehensive*, in the sense of including beliefs about all human-condition issues. For example, an inquirer's minimal worldview might include a belief about libertarian freedom of will, but not a belief about the mind–body issue, the ultimate nature of the world, or other human-condition issues the inquirer failed to think about.

Fourth, a minimal worldview typically will not be internally ordered, in the sense of not only containing no internal contradictions, but including

---

[19] Hocking, *Types of Philosophy*, 4.
[20] We do not intend to say that Hocking would necessarily disagree with what we are about to say, but only that what we say goes beyond what Hocking explicitly says.
[21] For a famous depiction of an individual with an inconsistent set of beliefs, along with a corresponding inconsistent set of motivations, see Dostoevsky's *Notes from Underground*, trans. Richard Pevear and Larissa Volokhonsky (New York: Vintage, 1993).

beliefs that are entailed by other beliefs in the worldview. For example, a minimal worldview might include a belief in libertarian freedom, and be internally consistent, but lack beliefs about the implications of that belief for, say, the belief that humans can't apprehend universals by means of concepts, or the belief in the existence of a Ground of Being.

By invoking the attribute *being a systematic worldview*, we intend to pick out those worldviews in which all four of these negative features of minimal worldviews are eliminated. A systematic worldview will be internally consistent, reasoned, comprehensive, and internally ordered. Of course, instantiations of that attribute will inevitably come in degrees, falling short of the ideal. Some will have the capacity to go further in the direction of reaching a systematic worldview than others, and even some with the same capacity as some others will fail to actualize their potentialities.

What is the minimum threshold for a worldview that qualifies as systematic? As is usual with such distinctions, the boundary is indeterminate to some extent. Distinguishing between minimal worldviews and systematic worldviews without so qualifying the distinctions is potentially misleading insofar as it suggests the existence of a nonarbitrary line dividing the two categories. Alternative worldviews are best understood as arranged on a spectrum, ranging from a *minimal* to a *systematic* end.

Summary to this point

At the beginning of the chapter, we proposed to explicate the nature of philosophical inquiry as a search for answers to ultimate questions. However, that is not helpful in the absence of an account of ultimate questions. In offering such an account, we took two approaches. First, we offered an *ostensive explication* consisting of a set of paradigmatic examples of the kinds of questions we have in mind. Second, we offered a *general characterization* of the questions in terms of the attribute *being a systematic worldview*. We proposed that the kind of ultimate questions at issue are those that ideally would be pursued by any philosophical inquirer who strives to formulate a systematic worldview, where that worldview is motivated by the two fundamental philosophical motivations: human-condition concern and Aristotelian wonder.

We conclude the preceding discussion with a twofold explication of the nature of philosophical inquiry. On the one hand, it can be understood as the sustained search for answers to the indeterminate set of paradigmatic questions we have ostensively provided. On the other hand, it can also be understood as the sustained search for answers to the questions that would ideally be pursued in any effort to formulate a systematic worldview for oneself.

Additional characteristics of philosophical inquiry

Is that all that can be said about the nature of philosophical inquiry? We think not. We now offer an account of additional characteristics that are essential components of philosophical inquiry.[22]

Philosophical inquirers proceed dialectically

What do we mean by "dialectical"? Imagine an inquirer trying to decide whether to affirm a proposition P. On the one hand, she might eventually choose to follow an authority, whether it be parents, friends, philosophers, scientists, or the culture. We will call such decisions *nondialectical* choices. In contrast, she might decide only after a sustained evaluation of arguments both for and against P. We will call such decisions *dialectical* decisions.

Like many ostensibly categorical distinctions, when more closely examined, this distinction can be resolved into a comparative distinction. Even those most strongly inclined to follow the dictates of an authority may devote at least some of their time to considering, however briefly and superficially, approaches that conflict with that authority. The significant issue is *to what degree* an inquirer engages in dialectical reflection.

The way in which we have drawn this distinction might be construed as suggesting that a seriously dialectical inquirer would never choose to follow an authority. That's not our intention. An inquirer might choose to follow an authority, even after sustained dialectical reflection. Imagine two inquirers pursing the same question. After sustained dialectical reflection, one resolves the question by appealing to a religious authority, while the other resolves it by appealing to an association that is strongly antireligious. Both would qualify as seriously dialectical inquirers in our intended sense.

With this distinction in hand, we maintain that part of the essence of philosophical inquiry is the sustained and systematic dialectical pursuit of issues. A serious inquirer will systematically search for, and evaluate, arguments on both sides of the questions he pursues.

Where should such an inquirer look for opposing considerations and arguments? There are at least three possible sources. First, there is the inquirer's own imagination. Indeed, any would-be philosophical inquirer who cannot imaginatively construct arguments on both sides of any given

---

[22] Given this description of these additional characteristics, readers might wonder why we did not include them in the previous section. We could have, but chose not to in the hope of achieving greater clarity by describing them separately.

issue is not likely to progress very far. Descartes[23] and Wittgenstein[24] are famous examples of inquirers who draw deeply from the first-person source. Second, there are the inquirer's contemporaries, including both those who have chosen the path of systematic philosophical inquiry and those who have not. Third, there are past inquirers who are now accessible only through their writings.

There is a sense in which any philosophical inquirer engaging in sustained dialectical reflection will inevitably focus upon the past with respect to all three of these sources. With respect to the first-person source, he will inevitably focus upon his own past reflections. As to his contemporaries, he will inevitably focus upon theirs. With respect to past inquirers, he will inevitably focus upon the past because those inquirers are no longer living. With respect to past inquirers, the question arises as to how far back an inquirer should go. Our short answer is that no nonarbitrary line that can be drawn. We will return to that issue later.

Philosophical inquirers are aware of their fallibility and of the inevitability of making choices under conditions of uncertainty

Any thoughtful inquirer should continually remind herself that none of her present beliefs, no matter how justifiable or certain they seem to be, are free from all possibility of error. They might turn out to be false, at least in part.[25] On the other hand, she should also continually remind herself that she must nevertheless act on the basis of such potentially fallible beliefs. She should be aware of the continuing inevitability of having to make choices, especially choices of an ultimate kind, in the absence of justified certainty. Philosophers who were keenly aware of the necessity of making such choices include Pascal,[26] Kierkegaard,[27] and James.[28]

---

[23] René Descartes, *Meditations on First Philosophy: With Selections from the Objections and Replies*, ed. and trans. John Cottingham (Cambridge: Cambridge University Press, 1996).

[24] Wittgenstein, *Philosophical Investigations*.

[25] The phrase "at least in part" is intended to address beliefs such as, "I now exist," where an inquirer asserting that sentence might eventually come to reject it on the grounds that the pronoun "I" does not refer to anything, or that the term "exist" has no application in this context.

[26] See Blaise Pascal, *Pensées and Other Writings*, trans. Honor Levi (Oxford: Oxford University Press, 1995).

[27] See Søren Kierkegaard, *Concluding Unscientific Postscript to Philosophical Fragments*, vol. I, ed. and trans. Howard V. Hong and Edna H. Hong (Princeton, NJ: Princeton University Press, 1992).

[28] See his essay, "The Will to Believe," in William James, *The Will to Believe and Other Essays in Popular Philosophy and Human Immortality: Two Supposed Objections to the Doctrine* (New York: Dover, 1956).

Philosophical inquirers do not forget the questions with which they began

In any particular instance, genuine philosophical inquiry begins with an inquirer raising *his own* questions. What would be the point of pursuing questions that are not his own, at least not yet?[29] A beginning inquirer should begin *exactly where he is*. He should not concern himself with whether others agree with, or even understand, his point of conceptual departure, at least not at the beginning.

Of course, if he pursues his own questions in a sustained way, he will likely eventually think of additional questions he also wants to pursue. However, no matter how far out the chain of such successively linked questions might stretch, he should never forget the questions that sparked his initial inquiries. Nor should he forget the importance of eventually linking his later reflections to his original questions, whatever that link might be, for example, concluding that his original questions were nonsensical; or, that they were meaningful, but false; or, that they were meaningful and true, although even then perhaps in a deeper sense than he initially realized.[30]

However, these comments don't apply to situations in which a philosophical inquirer never had her own personal philosophical questions to begin with, but instead made choices for the sole objective of advancing her academic career by pursuing questions that happen to be fashionable in her academic environment. It might be better for such an inquirer to forget about the questions assigned by other professional stalwarts and begin all over again with her *own* questions, unless, of course, she manages to make one of the fashionable questions truly her own. Making an inherited question her own should be accompanied by sustained self-reflection. Suppose that the inherited fashionable question is, "What is the best analysis of the existential quantifier?" She will quickly realize that any mathematically competent inquirer could build an entire academic career expounding the topic in article after article, book after book. That's all fine, but she should ask herself how spending the rest of her life writing about the existential quantifier relates to the personal questions with which she began.

---

[29] Of course, students might be asked to address certain questions as part of a course assignment. This does not preclude them from starting from their own questions, so long as they make the questions their own, as contrasted with simply going through the motions of trying to write an A essay. Even if the essay wins an A, it is no guarantee that the student made the question his own. What we have in mind is *authentic* inquiry.

[30] For an illuminating discussion of the importance of holding in mind one's initial questions, see Kierkegaard's "Introduction" to his *Concluding Unscientific Postscript*, 9–17.

Philosophical inquirers avoid Kierkegaardian infinite parentheses

Kierkegaard introduces the term "infinite parenthesis" in chapter 1 of the *Concluding Unscientific Postscript*. His use of the term is complex, but suggestive. As usual, he offers no definition. He focuses upon the question whether to become a Christian and offers an example of a hypothetical inquirer trying to decide that question for himself. Finding after a long period of reflection that he cannot reach absolute certainty whether Christianity is true, he postpones his decision until he resolves the logically prior question— What *is* Christianity?—reasoning that he can't be reasonably expected to decide the first question without first achieving absolute certainty about the second.[31] Then he reasons that, in order to achieve certainty about the second question, he must (1) undertake a comprehensive examination of the Christian Scriptures in order to ascertain with absolute certainty exactly what they say about Christianity, and (2) ascertain with absolute certainty the epistemic reliability of those Scriptures.[32] As a consequence of this chain of reasoning, the inquirer spends the rest of his life pursuing Scripture studies. As Kierkegaard puts it:

> he takes the work in hand, the enormous studies, to which he himself makes new contributions until his seventieth year. A fortnight before his death, to be exact, he is looking forward to a new publication that will shed light upon an entire aspect of the discussion[33] [and thus dies without ever having returned to the original question with which he began—"Should I become a Christian?"].

We will not try to parse every nuanced step in Kierkegaard's elaborate discussion, nor shall we try to explicate with precision his conception of infinite parentheses. In line with our approach to interpreting past philosophical texts, we shall instead propose a characterization that we think is reasonably suggested by his words.

Imagine an inquirer trying to resolve an issue personally important to her. What kind of issue? One might be inclined to say that the issue could be just one of two kinds: whether to believe some proposition, or whether to engage in some activity. However, invoking this traditional distinction between

---

[31] Kierkegaard's "Introduction," 23.
[32] For both points, see "If Christianity is viewed as a historical document, the important thing is to obtain a completely reliable report of what the Christian doctrine really is." Kierkegaard's "Introduction."
[33] Kierkegaard's "Introduction."

believing and acting is potentially misleading. On the one hand, it might be interpreted as falsely suggesting that a personally important decision to believe a proposition can't carry with it implications for action. On the other, it might be construed as falsely suggesting that choosing a pattern of action can be done without having beliefs about that pattern.

We shall avoid such potentially misleading implications by describing the inquirer as trying to resolve a personally important question that will involve both belief and action. Introducing a word to express this dual aspect, we shall describe the inquirer as trying to resolve the question whether to engage in an *undertaking*, where an undertaking necessarily involves a complex of belief and action. Examples are: marrying, raising children, becoming a Christian, becoming a Buddhist, becoming an atheist, writing a book, becoming a lawyer, or becoming a wine expert.

Now suppose that this inquirer is not absolutely certain about pursuing an undertaking. Suppose further that she is unwilling to make the decision without first achieving absolute certainty that choosing that undertaking would be the *right* decision. What does she mean by the "right" decision? That depends on the context. She might worry that at least one of the presuppositions of the undertaking is false, for example, worrying that at least one of the propositions presupposed by atheism is false. She might worry that she might find the undertaking unfulfilling, for example, worrying that she might find the life of a lawyer anxiety-ridden and morally degrading. She might worry about taking on more responsibility than she can bear, for example, worrying that she might not be able to bear the anxiety of the life of a physician. She might worry that she would fail in the undertaking, for example, worrying that publishing a book would result only in reviewer ridicule and realizing that the reviewers are correct. We will describe our inquirer as seeking absolute certainty that *no* such worries are possible.

So, she treads water, postponing an ultimate resolution of her original question until she completes *preliminary* inquiries. When she has resolved those with absolute certainty, then, and only then, will she be able to resolve her original question with absolute certainty. Indeed, at that point she believes that her original question will be automatically resolved. She will function solely as an innocent bystander, who mercifully does not have to assume the individual responsibility of making a decision under conditions of uncertainty, taking the risk that she might have been mistaken. Thus, she assumes that her ultimate decision will have been *made for her* by preliminary inquiries that are themselves resolved with absolute certainty.

Suppose, further, that she undertakes such preliminary inquiries. However, the longer she pursues them, the more she becomes aware of difficulties springing up in those preliminary inquiries themselves. She resolves to forge ahead anyway, expecting that all such difficulties will eventually be resolved. She spends the rest of her life running on the treadmill of these preliminary inquiries, never able to step off because of her assumption that, so long as even the slimmest shadow of doubt inheres in any of the preliminary inquiries, absolute certainty has not been achieved. So, she eventually dies, never having returned to her original question. In such a case, we shall say that the inquirer has *entered into an infinite parenthesis.*

In that hypothetical, the inquirer dies without ever returning to her original question. However, death is not necessary for the creation of an infinite parenthesis. Sometimes an inquirer's opportunity to return to his original question evaporates before his death. Imagine an inquirer trying to decide whether to marry a particular person and dithering with a set of preliminary questions that themselves trigger a host of preliminary inquiries. What is the essence of marriage, anyway? Should I wait until I get to know this person more fully? Should I undergo two years of psychotherapy in order to make sure that I'm suited for marriage? The open door to marry that person will probably shut long before the inquirer's death. Such inquirers also enter infinite parentheses.

Both of these hypotheticals highlight the fact that our use of "infinite" must be understood in a sense distinct from the "actual" infinity of Cantorian set theory. Infinite parentheses are simply patterns of activity that, if not limited in duration by deliberate choices of the inquirer, will extend indefinitely in time so as to preclude the inquirer from ever resolving his original issue. The only kind of infinity at issue here is the Aristotelian potential infinity, the infinity of pre-Cantorian mathematics.

We shall say that an inquirer confronting an issue she deems personally important *enters into an infinite parenthesis* if (1) she is not able to resolve the issue with absolute certainty; (2) she is not willing to resolve the issue in the absence of absolute certainty; (3) she chooses to pursue one or more preliminary inquiries she assumes will eventually generate absolute certainty in their own right and, thereby, will automatically generate absolute certainty about resolving her original question; and (4) she is mistaken about (2) and (3).[34]

Although the concept of an infinite parenthesis can be applied to an indefinite number of situations, we are concerned only with its application

---

[34] Of course, there are many situations in which inquirers reasonably enter infinite parentheses of a different kind. For example, situations in which an inquirer realizes beforehand that she is engaging in an activity that has no built-in termination point, but is justifiably at ease because doing so does not conflict with any of her other objectives, unlike the cases we are focusing upon. Examples include activities such as trout fishing or studying the history of philosophy for its own sake, without any expectations of using it to advance one's own first-order inquiries.

to philosophy. Philosophical inquirers should avoid infinite parentheses. But how does that recommendation apply in particular cases? How is any inquirer to know when he is confronted with the possibility of entering an infinite parenthesis?

It is difficult to formulate anything even approximating a comprehensive set of criteria, but perhaps we can begin with this suggestion. Imagine struggling for a long time with a personally important philosophical issue. You finally decide to postpone resolving your original issue while you undertake preliminary inquiries, which you believe must be resolved with absolute certainty before resolving your original issue. We suggest that, before pushing ahead with these preliminary inquiries, you think about this question: "Suppose that I never resolve these preliminary inquiries with absolute certainty and, consequently, never resolve my original question. If that happened, would I deeply regret it?" If your answer is affirmative, we suggest you are about to enter an infinite parenthesis.

There are many examples of potential infinite parentheses in philosophical inquiry. Here is just one. Imagine an inquirer who is personally concerned with the question of whether humans are wholly physical, but is still undecided about the answer. She chooses to pursue an undertaking consisting of two projects: (1) resolving the question for herself, and (2) publishing a book defending that resolution. However, she has two continuing concerns. Regarding the first project, she worries that, no matter what resolution she might ultimately reach, she will inevitably reach it in a condition of uncertainty. She fears that she may never achieve a state of self-perceived demonstrative certainty. Regarding the second project, she has two anxieties. First, perhaps no matter what resolution she makes of the first project, she will fail to adequately express and defend it in print. Second, perhaps if she resolves the first project by opposing physicalism, she will be ostracized by take-no-prisoners physicalists.

In order to extinguish these anxieties, she decides to pursue two *preliminary undertakings* she hopes will resolve themselves with absolute certainty and, thereby, automatically resolve her ultimate issue with absolute certainty. She will undertake both a systematic study of neuroscience and a second systematic study of everything significant that has been published on physicalism.

In choosing to pursue these preliminary undertakings, she has just whizzed by the left parenthesis of an infinite parenthesis. She will find that neither undertaking will yield the desired absolute certainty. Neither has a principled stopping point. As for the neuroscience project, she will never find a permanent consensus about the brain's relation to consciousness. There will always be one more contrarian to read. As for the second undertaking, not only will there be no principled stopping point for reading all relevant sources, but even with respect to sources the inquirer has already read, there will be unending uncertainty and debate about, for example, what Aristotle, Kant, or Davidson *really* held, and therefore always one more recent "groundbreaking" interpretation that "must" be read.

Philosophical inquirers draw upon multiple sources, including a priori insights, the inquirers' own intuitions and experiences, the intuitions and experiences of others, and scientific and mathematical inquiries

Philosophical inquiry draws upon several epistemic sources that provide evidence for or against philosophical claims.

A priori *insights*

A priori insights are judgments arising from a cognitive power that functions independently, in a sense, of the powers of sensation, introspection, and memory. We distinguish between *a priori judgments* and *a priori powers*. An *a priori power* is an innate power we have in virtue of being humans. Although learning Chinese is a power acquired after birth, the power to learn languages is innate. Again, although learning to identify instances of the type *being a Shetland pony* is a power acquired after birth, the power to identify instances of types is a power with which we enter the world. There are important relations between these two categories, but we shall focus upon *a priori* judgments.

We begin with examples of judgments that are self-evident in themselves. Once fully understood, they are apprehended as true without an essential appeal to sensory, introspective, or memory experience. Here are a few: (1) the judgment that for any x and y, if x is identical to y, then y is identical to x; (2) the judgment that anything is identical with itself; (3) the judgment that no physical object could be simultaneously black all over and white all over; (4) the judgment that if some Fs are Gs, then some Gs are Fs; (5) the judgment that every natural number has a successor; (6) the judgment that if P entails Q, and if P is true, then Q is true; (7) the judgment that for any property P and any entity E, it is not possible for E to possess both P and not-P at the same time and in the same respect; (8) the judgment that one is presently referring to some particular thing, as opposed to something else; (9) the judgment that being north of a location precludes being south of that location at the same time; and (10) the judgment that 2 + 1 = 3.

There is also a large class of *a priori* judgments that, although not self-evident in their own right, can be deductively derived from self-evident premises. Thus, given the plausible assumption that the Aristotle's First-Figure syllogistic forms are self-evident, his derivations of the forms in the other Figures from the First-Figure forms confer an *a priori* status on those others, even though at least some of them are not be self-evident in their own right.

Third, there are *a priori* judgments made in contexts in which conclusions are deductively drawn from premises that are not self-evident in themselves. For example, there are mathematical axiom systems whose axioms no one claims to be self-evident. Nevertheless, mathematicians will claim that the axioms entail the theorems. In such cases, it is *conditionals* of the form, "The set of axioms A deductively entails Theorem T" that are *a priori*. Assuming for the sake of discussion that the axioms of Zermelo-Fraenkel set theory are not self-evident, mathematicians can still appropriately claim that the *derivations* of the theorems from those axioms are *a priori* conditionals.

Some might be willing to concede the existence of *a priori* judgments, but deny that they play any significant role, at least outside of mathematics. That would be a mistake. Invoking *a priori* judgments can't be avoided altogether. Consider the class of judgments whose *supporting justifications* rely upon *a priori* judgments. For example, the standard proof for the proposition that the square root of two is not a rational number contains as a premise the conditional, "If a natural number, n, is an even number, then n = 2c, for some natural number c." The epistemic justification for that conditional is an *a priori* judgment. Grasping its truth does not require any essential appeal to sensory, introspective, or memory experience.

In addition, many ordinary and scientific judgments depend upon inductive premises of the form, "The fact that there are Fs which are also Gs is evidence for the proposition that all Fs are Gs." Obviously, such evidence is rebuttable and may sometimes confer only a tiny degree of support for the conclusion. Nevertheless, it constitutes at least *some* degree of evidence. The point is that such premises are justifiable on *a priori* grounds.

Arguments are not the only things that often depend upon *a priori* judgments. *Descriptions* often do as well: "Yesterday I drove along the Gallatin River for a few minutes and saw three fishable riffles, one that is two miles north of Big Sky, and two that are about two miles south of Big Sky." Here are some of the *a priori* judgments implicitly embedded in this narrative description: (1) the speaker's judgments that she is referring to certain things, as opposed to others, for example, "Yesterday," "I," "the Gallatin River," "Big Sky"; (2) her judgments instancing the Principle of Identity, "Yesterday," "I," "the Gallatin River," and "Big Sky"; (3) her judgments instancing the Principle of Non-Contradiction, for example, "I drove along the Gallatin River," thereby excluding the possibility that the speaker did not drive along the Gallatin River, and "saw three fishable riffles," thereby excluding the possibility that she did not see three fishable riffles; (4) her judgment that 2 + 1 = 3 ("saw three fishable riffles, one two miles north of Big Sky, and two about two miles south of Big Sky"); and (5) her judgment that being north of a given location excludes the possibility of being south of that same location at the same time, for example, "one is two miles north of the town of Big Sky, and two are about two miles south of Big Sky."

Such examples support our claim that invoking *a priori* judgments is common in both ordinary and scientific *reasoning* and *description*. Even so, there is an additional issue. The pervasive presence of *a priori* judgments in discourse has been explained in more than one way. The traditional explanation is the *rationalist* view. Here is Laurence Bonjour's formulation:

> The central idea of the rationalist view concerning the nature of *a priori* justification is at least initially extremely simple and straightforward: *a priori* justification involves a direct insight (or apparent insight) into the nature and structure of reality—where successful, one whose content is *necessary*, reflecting features and relations that could not fail to obtain.[35]

In contrast, *antirealist* reductive accounts concede the existence of *a priori* judgments, but replace the rationalist account with accounts explaining *a priori* judgments on the basis of sources other than the world, for example, linguistic conventions or relationships between human concepts. According to such reductive accounts, whatever *a priori* judgments reveal, they do not reveal mind-independent reality.[36] It seems that antirealist accounts are favored by a large proportion of analytical philosophers. We shall make no effort to challenge such reductive approaches here. Our present purpose is simply establishing that everyone, whether scientist or not, invokes *a priori* judgments on an everyday basis.

The inquirer's own intuitions and experiences

Another source of philosophical inquiry is the intuitions and experiences of the inquirers themselves. This is controversial. Many reject the claim that it is legitimate for philosophical inquirers to draw upon their own intuitions and experiences. The typical justification for the rejection is that such reliance is merely "subjective," in contrast to the "objective" results of genuine science,

---

35 Laurence Bonjour, *Epistemology: Classic Problems and Contemporary Responses* (Lanham, MD: Littlefield, 2002), 95.
36 For helpful expositions and evaluations of such antirealist accounts, see Bonjour *Epistemology*, chapter 5; Bonjour, *In Defense of Pure Reason*; Roderick M. Chisholm, *Theory of Knowledge*, 2nd ed. (Englewood Cliffs, NJ: Prentice-Hall, 1977), chapter 3.

such as physics and neuroscience. Only the latter qualify as legitimate sources for philosophical inquiry. Listen to Daniel Dennett:

> I declare my starting point to be the objective, materialistic, third-person world of the physical sciences. This is the orthodox choice today in the English-speaking philosophical world ... .[37]

Many share Dennett's view, rejecting the traditional expectation that inquirers attend to their own intuitions and experiences and replacing it with an exclusive reliance upon scientific methods, which they assume reject first-person experiential sources of evidence in favor of third-person experimental results cleansed of every taint of subjective poison.[38]

The consequences are dramatic. For example, the strongest evidence for the existence of consciousness is one's own experience. If reliance upon personal intuition and experience is ruled off-limits, so is this evidence for consciousness. Consequently, as the current physicalist trend shows so clearly, it becomes psychologically easier and easier to stoutly deny the existence of consciousness altogether. (Physicalist: "I've spent an hour studying X's brain fMRI, but haven't seen a trace of X's consciousness.") Our immediate awareness of our own consciousness is simply the product of a mass delusion, foisted upon us by the mythological superstitions embedded in our ordinary language. Of course, no one can consistently maintain the rejection of consciousness, whether in day-to-day life (Physicalist: "I just had an idea for another book."), or even in academic publications (Physicalist: "Take it from me, I know that none of us is conscious.").

---

[37] Daniel C. Dennett, *The Intentional Stance* (Cambridge, MA: MIT Press, 1987), 5.
[38] There are many sources for this point of view. See, for example, James Ladyman and Don Ross with David Spurrett and John Collier, *Everything Must Go: Metaphysics Naturalized* (Oxford: Oxford University Press, 2007), 1: "The aim of this book is to defend a radically naturalistic metaphysics. By this we mean a metaphysics that is motivated exclusively by attempts to unify hypotheses and theories that are taken seriously by contemporary science"; Tim Maudlin, *The Metaphysics Within Physics*, 1:

> The basic idea is simple: metaphysics, insofar as it is concerned with the natural world, can do no better than to reflect on physics. Physical theories provide us with the best handle we have on what there is, and the philosopher's proper task is the interpretation and elucidation of those theories. In particular, when choosing the fundamental posits of one's ontology, one must look to scientific practice rather than to philosophical prejudice.

John Bickle, *Philosophy and Neuroscience: A Ruthlessly Reductive Account* (Dordrecht: Kluwer Academic, 2003), xiii: "this entire book is at bottom an extended argument that higher-level theorists of mind, especially philosophers, should reorient their interest 'down levels' in the neurosciences."

There are many other traditional philosophical issues whose resolutions would be hamstrung if evidentiary appeals to first-person intuitions and experiences were abandoned. Do we have libertarian freedom of will? Is there a personal Ground of Being? Is there agent causality? Does the future already exist? Do we have concepts? Can we apprehend universals? Is there a fundamental conflict in everyone between malice and love? Do our lives have an ultimate metaphysical meaning? Is there beauty? Is there a nonrelative distinction between good and evil? Such questions motivate inquirers to look within, wherever else they might also look. Without recourse to first-person sources of insight and illumination, there is a drastically reduced chance of adequately resolving such issues for oneself. Imagine an inquirer asking whether types exist, in some significant sense. Presumably, at a very early stage she will experimentally focus upon her own mental activities. When she does, it will become at least *prima facie* obvious to her that no conscious moment passes without apprehending things and events as instances of types. Of course, such introspective evidence will probably not be the end of her inquiry, but it is an important first stage, one she should not forget.

Two paragraphs back, we expressed our own first-person suspicion that individuals can't consistently reject consciousness. Let us examine our suspicion more closely by raising a general question about the current pervasive hostility to using first-person intuition and experience as a philosophical source. Can anyone consistently maintain that attitude in his day-to-day life? One way of expressing the question is by asking whether such an approach violates what we will call *Kierkegaard's Principle of Existential Coherence*—the normative principle that if one can't on a daily basis live consistently with a philosophical thesis, one ought to reject the thesis. The term is ours, not Kierkegaard's, but the principle is a constant theme of all his writings. Here is one of his examples:

> A thinker erects a huge building, a system, a system embracing the whole of existence, world history, etc., and if his personal life is considered, to our amazement the appalling and ludicrous discovery is made that he himself does not personally live in this huge, domed palace but in a shed alongside it, or in a doghouse, or at best in the janitor's quarters. Were he to be reminded of this contradiction by a single word, he would be insulted. For he does not fear to be in error if he can only complete the system—with the help of being in error.[39]

---

[39] Søren Kierkegaard, *The Sickness Unto Death: A Christian Psychological Exposition for Upbuilding and Awakening*, ed. and trans. Howard V. Hong and Edna H. Hong (Princeton, NJ: Princeton University Press, 1980), 43–44.

As to the prevailing hostility to first-person experience, the question is whether anyone can consistently maintain it. There are at least three reasons for doubting the possibility.

First, consider the evangelistic zeal with which many scientistic philosophers proclaim their gospel of philosophical denial: no libertarian freedom of will, no metaphysical meaning, no Ground of Being, no consciousness, no nonphysical entities. The evangelical fervor with which they proclaim their denials suggests that they are motivated by their own first-person intuitions and experiences of redemption and fulfillment through science. Their rejection of first-person intuitions and experiences is itself grounded in their own first-person intuitions and experiences, a violation of Kierkegaard's Principle of Existential Coherence.

Second, consider the inevitability of *interpreting* the experimental results of scientific inquiry. Experimental results are what they are, but interpreting them is an unavoidable task that requires invoking the first-person intuitions and experiences of the interpreter, whether she be scientist or philosopher. Witness the controversies over the interpretation of the Stern-Gerlach experiments. Some argue that the experiments must be explained on the basis of the principle that no physical events can be uncaused, whereas others argue that the experiments must be explained on the basis of the principle that some purely physical events are uncaused.[40] The explanation for this controversy is the fact that different interpreters of the experiments bring to their interpretive task their own personal intuitions and experiences regarding causation and its role in the universe.

Third, consider the inevitability for both scientists and philosophers of relying upon their own intuitions and experiences in *thinking up* theories to explain things. Creative ideas about possible theories do not just roll by on cognitive conveyor belts, waiting to be picked up. They require a creative impulse springing from the imaginative powers of inquirers. According to G. Polya:

> The first rule of discovery is to have brains and good luck. The second rule of discovery is to sit tight and wait till you get a bright idea.[41]

According to Serge Lang:

> What distinguishes someone with talent for mathematics from someone without talent is that the first person will be able to discover such

---

[40] See, for example, Daniel F. Styer, *The Strange World of Quantum Mechanics* (Cambridge: Cambridge University Press, 2000).

[41] G. Polya, *How to Solve It: A New Aspect of Mathematical Method*, 2nd ed. (Princeton, NJ: Princeton University Press, 1973), 172.

beautiful formulas and the second person will not. However, everybody is able to plug numbers in the formula once it is written down. That does not take much talent.[42]

According to Henri Poincare:

> Pure analysis puts at our disposal a multitude of procedures whose infallibility it guarantees; it opens to us a thousand different ways on which we can embark in all confidence; we are assured of meeting there no obstacles; but of all these ways, which will lead us most promptly to our goal? Who shall tell us which to choose? We need a faculty which makes us see the end from afar, and intuition is this faculty. It is necessary to the explorer for choosing his route; it is not less so to the one following his trail who wants to know why he chose it. … Thus logic and intuition have each their necessary role. Each is indispensable. Logic, which alone can give certainty, is the instrument of demonstration; intuition is the instrument of invention.[43]

Scientific inquirers' reliance upon their own intuitions and experiences shows itself not only in the creative act of thinking up theories, explanations, and theorems. As Michael Polanyi argues, this inevitable reliance upon "personal knowledge" is an essential part of every aspect of scientific inquiry. Even the activity of confirming a scientific theory involves an infusion of the inquirer's first-person experience:

> There is an even wider area of personal judgment in every verification of a scientific theory. Contrary to current opinion, it is not the case that a proven discrepancy between theoretical predictions and observed data suffices in itself to invalidate a theory. Such discrepancies may often be classed as anomalies. The perturbations of the planetary motions that were observed during 60 years preceding the discovery of Neptune, and which could not be explained by the mutual interaction of the planets, were rightly set aside at the time as anomalies by most astronomers, in the hope that something might eventually turn up to account for them without impairing—or at least not essentially impairing—Newtonian gravitation. Speaking more generally, we may say that there are always some conceivable scruples which scientists

---

[42] Serge Lang, *Basic Mathematics* (New York: Springer-Verlag, 1988), 208.
[43] Henri Poincare, *The Value of Science: Essential Writings of Henri Poincare*, ed. Stephen Jay Gould (New York: Modern Library, 2001), 205–207.

customarily set aside in the process of verifying an exact theory. Such acts of personal judgment form an essential part of science.[44]

The intuitions and experiences of others

In addition to relying upon their own first-person intuitions and experiences, philosophical inquirers also rely upon the experiences of others. One's own first-person intuitions and experiences will never completely overlap with another's. Hence, an inquirer's inquiry can often be helped by paying attention to the first-person intuitions and experiences of others.

Imagine an inquirer who has never had religious experiences, at least none that he recognized as such. Paying attention to the reports of others' religious experiences might motivate him to look more closely at this potential source of insight and perhaps even into self-recognized religious experiences. Similar examples involve others' first-person experiences of music, poetry, literature, scientific and mathematical inquiry, modes of cooperation, marriage, and raising children.

Cases of others' first-person intuitions and experiences can serve as *positive* inducements for an inquirer to pursue activities she might not otherwise have pursued. They can also serve as *negative* inducements for an inquirer to avoid activities she might have otherwise pursued. Witnessing the consequences of another's drug addiction might persuade an inquirer who has never used drugs to infer that drug addiction is not a worthwhile activity. Witnessing another's entanglement in an infinite parenthesis might persuade an inquirer who has never been in one to conclude that it is not a productive way to pursue philosophy. Such negative inducements can serve as a way of avoiding at least some of the effects of being metaphysically compelled to *live life forwards*. As Kierkegaard puts it:

It is quite true what philosophy says: that life must be understood backwards. But then one forgets the other principle: that it must be lived forwards. Which principle, the more one thinks it through, ends exactly with the thought that temporal life can never properly be understood precisely because I can at no instant find complete rest in which to adopt the position: backwards.[45]

---

[44] Michael Polanyi, *Personal Knowledge: Towards a Post-Critical Philosophy* (Chicago: University of Chicago Press, 1962), 20.

[45] Alastair Hannay, ed. and trans., *Søren Kierkegaard: Papers and Journals: A Selection* (London: Penguin, 1996), 161.

Everyone is compelled to live life forward in the sense of having to make choices without certainty about the consequences. However, instead of making choices under conditions of uncertainty and then waiting anxiously to evaluate their consequences, it is sometimes easier to evaluate choices by looking at the consequences of others' choices.[46] If we were all forced to make our own choices without awareness of the consequences of the choices of others, the chasm of uncertainty between *having to live life forward* and *understanding life only backward* would be much wider.

Scientific and mathematical inquiries

Philosophy also focuses upon scientific and mathematical concepts and results. This does not mean that philosophical inquiry is identical to scientific and mathematical inquiry, but it does mean that the modes of inquiry are not mutually exclusive.

Consider the relation between philosophical and scientific inquiry. Since physics is a paradigmatic instance of scientific inquiry, we shall focus upon the relation between philosophy and physics. The distinction between the two modes of inquiry is a function of two essential characteristics of physics inquiry, neither of which is shared by philosophical inquiry. Physics relies upon systematic and controlled empirical experimentation, which, in turn, relies upon mathematical methods whose application presupposes a *quantitative* approach to investigating nature. The experiments of physics yield quantitative results expressible in the language of mathematics. In contrast, philosophy does not engage in experimentation of that kind and does not restrict itself to quantitative analyses. Of course, some philosophers engage in physics, but they do so as physics inquirers.[47]

To be sure, there are introspective experiments that philosophical inquirers sometimes perform, *qua* philosophers. An inquirer evaluating the thesis that humans lack freedom of will might himself try experiencing a lack of freedom of will for, say, 48 hours. If he cannot make it through the test period successfully, he might conclude that the denial of libertarian

---

[46] Unfortunately, many of us often do not choose to do so.

[47] This is how we interpret the recent fashion of "experimental" philosophy. On the one hand, if "experimental" philosophy means interpreting empirical experiments performed by others, then it is nothing more than philosophers have traditionally done in focusing upon the methods and results of science. On the other hand, if "experimental" philosophy means that philosophers are performing, say, physics experiments on their own, then, in that mode of activity, they are functioning as physicists.

freedom is at least pragmatically incoherent. Such experiments, however, do not involve the kind of mathematically sophisticated quantitative analysis intrinsic to physics.

We just argued that physics and philosophy are not identical; there are areas of nonoverlap. However, it doesn't follow that the boundary lines between the two are always obvious. In particular, it doesn't preclude the possibility that some inferential patterns of inquiry can be understood *both* as instances of philosophical inquiry *and* as instances of physics inquiry. There are potential areas of overlap between the two modes of inquiry. First, physics relies essentially upon the principles of deductive and inductive reasoning. However, the formulation and evaluation of neither set of principles falls exclusively within the domain of physics, or exclusively within the domain of any other empirical science, for that matter. On the contrary, the formulation and evaluation of deductive and inductive principles are paradigmatic subjects of philosophical inquiry. They are *topic-neutral*, applying to all types of inquiry, including philosophy itself. Thus, philosophy is a cognitive source for the principles of inference upon which all other modes of inquiry rely. There is at least one overlap between philosophy and physics.

Second, although quantitative empirical experimentation is not itself an essential component of philosophical inquiry, *thinking up and designing* such experimentation is an activity that invokes philosophical considerations, at least in part. Of course, this initial phase also typically uses mathematical methods. However, the reliance upon mathematics does not preclude the possibility that the initial phase is also grounded upon philosophical considerations. *Mathematics can be used philosophically.*

Third, interpreting the quantitative results of experiments is a process that typically invokes philosophical considerations, at least in part. Although this post-experiment phase also typically uses mathematical methods, that doesn't preclude using philosophical methods. Again, mathematics can be used philosophically.

What about the relation between philosophy and pure mathematics? The observations just made about the relationship between philosophy and physics apply to this relationship as well. Like physics, mathematics relies upon principles of deductive logic, principles that are not within the exclusive province of mathematics. Rather, they are topic-neutral principles that, although applying to all modes of inquiry, fall paradigmatically within the scope of philosophy, the scope of which includes all other patterns of inquiry as potential objects-of-focus.

In addition, as Polya has argued, even pure mathematical inquiry uses principles of patterns of inductive inference as a way of discovering theorems.[48] Like deductive logic, the principles of inductive logic are not the exclusive property of pure mathematical inquiry, but rather, topic-neutral principles applying to all modes of inquiry, including the modes of deductive inquiry used in pure mathematics.

We have argued that physics is infused with philosophical inquiry in two respects: in the phase of *thinking up* experiments with which to test theories and in the phase of *interpreting* the results of those experiments. This can be expressed in terms of the metaphor of the *poles* of a physics experiment. One can think of the experiment as having two poles, one the creative and inventive activity of designing the experiment in the first place, the other the creative activity of interpreting its result. The *core* separating the two poles is the experiment itself. Often both poles are anchored, at least partially, in philosophical considerations.

A similar metaphor applies to mathematics. Of course, because pure mathematics does not involve physical experimentation, we cannot appropriately speak of the "poles" of a core consisting of an empirical experiment. However, we can appropriately talk about the *mathematical core* of an instance of mathematical inquiry as being a *mathematical proof* and then go on to refer to the *poles* of that proof core.

On the one hand, there is the creative pole of thinking up a proof in the first place. As in the case of physics, often that pole is embedded, at least partially, in philosophical considerations. Consider Frege's (failed) attempt to derive arithmetic from logic. The derivations themselves are products of pure mathematical inquiry, but the motivations and ideas for those derivations articulated in his earlier work, *The Foundations of Arithmetic*, are philosophical.

On the other hand, there is the creative pole of interpreting the concepts and theorems of pure mathematical inquiry. Again, as in the case of physics, that pole is anchored, at least partially, in philosophical considerations. Interpreting such concepts and theorems often involves philosophical inquiry. Frege's definition of the natural numbers raises the question whether his definition is a philosophically adequate analysis of the attribute, *being a natural number*. Cantor's definitions and derivations of the infinite cardinals and ordinals raise philosophical questions, such as whether the infinite ordinal $\omega + \omega$ exists, and, if so, in what sense.[49]

---

[48] Polya, *How to Solve It*.
[49] Helpful accounts of the infinite cardinal and ordinal numbers can be found in Abraham Fraenkel, *Abstract Set Theory*, 3rd ed. (Amsterdam: North-Holland, 1968); Joseph Breuer, *Introduction to the Theory of Sets* (Mineola, NY: Dover, 2006); and Paul Halmos, *Naive Set Theory* (New York: Springer-Verlag, 1974).

These observations presuppose discernible points at which scientific and mathematical inquiries involve philosophical inquiry. How can one recognize such points? Here is a suggestion. In physics, once questions are raised that go beyond the details of an experiment and its quantitative results, philosophical inquiry has been potentially invoked. Similarly, in mathematics, once questions are raised that go beyond the details of a proof or derivation, philosophical inquiry has again been potentially invoked. We shall later take up this issue in greater detail, along with others mentioned in this section.

Philosophical inquirers use the methods of argument, explanation, distinction, definition, and generalization in their own inquiries—in addition, they formulate guiding principles for using those methods

One of the essential characteristics of philosophy is its systematic use of five methods—argument, explanation, distinction, definition, and generalization. Like everyone else, philosophers make assertions, but unlike many, they support their assertions with arguments, explanations, distinctions, definitions, and generalizations.

Clarifications of terms are in order. An *argument* is a set of propositions marshaled to support the claim *that* a proposition is true. There are two categories of arguments: (1) those intended to be deductively valid, and (2) those intended to be inductively valid. What precisely it is to be deductively valid is controversial. According to the standard account, an argument is deductively valid if and only if it is not possible for the premises to be true and the conclusion false. However, the standard account is debatable. Everyone agrees with the "only if" component, but not everyone agrees with the "if" component. That is, everyone agrees that the impossibility of the premises being true and the conclusion false is a necessary condition for deductive validity, but not everyone agrees that it is also a sufficient condition. Among the dissidents are the relevance logicians who, following Aristotle, argue for an additional requirement of some kind of semantic connection between premises and conclusion serving to make the conclusion follow *from, or by means of,* the premises. Such a connection is lacking in any argument qualifying as deductively valid simply because its premises are mutually inconsistent.

Arguments intended to be only *inductively* valid do not claim that it is impossible for the premises to be true and the conclusion false. They claim only that the premises provide some degree of support for the conclusion. There are several species of inductive arguments—generalizations based upon finite sets of data, arguments based upon sensory perceptions, arguments by analogy, inferences to the best explanation, and many others.

An *explanation* is a set of propositions marshaled to show *why* a proposition is true, where it is assumed that the proposition is true. A more modest form is a set of propositions marshaled to show *why* a proposition *would* be true if it *were* true, where it is not assumed that the proposition is true. Some explanations purport to be deductively valid. Others claim just inductive validity.

A *distinction* is the product of an act of distinguishing things that tend to be merged together in people's thinking, but should not be. A typical case is distinguishing senses of a linguistic expression. Many philosophers have noted that "thought" is ambiguous as between an act of thinking and the object of that act. Similarly, following Aristotle, many have distinguished different senses of "exists," arguing that, say, what it means to assert that oak trees exist is different from what it means to say that attributes and relations exist, and that both of those senses are different from what it means to say that numbers exist.

A *definition* is an analysis of the nature of something, whether it be an attribute, relation, or a particular. We have in mind what are traditionally called "real" definitions, as opposed to "linguistic" definitions. As usually understood, linguistic definitions express only a decision to use words in certain ways, rather than others. They are not intended to assert anything about the nonlinguistic realm. In contrast, real definitions purport to assert something about the nonlinguistic realm itself. Real definitions come in two forms. There are definitions purporting to explicate only part of the essence of something, and there are definitions purporting to explicate the entire essence of something.

As for generalizations, we focus upon generalizing terms and sentences, understood as linguistic types. Since on the mind's side of the cognitive relation between thinker and world, terms can be understood as expressing mental concepts and sentences as expressing mental judgments, one can also talk about generalizing concepts and judgments, but that will not be our focus.

It is necessary to discuss generalizing both terms and sentences. Since sentences are composed at least partially of terms, in order to discuss generalizing sentences, one must also discuss generalizing terms. On the other hand, since the only reasonable purpose of generalizing terms is thinking about how generalized terms function in sentential contexts, generalizing terms cannot be an end-in-itself. One must go on to consider sentential contexts in which generalized terms occur as constituents.

Generalizing a term involves replacing a term with a greater possible extension than the extension of the term being replaced. In general, it also requires replacing the intension of the original term with a different intension.

Generalizing a sentence involves formulating a second sentence that generalizes the intended-subject term of the original sentence, generalizes the intended-predicate-attribute term of the original sentence, or both. The intended-subject term of a sentence is the linguistic item a speaker uttering the sentence uses to refer to whatever the speaker is talking about. The intended-predicate attribute term of a sentence is the linguistic item a speaker uses to predicate something of the thing the speaker is talking about. Contrary to what might be thought, this intentional analysis is adequate for relational assertions, as well as nonrelational subject–predicate assertions.[50]

There are at least two kinds of contexts in which one might want to generalize sentences—argumentative contexts and definitional contexts. With respect to argumentative contexts, there are constructive uses and destructive uses. In constructive uses, one asserts that the original sentence is true and then argues as follows: If the original sentence were true, then its generalization would be true. The original sentence is true. Hence, its generalization is true. The underlying pattern of reasoning is *modus ponens*: If P were true, then Q would be true. P is true. Hence, Q is true. In destructive uses, one asserts that the original sentence is false and then argues in support of that assertion as follows: If the original sentence were true, then its generalization would be true. The generalization of the original sentence is false. Hence, the original sentence is false. The underlying pattern of reasoning is *modus tollens*: If P were true, then Q would be true. Q is false. Hence, P is false. With respect to definitional contexts, one selects a definition and then generalizes both the intended-subject term and the intended-predicate-attribute term.[51]

We are not suggesting that philosophers are the *only* inquirers who use these methods. Inquirers in other practices do so as well—mathematics, physics, engineering, biology, literary criticism, history, psychology, economics, and medicine, to mention just a few. Indeed, there is an extended sense in which even works of literature and art *suggest* (as contrasted with *assert*) arguments, explanations, distinctions, definitions, and generalizations. Recall Dostoevsky's *Crime and Punishment*, Bach's *Mass in B-Minor*, Shakespeare's *King Lear*, or Yeats's *The Second Coming*. Using these methods does not uniquely characterize philosophy.

---

[50] For details, see our article, "Mindful Logic: How to Resolve Some Paradoxes of Identity," *Notre Dame Journal of Formal Logic* 29 (1988): 246–266.

[51] A good way to begin thinking about generalizing propositions is by reading Aristotle's *Topics*, Bk.1, Ch.14 in *The Complete Works of Aristotle*, vol. 1, ed. Jonathan Barnes, transl W.A. Pickard-Cambridge (Princeton: Princeton University Press, 1984); and his *Sophistical Refutations*, chapters 5 and 25, in *The Complete Works of Aristotle*, vol. 1, ed. Jonathan Barnes, trans. W.A. Pickard-Cambridge (Princeton: Princeton University Press, 1984).

Nevertheless, these methods are essential to philosophical inquiry. What distinguishes philosophy from other practices using the same methods is that philosophers use them in the pursuit of philosophically ultimate questions. That should not be surprising. Using mathematics is essential to the practice of physics, but it is not unique to physics. Physics can be distinguished from other disciplines that also use mathematics on the ground that physicists use mathematics as a means of pursing a distinctive class of questions about the physical realm.

Even within the philosophical tradition, there is a jungle-like variety of ways of formulating arguments, explanations, distinctions, definitions, and generalizations. At one end of the spectrum, there are those who prefer expressing them in the language of classical first-order quantification theory, for example, arguments expressed with numbered premises and statements of the logical rules justifying each line of an inference from a set of premises. At the other end, there are those who, like Augustine, Montaigne, Pascal, Nietzsche, Kierkegaard, and William James, express them in less-precise terms that are often more difficult to interpret, but also sometimes more suggestively illuminating than more rigorously formulated offerings. This is not to say that expressive obscurity is entirely on the side of the "nonanalytic" tradition. Anyone who has ever struggled to explicate the *exact* structure of an argument of, say, Wittgenstein, Quine, Sellars, or Davidson, should agree. In any case, this unruly tangle of historical variations in formulating arguments, explanations, distinctions, definitions, and generalizations does not falsify our claim that philosophy is essentially characterized by the systematic and sustained use of these methods. Philosophy essentially uses them, although there is a broad range of ways of using them.

However, philosophical inquirers do not just *use* these methods. They also make sustained and systematic efforts to formulate *guiding principles* for their use. Aristotle does not just use these methods in his own inquiries; he also proposes elaborate guiding principles for their use. The same is true for many others, for example, Bolzano, Husserl, Frege, Peirce, Russell, Carnap, and Quine. However, as with using these methods, philosophy is not the only practice that formulates guiding principles for their use. Mathematics and physics illustrate the point. Nevertheless, there is something distinctive about philosophy's project. The efforts of other disciplines are topic-specific, focusing upon their own particular subject matters. Philosophical efforts tend to be topic-neutral in the sense of focusing upon guiding principles applying to all subject matters.

3

Arguments for Taking Past Philosophers Seriously

Introduction: The distinction between direct and indirect arguments for a thesis

In this chapter we propose arguments supporting our thesis that studying past philosophical sources is an excellent means of promoting one's own first-order philosophical inquiries. Two types of arguments can be made in support of any given thesis. First, there are arguments intended to support it *directly*, insofar as they are formulated *without detouring* through arguments intended to refute the thesis. Second, there are arguments intended to support the thesis *indirectly*, insofar as they are formulated *precisely by detouring* through arguments intended to refute it.

Aquinas's procedure in the *Summa Theologica* illustrates the distinction. In any given article he proceeds in phases. In the first phase, he states an issue. In the second, he presents objections to the resolution of the issue he will ultimately propose in the third phase. In the third phase, he presents his own resolution, without reference to the objections presented in the second phase. This phase consists of *direct* supporting arguments for his thesis. In the fourth phase, he responds to each of the objections stated in the second phase with additional arguments. This phase consists of *indirect* supporting arguments for it.

There is a sense in which this distinction is not stable. Given any thesis, any supporting argument can be formulated either directly or indirectly, depending on the proponent's argumentative strategy. On the other hand, there is also a sense in which the distinction *is* stable. Given any particular formulation of a supporting argument, the question whether it supports its thesis directly or indirectly is determinately resolvable. Either it is formulated by detouring through arguments opposing the thesis, or it is not. If it is not, it directly supports the thesis. If it is, it indirectly supports it.

How does this distinction apply here? In this chapter, we propose *direct* supporting arguments for Thesis T—that investigating past sources of philosophical inquiry is an excellent means of promoting one's own first-order philosophical inquiries. These arguments are based on the analysis of philosophical inquiry proposed in Chapter 2 and, accordingly, are formulated without detouring through arguments opposing Thesis T. In contrast, in Chapters 4, 5, and 6 we shall propose *indirect* supporting arguments for Thesis T that are formulated in response to arguments opposing Thesis T.

Practical arguments

Preliminary clarification of the nature of practical arguments

We shall express both the direct and indirect arguments for Thesis T in the form of *practical arguments*. Practical arguments are *normative* arguments, arguments for conclusions intended to guide choices. In every conscious moment everyone is confronted with choice situations that instantiate the fundamental human-condition question, "What should I do with my time?" Practical arguments are responses to that question. In any given choice situation, some alternatives are better than others. Practical arguments are used because people want to make good choices. As we will see, such arguments may be directed to oneself, to others, or to both.

Accordingly, practical arguments can be characterized as arguments whose conclusions contain *normative linguistic constituents*, such as, "ought to," "should," "a good reason for," "a conclusive reason for," "permissible," "good," and "preferable."[1] This short list is not a definition, but only a semantic gesture toward a *class* of arguments. However, though only a gesture, it partially illuminates the nature of practical arguments. Their conclusions contain such normative expressions because they have the primary function of *guiding human choices*.

---

[1] Practical arguments are often distinguished from *theoretical* arguments. The usual bases for that distinction are the claims (1) that whereas practical arguments purport to guide *actions*, theoretical arguments purport to guide *beliefs*; and (2) that actions are distinct from beliefs. According to this approach, the conclusions of theoretical arguments use only verbs such as "is true," "is not true," without normative qualifiers, in contrast to the conclusions of practical arguments. However, the distinction drawn in this way might mislead. A belief accepted as a consequence of accepting a "theoretical" argument is itself an action of a certain kind—a mental action. Thus, at best, this way of distinguishing between "practical" and "theoretical" arguments is only a distinction of species falling under an overarching genus of "practical" arguments, understood in a broader sense. This conclusion is further supported by the fact that the conclusions of even "practical" arguments, as customarily understood, can be formulated trivially with locutions such as, "It is true that … ought to be done". Similarly, the conclusions of "theoretical" arguments, as customarily understood, can also be formulated in terms such as, "One ought to believe that … is true". Indeed, even without any such explicit reformulation, any "theoretical" argument can be appropriately understood as implicitly recommending an act of belief. However, we refrain from taking up this difficult issue here.

We formulate our arguments for Thesis T as practical arguments because Thesis T is itself normative. Hence, arguments supporting Thesis T should have normative conclusions. However, although reasonable, this approach faces difficulties of its own. There are long-standing controversies about both the logical structure and the logical force of practical arguments.[2] A resolution of those controversies is important, but we do not have room to take up such controversies here. We shall articulate our conception of practical arguments without comparing and contrasting it with alternatives.

A minimal condition for being a practical argument

A *minimal* condition for an argument to be a practical argument is having a conclusion containing at least one normative expression. However, since many differing practical argument forms satisfy that condition, it cannot by itself serve to sort the entire class of practical arguments into illuminating subclasses. The class is conceptually unruly, capable of being sorted in an indefinite variety of ways. For example, practical arguments can be sorted on the basis of the number of premises. They can be sorted on the basis of whether their premises contain at least one normative expression. Even within the class of practical arguments whose premises contain at least one normative expression, subclasses can be distinguished on the basis of the types of normative expressions used, to mention just a few examples. Given that the minimal condition provides no basis for any such alternative sorting methods, how should the class of practical arguments be sorted? Among several possibilities, we shall focus upon two.

---

[2]   In support of this claim, selecting titles at random, readers might look into Garrett Cullity and Berys Gaut, eds., *Ethics and Practical Reason* (Oxford: Clarendon, 1997); Joseph Raz, *Practical Reason and Norms* (Princeton, NJ: Princeton University Press, 1990); Robert Audi, *Practical Reasoning and Ethical Decision* (London: Routledge-Taylor and Francis, 2006); J. David Velleman, *The Possibility of Practical Reason* (Oxford: Clarendon, 2000); Georg Henrik Von Wright, *Practical Reason* (Ithaca, NY: Cornell University Press, 1983); Joseph Raz, ed., *Practical Reasoning* (Oxford: Oxford University Press, 1978); Elijah Millgram, *Practical Induction* (Cambridge, MA: Harvard University Press, 1997); Michael E. Bratman, *Intentions, Plans, and Practical Reason* (Cambridge, MA: Harvard University Press, 1987); R.M. Hare, *Practical Inferences* (London: Macmillan, 1971); Henry S. Richardson, *Practical Reasoning About Final Ends* (Cambridge: Cambridge University Press, 1994); Nicholas Rescher, *Pascal's Wager: A Study of Practical Reasoning in Philosophical Theology* (Notre Dame: University of Notre Dame Press, 1985); Hector-Neri Castaneda, *The Structure of Morality* (Springfield, IL: Charles C. Thomas, 1974); William James, *The Will to Believe and Other Essays in Popular Philosophy and Human Immortality: Two Supposed Objections to the Doctrine* (New York: Dover, 1956); Martin Peterson, *An Introduction to Decision Theory* (Cambridge: Cambridge University Press, 2009). We will not even begin to cite relevant sources preceding the twentieth century, for example, Plato, Aristotle, Aquinas, Pascal, Hume, Kant, and Kierkegaard.

Sorting on the basis of the classes to which they are addressed

The first method distinguishes between the classes of persons to whom practical arguments are *addressed*. Given a particular practical argument, we shall call the addressed class the *intended-recipient class*, which can be identified by asking the argument's proponent to describe the class of persons to whom she is directing her argument.

We distinguish three cases, without purporting to exhaust the alternatives. Given an argument satisfying our minimal criterion, the proponent may intend to direct her argument to: (1) herself, in which case the intended-recipient class contains just one member; (2) a proper subset of all persons, which may or may not include the proponent; or (3) everyone, including the proponent. The availability of these three alternatives suggests prefacing every practical argument with an address heading of the general form: *Addressed to: The class X*, where *X* is a variable whose substitutions are descriptions of intended-recipient classes.

Exclusively self-directed practical arguments

The most fundamental practical arguments are those one adopts for one's own choices. We shall call them *exclusively self-directed practical arguments*. In every moment of conscious life, each of us is confronted with alternative courses of action. Choices must be made. They are made upon the basis of rationales, which can be expressed in the form of practical arguments. For example, an inquirer interested in the concept of essence might accept a practical argument that concludes that anyone investigating the concept of essence should study Aristotle's *Metaphysics*, on the ground that Aristotle's account, although difficult, is one of the most profound.

Some might point out that motivating considerations are often chosen on a level of consciousness that is not fully explicit. We agree. We also acknowledge that bringing such motivating considerations to full consciousness is important, even crucial. But that does not negate the fact that practical arguments are invoked continuously by each of us, on some level of consciousness.

Selectively directed practical arguments

The second category includes all, and only all, those arguments intended to guide the choices of at least one person other than the proponent herself (but not everyone), and may or may not include her own choices. We shall call them *selectively directed practical arguments*. Imagine that A asks B for advice about a choice situation that A must resolve, and B directs a practical argument addressed to only A. The intended-recipient class would include just A. Alternatively, suppose that B discovers a method for solving a significant class of mathematical problems and publishes her method in a mathematical journal. The intended-recipient class would include an indefinite number of members (but not the class of everyone, since not everyone practices mathematics). The question of whether B directs the argument to herself, as well, would depend upon the context. Perhaps she recently abandoned mathematics, in which case she would not direct the argument to herself. On the other hand, if she is still mathematically active, she would include herself within the argument's intended scope.

Universal practical arguments

Universal practical arguments are directed to everyone, including the proponents themselves. Imagine a theist arguing that everyone ought to pursue the objective of spiritual union with God. Then imagine an atheist arguing that no one should pursue the theist's objective. Both arguments qualify as universal practical arguments.

Sorting practical arguments on the basis of the different types of arguments that could be directed to a given intended-recipient class

The second method of sorting practical arguments reverses the first method. The first method starts with a given practical argument and then moves on to distinguish the possible intended-recipient classes. The second method starts with a given intended-recipient class and then moves on to distinguish between the different kinds of practical arguments that might be addressed to that class. Thus, we are now using the term "intended-recipient class" in two ways, depending upon whether the sorting analysis begins with a given practical argument or with a given intended-recipient class.

The second method sorts practical arguments by distinguishing *conditional* from *unconditional* practical arguments.[3] This is a distinction between two kinds of *intended normative force* a practical argument could have. If the intended normative force is conditional, we shall call it a *conditional* practical argument. If the intended normative force is unconditional, we shall call it an *unconditional* practical argument.

---

[3] We choose to use the dichotomy *conditional/unconditional* rather than the traditional dichotomy, *hypothetical/categorical*, because the latter phrasing does not explicitly bring out the necessary incompatibility of the pairs.

Conditional practical arguments

Recall that applying the conditional/unconditional distinction presupposes an antecedent fixing of an intended-recipient class. In offering general schematic examples, we shall refer to the given intended-recipient class by the variable *X*, which is replaceable in any particular context by a specific class description.

It helps to understand the nature of conditional practical *arguments* by beginning with a subclass of the class of conditional *propositions*. Conditional propositions have the general form, *If P then Q.* P is the *antecedent* of the conditional, and Q is its *consequent.* The subclass of the class of conditional propositions on which we focus is the subclass of *normative* conditional propositions. What are they?

Imagine advising someone who wants to accomplish objective O. You could express your advice in a conditional proposition of the form: "If anyone wants to accomplish objective O, then she/he ought to perform action M." Conditionals instantiating that form are normative conditionals because they contain a normative term in their consequents. Although normative conditionals are not themselves arguments, they can be converted into arguments. Consider the following conversion of that normative conditional:

Addressed to: All members of the class X.

[1] Assume that you want to accomplish objective O.
[2] Performing action M is a necessary means for accomplishing O.
[3] Hence, you ought to perform action M.

Although in this example we used the terms "necessary means" and "ought," we don't intend to suggest that these terms are necessary constituents of all conditional practical arguments. Other terms may be used, depending upon the proponent's intent. Consider an alternative formulation:

Addressed to: Members of the class X.

[1] Assume that you want to accomplish objective O.
[2] Performing action M is a useful means of accomplishing O.
[3] Hence, you would have a good reason for performing action M.

Of course, making either of these argument forms determinate for a specific context would require substituting class descriptions for the variables.

Note five things: First, do not be misled by the unconditional form of the conclusions of the argument forms. They are *conditioned upon hypothetical assumptions*—that at least some of the persons addressed "want" to accomplish objective O. Considered as wholes, the argument forms are conditional forms. Those familiar with Conditional-Proof argument patterns in natural deduction systems will recognize the pattern, although, to keep things simple, we will not bother to "discharge" the assumptions.

Second, the always-present possibility of converting normative conditional propositions into conditional practical arguments is based on the fact that the latter are *supporting arguments* for their corresponding normative conditionals.

Third, the sense in which normative conditional *propositions* are conditional is related to the sense in which conditional practical *arguments* are conditional. Consider the class of normative conditional *propositions*. As just noted, their general structure is illustrated by the following form: *If anyone wants to accomplish objective O, then she/he ought to perform action M*, where "ought to" can be replaced by any other appropriate normative phrase, for example, "have an excellent reason for." By their terms, propositions instantiating such forms apply to only those who satisfy the *antecedent* condition of wanting to accomplish objective O. So, the applicability of the normative *consequent* of any such conditional proposition is conditioned upon satisfying the proposition's antecedent condition—wanting to accomplish O.

Now, consider the class of conditional practical *arguments*. Their conclusions are normative propositions, as are their corresponding normative conditional propositions. Further, just as the consequents of those corresponding normative conditional propositions apply to only those satisfying their antecedents— wanting to accomplish objective O—the conclusions of the corresponding conditional practical arguments apply to only those satisfying the argument's first premise—wanting to accomplish objective O. Consequently, just because an individual belongs to an intended-recipient class X, it does not follow that she need concern herself conditional practical arguments directed to members of X. As long as she does not satisfy the hypothetical assumption of those arguments, she is outside its intended normative boundaries.[4] It follows that there is a sense in which conditional practical arguments are "directed" to all members of their intended-recipient classes and a sense in which they are not. On the one hand, their "address lines" are directed to all members of the intended class, which simply means that the proponents intend that all members be made aware of the argument. But, on the other hand, the proponents intend their substantive arguments be *action-guiding* only for those members of the class who "want" to pursue the posited objective, and,

---

[4]   Of course, in making this observation, we are assuming that the condition of wanting to accomplish objective O has not been built into the very description of the intended-recipient class. Thus, if the intended-recipient class is described as, "All those who want to accomplish objective O," then every member of *that* class would necessarily be within the scope of both the normative conditional and its corresponding conditional practical argument.

as the proponents realize, that class will most likely be only a proper subset of the whole class. If they intend their argument to be action-guiding for the entire class, they should use an *unconditional* argument form, which will be discussed shortly.

Fourth, recall that the two examples of general forms of practical arguments share as their first premises the very modest: "Assume that you want to accomplish objective O." The proposition contains no suggestion that there is anything normatively objectionable about either wanting to accomplish O or not wanting to accomplish O. Conditional practical arguments take no normative position about their objectives' normative status. They present objectives in a purely take-it-or-leave-it fashion, with no normative strings attached. We shall say that conditional practical arguments present their posited objectives in a *normatively neutral way*.

Conditional practical arguments can be misused by positing objectives that are not normatively neutral. Consider the premise, "Assume that you want to murder someone," or the premise, "Assume that you want to avoid being a coward." Such examples show that it is not appropriate for proponents of conditional practical arguments to use a conditional form unless they believe that their posited objectives do not raise normative issues. Of course, even though it is logically inappropriate, some will inevitably misuse the form, which can happen in either of two ways: bad faith or ignorance. In either case, it behooves those addressed by conditional practical arguments to evaluate for themselves the proponents' claims that the posited objectives are normatively neutral.

Fifth, neither of the forms of conditional practical arguments is deductively valid, as stated. We express the forms in a way that we think adequately represents how such arguments are typically formulated in ordinary discourse. We are not suggesting that all conditional practical arguments, much less all practical arguments, must be formulated in deductively invalid patterns. Indeed, deductively valid patterns are often preferable, especially in philosophical contexts.

Unconditional practical arguments

The second class of practical arguments is the class of *unconditional* practical arguments. However, instead of beginning with normative *conditional* propositions, as we did with respect to conditional practical arguments, we now begin with *unconditional* normative propositions. What are they?

Imagine advising a class of intended recipients in unconditional normative terms, for example, "You ought to accomplish objective O." Like conditional normative propositions, this is a normative proposition in virtue of containing a normative term. However, in contrast to conditional normative propositions, it is an *unconditional* normative proposition, in the sense that it does not contain an antecedent that identifies a proper subset of the intended class, such as, "if you want to accomplish objective O, then ...." Suppose that you believe that performing action M is a necessary means for accomplishing O. Then your unconditional normative proposition could be converted into a corresponding practical argument of the following form:

Addressed to: Members of the class X.

[1] You ought to accomplish objective O.
[2] Performing action M is a necessary means for accomplishing O.
[3] Hence, you ought to perform action M.

As we mentioned in relation to conditional practical arguments, in offering this example of a general form, we are not suggesting that "ought to" and "necessary means" must be constituents of all unconditional practical arguments. Other terms are admissible. For example,

Addressed to: Members of the class X.

[1] You have an excellent reason for accomplishing objective O.
[2] Performing action M is a useful means of accomplishing O.
[3] Hence, you have an excellent reason for performing action M.

Unconditional argument forms and the conditional argument forms discussed earlier differ in two ways. First, in contrast to conditional practical arguments, unconditional practical arguments do not contain first premises that assume that *only some* members of the intended class might *want* to accomplish O. Rather, they make a recommendation to all members of X, regardless of whether they want to pursue O.

Second, in contrast to conditional practical arguments, unconditional practical arguments carry a *normative* implication that members of X would be *blameworthy* if they did not pursue O. Asserting that the members of the intended-recipient class X *ought* to accomplish O, or *have a good reason* to accomplish O, and so on, implies that they would be blameworthy if they chose not to pursue O.

Why do we need both methods of sorting practical arguments?: The two senses of "conditional"

We proposed two methods of sorting practical arguments: (1) sorting them based on the classes of persons to which they are addressed, and (2) sorting them based on the kinds of practical arguments directed to those classes. Some might ask why both methods are needed. For example, why isn't it sufficient to use just the distinction between conditional and unconditional practical arguments?

Using only a conditional/unconditional distinction would create ambiguities. Imagine directing a practical argument to the entire class of lawyers and expressing your argument in an unconditional form. If one were limited to using only the distinction between conditional and unconditional practical arguments, the analysis of the structure of your argument would be unclear. On the one hand, it could be analyzed as an unconditional practical argument because it is expressed in an unconditional form. On the other hand, it also could be analyzed as a conditional practical argument because it is addressed to the class of lawyers, which is only a proper subset of all persons. Using both distinctions avoids such potential ambiguities.

Using both distinctions also enables a further distinction between two senses of "conditional." One sense grounds the distinctions between alternative intended-recipient classes. The other grounds the distinction between conditional and unconditional practical arguments. Invoking both senses, we can intelligibly say that a practical argument expressed in an unconditional form and addressed to everyone is an argument belonging to that subclass of practical arguments possessing the highest-possible degree of *being unconditional*.

The determination of which distinction to apply first in the analysis of a particular practical argument context is a function of the nature of the context. Given an antecedently fixed practical argument, apply the intended-recipient class distinctions in order to identify the intended-recipient class. Given an antecedently fixed intended-recipient class, apply the conditional/unconditional distinction in order to identify the type of practical argument.

How do these two distinctions apply to our project?

All the practical arguments for Thesis T we propose are directed to the intended-recipient class: *Those who are inclined to engage in philosophical inquiry*. So, our arguments are conditional in one of the two senses we just distinguished—they are not directed to everyone. On the other hand, they are not conditional in the other sense. Having fixed that intended-recipient class, we formulate all our practical arguments in unconditional form.

What do we mean by referring to "those who are inclined to engage in philosophical inquiry"?

Predictably, we include within the scope of "those who are inclined to engage in philosophical inquiry" academics already engaged in philosophical inquiry. We also include anyone who is inclined toward philosophical inquiry, whatever her occupational situation.

Of course, our specified scope generates a large and unruly class, whose boundaries are somewhat indeterminate. What exactly is it to be inclined to pursue philosophical inquiry? We concede the term's vagueness, but aside from the abstract discourse of pure mathematics or physics, terms that are not vague to some degree are difficult to find. Ultimately, we appeal to readers' self-appraisals. We encourage anyone who experiences even occasional inclinations to pursue philosophical inquiry to regard himself as belonging to our intended-recipient class, at least for the time being. Short of death, there will always be time enough to discard earlier self-appraisals, if thought necessary.

But doesn't our description of the intended-recipient class effectively include everyone, contrary to our stated intention?

Readers might wonder whether the elastic boundaries of our intended-recipient class mean that, in effect, we are addressing everyone, contrary to our declared intent. We think not. In Chapter 1 we argued that everyone lives on the ongoing basis of some philosophy of life, on some level of consciousness. In virtue of the human condition, everyone is compelled to take a position, however implicit and unsystematic, about human-condition questions, such as, "What, if anything, is the purpose of human existence?" But the claim that everyone lives on the ongoing basis of a philosophy of life in that minimal sense falls far short of the claim that everyone has an inclination, much less an obligation, to pursue philosophical inquiry in a systematic and sustained way. We reject the latter claim. We exclude those who, in virtue of their inherited temperaments, are not drawn to sustained philosophical inquiry, as well as those who, in virtue of familial, social, or economic situations, are unable to devote the time and effort required for sustained philosophical inquiry.

We address our arguments to two classes of readers

Nevertheless, despite that last disclaimer, we do not intend to exclude a subclass of readers who, though unaware of a strong inclination toward philosophical inquiry, are at least curious about what it would be like to pursue it. Indeed, such curiosity may itself be evidence of an inclination to philosophize. So, we address this book to two classes of readers: those who are already consciously inclined to engage in philosophical inquiry, whether academics or not; and, those who, although not consciously inclined to pursue philosophical inquiry, are at least curious about what it would be like to live in that mode.

The practical argument from the dialectical nature of philosophical inquiry

In Chapter 2 we argued that one of the essential characteristics of philosophical inquiry is its *dialectical* nature. Philosophical inquirers systematically assemble and evaluate arguments that both support and oppose propositions they deem philosophically important.

Dialectical inquiry can be pursued in more than one way. One consists of juxtaposing, supporting, and opposing arguments for any given thesis in an interlocking series in the following fashion: Begin with a proposition P that is of philosophical interest to you, the inquirer. Formulate an argument supporting P. Call it argument A-1. Juxtapose to A-1 another argument A-2, which opposes P and responds to A-1. Juxtapose to A-2 another argument A-3, which supports P and responds to A-2, and so on. Of course, you could also begin with an argument opposing P. Another procedure is this: Assemble all of the arguments you can think of supporting proposition P, assemble all of the arguments you can think of opposing P, and make an overall judgment as to which set of arguments is stronger.

We are not concerned with which dialectical procedure an inquirer chooses, so long as it works to collect as many of the arguments for and against a given proposition the inquirer can find. Given an adequate conception of dialectical inquiry, the examination of past philosophical sources is highly useful for engaging in such a dialectical pattern of inquiry. How should we express that claim in an argumentative form? Following is a practical argument for Thesis T, based on the dialectical nature of philosophical inquiry:

Addressed to: Those who are inclined to engage in philosophical inquiry.

[1] You have an excellent reason for engaging in dialectical philosophical inquiry for your own first-order philosophical purposes.
[2] If you have an excellent reason for engaging in dialectical philosophical inquiry for your own first-order philosophical purposes, then you have an excellent reason for investigating past sources of philosophical inquiry for your own first-order philosophical purposes.
[3] Hence, you have an excellent reason for investigating past sources of philosophical inquiry for your own first-order philosophical purposes.

Note three things: First, the argument is an unconditional practical argument because its first premise is an unconditional normative assertion, rather than a hypothetical assertion about what someone might want to do. Second, the argument is expressed in a deductively valid form. Third, since the argument is deductively valid, the only remaining task is providing justifications for the premises.

Consider the first premise: You have an excellent reason for engaging in dialectical philosophical inquiry for your own first-order philosophical purposes. Some might ask why everyone should accept that claim. But that question would be misguided. The argument is not addressed to everyone; it is addressed to only those who are already inclined to engage in philosophical inquiry.

What about a similar question put by a member of the intended-recipient class: Why should I believe that I have an excellent reason for engaging in dialectical philosophical inquiry for my own first-order philosophical purposes? We repeat what we argued in Chapter 2. Dialectical inquiry is part of the essence of philosophy. Hence, anyone who is engaged in genuine philosophical inquiry is necessarily engaged in dialectical inquiry. If you doubt this, ask yourself whether, as one inclined to philosophize, you can justifiably reach conclusions without making a sustained effort to evaluate arguments both for and against those conclusions. Doing that *is* dialectical inquiry.

Consider the second premise: If you have an excellent reason for engaging in dialectical philosophical inquiry for your own first-order philosophical purposes, then you have an excellent reason for investigating past sources of philosophical inquiry for your own first-order philosophical purposes. Why should a member of the intended-recipient class accept that? First, many past sources of philosophical inquiry are excellent examples of dialectical inquiry and thereby provide insight into both the nature and scope of dialectical inquiry itself. Consider some paradigmatic examples: Plato, Aristotle, Aquinas, Duns Scotus, Ockham, Descartes, Leibniz, Spinoza, Locke, Berkeley, Hume, Kant, and Bradley, among many. Second, many past sources of dialectical philosophical inquiry are relevant to the issues you are pursuing. If you are pursuing, say, the topic of essences, you should not neglect Aristotle's dialectical discussion in his *Metaphysics* or Aquinas's dialectical discussion in *Being and Essence*.

Suppose that the questioner persists, "I concede all that. But give me a good reason why I can't just confine my inquiries to *present* examples of dialectical inquiry?" The response concedes too much. Of course, many living philosophers, including the persistent inquirer himself, engage in dialectical inquiry. But the vast majority of their dialectical exercises are already in the *past*. Thus, even restricting oneself to the publications of living philosophers requires inquirers to look to the philosophical past. Given that inevitability, what good reason can there be to restrict one's inquiries to living philosophers? After all, there may be illuminating examples of dialectical reasoning, as well as reflections on the nature of dialectical reasoning itself, that reach further back into the past than recent philosophical efforts. How could one possibly know without first investigating?

Some might respond by noting that there is always the possibility of communicating with living inquirers in order to get clarifications of their views, unlike the situation with inquirers who are no longer alive. Granted, consulting living philosophers is a possibility. However, in many cases it is not a realistic possibility. Imagine this telephone introduction: "Hello, Professor X. My name is Y. You don't know me, but I would like to meet with you for a day or two to ask questions about an essay you published thirty-five years ago."

In addition, the fact that an inquirer who created an illuminating dialectical reflection has died should not substantially hinder the efforts of a living inquirer to resolve obscurities in that past reflection. There will often be commentators on that past reflection who offer helpful analyses of those issues, and, in any case, an inquirer can always analyze the text herself by distinguishing alternative interpretations and choosing the strongest in light of the Principle of Charity.

Consider this absurdity. Imagine an inquirer who has determined to not read anything written by a philosopher who is no longer alive. She has struggled for months studying a book written by a living philosopher P, but has never had a chance to ask P questions about his book. Just as she finishes the final draft of an insightful analysis of P's book, she learns that P died yesterday. What is she to do? Given her own principle, she should put her essay in a paper shredder and forget about it. But that would be perverse. Once she permits herself to look into the philosophical past to any degree at all, there is no principled stopping point. If she draws any temporal boundary she likes, say, 1965, and then resolves to ignore any dialectical analyses published before that year, there will be indefinitely many dialectical analyses antedating 1965 that she would ignore at the risk of hindering her own philosophical progress.

Generalization of the argument from the dialectical nature of philosophical inquiry

The practical argument just offered focuses upon just one of the essential elements of philosophical inquiry identified in Chapter 2—being dialectical. But that argument can be generalized to invoke any of the essential attributes of philosophical inquiry taken up in Chapter 2. Here is a brief summary of them:

(1) Philosophical inquirers focus upon a set of *ultimate issues*, for example, the nature of the world, human nature, whether some patterns of living are preferable to others, the question of a Ground of Being, the question of universals and particulars, the nature of time, the nature of space, the nature of causation, and the nature of thinking. Some of these questions are primarily motivated by a concern to pursue *human-condition questions*, others by *Aristotelian wonder*. Ideally, all such questions would be simultaneously motivated by both.

(2) Philosophical inquirers strive to formulate *systematic* worldviews.

(3) Philosophical inquirers are *self-consciously fallible* and aware of the *necessity for making choices under conditions of uncertainty*.

(4) Philosophical inquirers do not forget their *original questions*.

(5) Philosophical inquirers avoid *Kierkegaardian Infinite Parentheses*.

(6) Philosophical inquirers draw upon *several sources of philosophical insight*, including *a priori* intuition and reasoning, the personal intuitions and experiences of the philosophical inquirers themselves, the intuitions and experiences of others, and scientific and mathematical concepts and results.

(7) Philosophical inquirers use at least five methods of inquiry—argument, explanation, distinction, definition, and generalization, and, in addition, formulate guidelines for using them.

Now, select any of these attributes and substitute its description for "X" in the following practical argument schema:

Addressed to: Those who are inclined to engage in philosophical inquiry.

[1] You have an excellent reason for engaging in philosophical inquiry that possesses attribute, X, for your own first-order purposes.

[2] If you have an excellent reason for engaging in philosophical inquiry that possess attribute, X, for your own first-order purposes, then you have an excellent reason for investigating past sources of philosophical inquiry for your own first-order purposes.

[3] Hence, you have an excellent reason for investigating past sources of philosophical inquiry for your own first-order purposes.

Each substitution generates a practical argument whose degree of strength is similar to the argument based on the dialectical nature of philosophy.

Considerations of space preclude our setting out arguments for each such substitution, but here a few examples.

In Chapter 2 we argued that the attribute *being systematic* is an essential component of philosophical inquiry. Substituting the description of that attribute into the general schema, we have

Addressed to: Those who are inclined to engage in philosophical inquiry.

[1] You have an excellent reason for engaging in philosophical inquiry that possesses the attribute, *being systematic*, for your own first-order purposes.

[2] If you have an excellent reason for engaging in philosophical inquiry that possesses the attribute, *being systematic*, for your own first-order purposes, then you have an excellent reason for investigating past sources of philosophical inquiry for your own first-order purposes.

[3] Hence, you have an excellent reason for investigating past sources of philosophical inquiry for your own first-order purposes.

As with the argument based upon the attribute, *being dialectical*, there are at least two considerations supporting premise [2]. First, examining past philosophical sources of systematic philosophical inquiry yields a deeper and more comprehensive understanding of what systematic philosophy is. Think of Plato, Aristotle, Aquinas, Locke, and Kant. Second, it will yield a deeper and more comprehensive understanding of the issues you have been pursuing.

By the way, arguments like this, which mention certain past philosophers and urge their relevance for one's own first-order purposes, must be understood in a special way. Of course, listing past sources of philosophical wisdom and asserting their contemporary relevance for first-order purposes are not likely to have much epistemic force for readers. They will not be able to evaluate such arguments unless they undertake to investigate those sources *for themselves*. This kind of argument is not unusual. Many practical arguments can be understood as being implicitly tied to an appeal of this basic form: "I've just offered you a practical argument, but I encourage you to try out its recommendation for yourself. If you do, I predict that you will apprehend the epistemic force of the argument. If you don't, you will have precluded yourself from potential illumination."

There are many examples. Here is just one, addressed to someone who has never heard Bach's music: "You ought to listen to Bach's music because it will deepen your musical understanding, deepen your experience of reality, and give you intellectual and emotional insights you might otherwise never find." Standing alone, this practical argument carries little, if any, epistemic force for its intended recipients. In order to evaluate its epistemic force, they must themselves listen to Bach's music. In general, any practical argument that appeals to personal experience in support of its recommendation cannot be adequately evaluated unless the intended recipients try it out for themselves, at least in imagination. We add this last qualification in light of practical arguments that recommend experiences the intended recipients might justifiably choose not to try out for themselves, for example, those of De Sade.

We also argued in Chapter 2 that philosophy essentially uses the methods of argument, explanation, distinction, definition, and generalization, and, in addition, formulates topic-neutral guiding principles for using those methods. Substituting the description of the attribute *using these five methods of inquiry and formulating guiding principles for their use* in the general schema, we have

[1] You have an excellent reason for engaging in philosophical inquiry that possesses the attribute, *using these five methods of inquiry and formulating guiding principles for their use*, for your own first-order purposes.

[2] If you have an excellent reason for engaging in philosophical inquiry that possesses the attribute, *using these five methods of inquiry and formulating guiding principles for their use*, then you have an excellent reason for investigating past sources of philosophical inquiry for your own first-order purposes.

[3] Hence, you have an excellent reason for investigating past sources of philosophical inquiry for your own first-order purposes.

What is the support for premise [1]? If what you are doing does not involve those five methods of inquiry, then, whatever it is you are doing, it is not philosophical inquiry. The support for premise [2] is the entire philosophical tradition. As to *using* arguments, explanations, distinctions, definitions, and generalizations, you could not do better than to read, say, Plato, Aristotle, Augustine, Aquinas, Duns Scotus, Ockham, Descartes, Berkeley, Leibniz, Spinoza, Locke, Hume, Kant, and Bradley. As to *formulating guidelines for using those methods*, Plato, Aristotle, Aquinas, Kant, Frege, Russell, Reichenbach, Carnap, C.S. Lewis, and Quine would be good places to start.

In this chapter we have proposed practical arguments for Thesis T for each of the essential attributes of philosophical inquiry set out in Chapter 2, although for reasons of space, we have not set out arguments for each one. Our procedure might lead some readers to assume that, unless they accept all of Chapter 2's enumerated attributes, they need not bother with the practical arguments in this chapter. But that is not so. Even those who accept only some of those attributes have an excellent reason for investigating past philosophical sources. Imagine yourself setting out to engage in philosophical inquiry, having accepting just some of the attributes set out in Chapter 2. Even in that case, in order to carry out your philosophical commitment to the attributes you do accept, you would still find it highly useful to examine seriously past philosophical sources that take up those attributes. Suppose that the only attribute you accept is the last one taken up in Chapter 2: philosophy's use of argument, explanation, distinction, definition, and generalization, together with the formulation of guiding principles for that use. You would profit by seriously examining past philosophical sources focusing upon those five methods, either by way of using them, by way of formulating principles for their proper use, or both.

4

Science, Scientism, and Philosophy

The problem and the plan

Blasts

Near the beginning of the twentieth century, celebrated quantum physicist Niels Bohr confided to a friend that he had "made a discovery, a very great discovery." It wasn't in physics. What then might the great discovery be? "All that philosophers have ever written is pure drivel."[1]

Half a century later, Hans Reichenbach argued rather more generously, but to the same overall effect, that philosophers writing before Bohr, Einstein, and other scientific revolutionaries who changed the world picture could be credited with raising important questions about the structure of the physical world and entities within it—but never with answering them. The means at their disposal were inadequate to the task. Reichenbach pointed to Kant, who built his theoretical philosophy on the foundations of the Newtonian physics of absolute space, time, and determinism in nature, with the result that the philosopher, who is considered by many to be the greatest of all time, "has nothing to say to us who are witnesses of the physics of Einstein and Bohr."[2]

Now, another half century later, Stephen Hawking and Leonard Mlodinow announce that philosophy "is dead," since philosophers have failed to keep up with developments in science. According to these eminent physicists, "scientists have become the bearers of the torch of discovery in our quest for knowledge."[3]

More than a century of such belittlements have worked their effect. Surely, many readers of Hawking and Mlodinow nod in agreement. And these readers draw further conclusions more or less in the direction taken by Bohr and Reichenbach, even if they have never heard of either and are unfamiliar with twentieth-century positivism. Perhaps without ever articulating the

[1] Remarked to Jens Lindhard after Bohr had attended a philosophers' meeting. Quoted in Abraham Pais, *Niels Bohr's Times in Physics, Philosophy, and Polity* (Oxford: Clarendon, 1991), 421.
[2] Hans Reichenbach, *The Rise of Scientific Philosophy* (Berkeley: University of California Press, 1951), 41.
[3] Steven Hawking and Leonard Mlodinow, *The Grand Design* (New York: Bantam, 2010), 5.

thought, even to themselves, they believe that the progress of science makes it quite clear that past philosophy is now worthless, and current philosophy is no better.

So it is widely believed. Are these beliefs warranted? Is it the case that because of the advance of science every philosopher from Thales to Kant and beyond is fit only for historical study, not for telling us anything important about the way things are?

The plan

Our aim in this chapter, and the next, is to confront the following two related issues: (1) Is philosophy *per se* passé?; and (2) Is our Thesis T false—is it false that investigating past sources of philosophical inquiry is an excellent means of assisting one's own philosophical investigations? If philosophy as such is worthless for answering our first-order questions—questions that arise out of the existential need or desire for fundamental answers about our lives and the world—then, of course, so is *past* philosophy. But the converse does not follow. It may be that past philosophy is best left in the dustbin of history, but philosophy today, revitalized by science, is well worth pondering. Though two interconnected questions are on the docket, the question of the truth of Thesis T remains the heart of the matter. We are concerned with the broader question because of its bearing on our thesis. Occasionally, it will be necessary to flag whether it is past philosophy or philosophy *per se* that is at issue. We trust, however, that context will usually suffice to make this clear.

Both questions, however, need to be refined. We also give reasons for thinking that scientistic attacks on the two propositions of central interest can be answered. The next chapter explores in greater detail such lines of scientistic attack and provides possible answers to them.

Scientistic arguments

Given widespread belief that science has displaced philosophy or that philosophy can do no more than wait on science, it is remarkable that in recent times there has been so little effort to demonstrate such claims in detail. No book in English appears to rival Reichenbach's work in the mid-twentieth century.

Three general scientistic arguments

Gathering bits and pieces, it seems safe to say that three arguments occupy center stage of a scientistic view of philosophy.

The Success Argument

First, science has been marvelously successful; by stark contrast, philosophy has not.

The Replacement Argument

Second, over time science has obliterated huge swaths of what once passed for philosophic wisdom. This strongly suggests that at some time in the future there will be little or nothing left of this ancient practice.

The Poverty of Means Argument

Third, philosophy lacks the means that science has developed to explore the world; therefore, philosophical speculation proves too unreliable to produce anything comparable to modern science when it comes to depicting and explaining the way things are.

These three general arguments should be borne in mind as we proceed, though we will return to them explicitly in the next chapter.

To be more precise about our project in this chapter and the next on science, let us define a few key terms.

Terms of the argument

"Scientism" and "scientistic"

Our concern is only with "scientistic" objections to Thesis T. These are objections that appeal to science for support, whether the invoked science is respectable or not. Let us say an objection to past (or present) philosophy is "scientistic" if and only if appeal is made either to the history of science, current reports of findings, or methods putatively employed only by science.

"Scientistic" is not here employed as an abusive epithet. Our use is intended to be purely descriptive and neutral in much the same way as supporters of scientism sometimes use the term.[4] Were we to call arguments that appeal to science to disparage philosophy "scientific," that would have the unfortunate consequence of making them sound plausible, when their plausibility is just what is at issue.

---

[4] See, for example, "In Defense of Scientism," Chapter 1 of Ladyman and Ross, *Everything Must Go*, 1–65.

"Science" and "science*"

So much for "scientistic." What about "scientific"? The effort in the twentieth century by Popper and others to "demarcate" science from pseudoscience and from different approaches to reality met with little success. Fortunately, our task does not require us to review these efforts or to formulate a definition of science. Since a case against the worth of earlier philosophy depends on the inadequacy of the means at the disposal of early investigators of the world, we can simply stipulate that that part of science making use of high powered mathematics, logic peculiar to science (e.g., quantum logic), or physical instruments to enlarge the human sensorium, or powerful devices for controlling the movements of the unseen world, or rigorous experimental techniques could be called "science*." "Science" without a star, then, will be used more broadly and vaguely, much the way so many terms in ordinary language are used, like the term "art." Though the distinction between "science*" and "science" in the next chapter proves to be exceedingly important, in some contexts we, again, need not be too fussy.

"Philosophy" and "pure philosophy"

Acknowledging that "philosophy" is just as vague and ambiguous as "science" and "art," we saw no unmovable obstacles to expressing the essence of the activity and product at the heart of what is called "philosophy." Assuming we have clarified the essence of philosophy, our attention here turns to "pure" and "mixed" philosophy. For emphasis, we will use "pure philosophy" to refer to philosophy independent of science*. This obviously includes all philosophy before the rise of modern science, but also current philosophy that makes no essential use of science*. "Mixed philosophy" (rarely used) will refer to philosophy that does make essential use of science*.

"Philosophy of nature," "metaphysics," and "ontology"

For reasons that will become clearer as we move along, our main concern will be with pure philosophy bearing on the physical world and, more broadly, all that might be called "reality," exclusive of norms. In earlier times, the philosophical study of the natural world was referred to as "natural philosophy." The expression is not in vogue these days, but it make sense to distinguish philosophical ponderings about the natural world from more general studies about being or existence as such, in the Aristotelian tradition called "metaphysics." Today "metaphysics" is usually thought of as a general study of reality broad enough to include the philosophy of nature, even though the etymology of "metaphysics" suggests going beyond the physical order. "Ontology" is now often used as a synonym for "metaphysics." Though we think there is considerable advantage to be had by distinguishing ontology (metaphysics) from the philosophy of nature (and of mind), we will follow current practice and almost always use "ontology" when discussing the way things are. Scientistic arguments usually take aim at ontology in our sense of the term, not ethics, politics, aesthetics, philosophy of logic, or mathematics, except insofar as these areas rest upon ontological assumptions.

More exact statement of the question

With these stipulations and distinctions, we can now state our main question: Do scientistic arguments show that pure philosophy, and in particular pure ontology, past or present, is not worth serious study? In one way, we have narrowed the focus of both questions to ontology. But the broader issues remain of interest. Thesis T remains the heart of the matter, while the question of philosophy *per se*, pure philosophy, is of concern insofar as it bears on the question of Thesis T.

Foregone responses

Before getting into the thick of the arguments, we should say how we do *not* intend to argue our case. Opponents of scientism take positions that strike us as quite unattractive, despite their popularity, and we want to be crystal clear about refusing to go down a number of paths.

Attacks on science

In our view, not a moment's thought should be given to any efforts to counter scientistic claims by discrediting science itself. Science is one of the glorious achievements of the human spirit. It has proved itself a hundred thousand times via marvelous observations and predictions of future events; it continues to produce wondrous results with blinding speed. No sensible person with cancer refuses treatment on the grounds that science is all pretense. The fantasy popular in some academic quarters, that modern science is merely a tool of power, will certainly not be part of our case against scientism. Nor will we call upon arguments of deconstructionists and postmodernists who see all discourse, including scientific, as deceit.

Disavowing the actual

A number of responses to scientistic rejections of philosophy, though respectful of science and intrinsically engaging, nonetheless seem to offer weak counters. Philosophic views that leave the physical world entirely to scientific theorizing cannot be relied upon to deal with the issues confronting us here. Nor do we wish to spend much time exploring philosophic work dealing mainly with our language and conceptual schemes. To the extent that such work brackets the world or leaves to the physical and social sciences the task of telling the truth about the world's origin, structure, and elements within it, we are left destitute of answers to scientistic challenges of the hour.

And, while we especially appreciate the aspirations and methods of a loose federation of thinkers willing to call themselves "analytic philosophers," it is best to put to one side a claim that seems to be gaining ground within that community: the proper task of analytic ontology is to investigate only possibilities. Confronting the question, "how we can attain knowledge of being, or of reality 'as it is in itself,' especially if ontology is conceived to be not empirical but an *a priori* science," one of the most astute among the analysts writes:

> The answer that I favour divides the task of ontology into two parts, one which is wholly *a priori* and another which admits empirical elements. The *a priori* part is devoted to exploring the realm of metaphysical possibility, seeking to establish what kinds of things could exist and more importantly, *co-exist* to make up a single possible world. The empirically conditioned part seeks to establish, on the basis of empirical evidence and informed by our most successful scientific theories, what kinds of things do exist in this, the actual world. But the two tasks are not independent: in particular, the second task depends upon the first. We are in no position to be able to judge what kinds of things actually *do* exist, even in the light of the most scientifically well-informed experience, unless we can effectively determine what kinds of things *could* exist, because empirical evidence can only be evidence for the existence of something whose existence is antecedently possible.[5]

We agree with much that the writer, E.J. Lowe, articulates so well before and after this passage. We hold, as he does, that ontology should treat the world, not merely our concepts. We too resist the Kantian idea, embraced by many contemporary thinkers, that limits ontology to the examination of our

---

[5]   E.J. Lowe, *The Four-Category Ontology* (Oxford: Oxford University Press, 2006), 4–5.

conceptual schemes. Furthermore, we are with him largely for the reason he elaborates: our conceptual schemes are themselves part of reality. Moreover, we are sympathetic to the conviction that ontology somehow bears on being as such, which binds Lowe to the Aristotelian tradition.

The following important passage, however, seems to point Lowe's readers in the wrong direction:

> We are in no position to be able to judge what kinds of things actually *do* exist, even in the light of the most scientifically well-informed experience, unless we can effectively determine what kinds of things *could* exist, because empirical evidence can only be evidence for the existence of something whose existence is antecedently possible.[6]

It is hard to see how to reconstruct this argument without supplying missing premises that look too implausible for Lowe to be asserting. Rather than set out our best effort, we will simply note that a reader could not be blamed for suspecting that in the passage Lowe forgets what he surely knows: ontological priority is one thing, epistemic quite another. Assuming that the possibility of F's being a fact is somehow ontologically prior to F's being a fact, it does not follow that we have no evidence for F until we have good *a priori* evidence for F's being possible. A biologist can determine that in the human elbow the humerus connects to the ulna without the help of an *a priori* argument establishing that such a connection is possible. Lowe's reader cannot be faulted for worrying that Lowe's argument, his contrary intentions notwithstanding, gives grounds for thinking that the pure philosopher mistakenly thinks that science must wait until the general ontology of possibilities is worked out, forgetting that the only way, sometimes, to secure the possible is by securing the actual.

Where does this leave us? With the sense that standard explanations of how philosophy can survive in an age of science may not work. In any event, we do not intend to attack science. We also do not intend to back away from ontology about the actual world, either in the manner of those who would bracket its existence, or those who would plead that we deal only with possibilities.

Confinement to values

Another unsatisfactory response to scientistic disparagements of philosophy is to hand over to science the world of facts, while reserving the world of values for philosophy. "Values" includes aesthetics, ethics, politics, epistemology,

[6] Lowe, *The Four-Category Ontology*.

and much else. All categories of "values" do have philosophical aspects, but to hole up in this realm, spacious and attractive as it is, is to yield far too much territory to the attacks of scientistic critics. Though Socrates eschewed philosophy of nature and ontology, it has become sufficiently clear that a deep philosophy of value requires grounding in an underlying philosophy dealing with non-normative facts. Restricting philosophy to "values" is an illusion because all positing of "values" presupposes ontological posits. Hence, limiting philosophy to "values" alone would have the effect of eliminating even those values themselves, leaving philosophy with literally nothing to do—not even treat values. We therefore concede that if the physical world must be handed over to science, pure philosophy is reduced to a pale shadow of its former self, with the result that, at a minimum, it must also be acknowledged that there is all too much that is true in the scientistic charges.

Our approach to scientistic objections

There are reasons to hope that the charges can be answered. We will list some of these immediately. Others, more probing, we will elaborate in the next chapter.

How are scientistic charges to be dealt with? What is to be said in defense of the idea that good-old-fashioned pure philosophy, and particularly ontology, can be conducted responsibly in an age of science? Answers to such questions must, of course, include direct rebuttals to scientistic objections. Before getting to these arguments and counters, however, there are things we can do to reassure ourselves that digging into the issues may well pay off. We can and should ask what the chances are that scientistic objections can be rebutted, if not by us, then by others more capable.

Reasons for hope

Counter-authority

The first reason for thinking that the probability of answering scientistic objections is not low is that great physicists have seen a deep connection between science and philosophy, and some have expressed appreciation of earlier philosophy. Newton entitled his contributions to physics *Philosophiæ Naturalis Principia Mathematica—The Mathematical Principles of Natural Philosophy*. Einstein is reported to have read with pleasure Plato, Spinoza, J.S. Mill, Poincare, and Karl Pearson.[7] Quite a few distinguished twentieth-century

---

[7] Gerald Holton, *The Advancement of Science and Its Burdens* (Cambridge, MA: Harvard University Press, 1998), 164.

physicists have written sympathetically about past philosophy, among them Werner Heisenberg.[8] According to noted historian of quantum mechanics Aage Petersen, Erwin Schrödinger reached radical conclusions about this fundamental science "through a logical and historical study of especially ancient Greek philosophy…".[9,10]

It might be replied that none of this means much, since these authorities belong to an earlier era. The education scientists received in the nineteenth century and the early part of the twentieth was generally broader than the training now offered to scientists, who tend to develop sub-sub-specialties early in their careers. Naturally enough, earlier scientists did not entirely lay aside this wider education. They continued to read philosophy for recreation, it seems, much as scientists today read history or fiction.

There is something to this counter. Educated at a different time and in a different way, scientists were more likely to say something good about philosophy. Yet, it remains true that eminences from an era not all that distant from ours did indeed value pure philosophy. Furthermore, they may have taken an interest precisely because their broad education had an effect akin to that of travel to another place or time, which allows one to see things anew.

Yet, if that consideration is unconvincing, there is a fact that should give pause to any scientistically minded critic of philosophy or earlier philosophy: Einstein told the world "the special theory of relativity was decisively furthered by reading Mach and Hume."[11] Who knows what twentieth-century physics would have looked like had Einstein not read Hume? Moreover, might not earlier philosophy, beyond retaining its power to entertain and startle the intellectually fatigued, awaken genius from dogmatic slumber and supply concepts key to furthering understanding of current theories and creation of new ones?

Scientistic hedging

There is something comforting about the way many critics of pure philosophy hedge their denigrations. Nobel laureate Richard Feynman, famous for his disparagements, is reputed to have quipped that philosophy of science is

---

[8] Werner Heisenberg, *Physics and Philosophy: The Revolution of Modern Science* (New York: Harper Torch, 1958).

[9] Aage Peterson, *Quantum Physics and the Philosophic Tradition* (Cambridge, MA: MIT Press, 1969), 7.

[10] Peterson, *Quantum Physics and the Philosophic Tradition*, 424; Even Bohr took a more cautious stance at times. Asked about what kind of contribution earlier philosophers had made, he replied, "It was hard to say." Pais, *Niels Bohr's Times*, 424.

[11] Albert Einstein, "Autobiographical Notes" in *Albert Einstein: Philosopher-Scientist*, vol. 1, ed. Paul Arthur Schilpp (New York: Harper Torch, 1951), 53.

about as useful as ornithology is to birds. Nobel laureate Steven Weinberg entitles a chapter of his *Dreams of a Final Theory*, "Against Philosophy."[12] It is noteworthy that they pull their punches. Feynman ridicules philosophy of science, but nowhere, so far as we know, does he commit himself to the proposition all philosophy is drivel. Indeed, speaking of philosophy, he says he has "no idea" whether their methods might work outside of science.[13] He asserts that while science influences many ideas in religion, "there is a kind of independence between ethical and moral views and the theory of the universe."[14] As for Weinberg, he allows that good philosophy is needed to combat bad philosophy, such as positivism.

Restricting their attacks on philosophy signals that at least some naysayers sense there are legitimate problems modern science cannot fully solve. Scientistic thinkers generally refrain from claiming that science undercuts all philosophizing about *value* and *norms*. Of course, science can bear on value and normative considerations, yet one must surely hesitate before declaring that science completely settles issues in ethics, politics, aesthetics, logic, or any other discipline that makes fundamental use of evaluative expressions such as permissible, impermissible, right, wrong, valid, invalid, lovely, ugly. Even if modern physics has obliterated the succession of older physical systems that earlier philosophers relied upon—and that is an oversimplification—many earlier contributions to logic, rhetoric, poetics, ethics, and politics are surely of lasting value. Aristotle's treatment of modality in the *Prior Analytics*, for example, differs from modern systems in the way he handles the concept of modal predication.[15] It is not clear that his conception is erroneous or that a discovery of the physical sciences is relevant to determining which combination of modal premises entails which modal conclusions. Or again, it would seem absurd to reject Lessing's distinctions in *Laocoön* between spatial properties of painting and temporal properties of poetry, solely because Lessing was ignorant of the theory of space-time physics.

Temptations of the naysayers

The claim that the torch of truth has been handed from philosophers to scientists can be understood in two ways. It may mean that science is the only road to truth, or it may mean that those who carry a union card in science are

---

[12] Steven Weinberg, *Dreams of a Final Theory: The Scientist's Search for the Ultimate Laws of Nature* (New York: Vintage, 1994), 166–190.

[13] Richard P. Feynman, *The Meaning of It All: Thoughts of a Citizen-Scientist* (Reading, MA: Perseus, 1998), 20.

[14] Feynman, *The Meaning of It All*, 41.

[15] For more on Aristotle's modal logic, see Richard Patterson, *Aristotle's Modal Logic: Essence and Entailment in the Organon* (Cambridge: Cambridge University Press, 1995).

the only ones on the path to truth. If the claim means the former, then those who make up the profession had better be careful not to do philosophy, on the pain of inconsistency. If it means the latter, then it says nothing damaging to pure philosophy, since *somebody* can do it and perhaps do it very well.

Scientistic naysayers like Hawking, Mlodinow, and Atkins seem to mean the former, but nonetheless fall victim to the temptation to do what everyone recognizes as philosophy, pure in some cases, mixed in others. Hawking and Mlodinow argue, for example, that simpler theories are preferable to more complex theories and, siding with Hume and Kant, that we cannot know things in themselves; all we can do is correlate observables. They thus take sides in age-old debates.[16] That is philosophy as pure as philosophy comes. And they argue that free will is part of an "effective theory," which is to be assumed, even though, in truth, they say, "This book is rooted in the concept of scientific determinism."[17] By "concept" they appear to mean belief, assertion, assumption, hypothesis, axiom, or some such bearer to truth. The "concept" rules out miracles.[18] Of course, these "concepts" have been debated philosophically for centuries. Hawking and Mlodinow's philosophical remarks take on the aura of science since their contentions are located in a science book, but they are philosophical nonetheless. Mixed philosophy is still philosophy, and pure to the degree it stands independent of the associated science. Yielding to the temptation to philosophize, the two authors credit what they scorn.

Need they? Is this just two scientistic thinkers' failure to remain consistent, like all of us do from time to time? *Must* scientistic thinkers blunder in this way? Why can't scientistic scientists just "shut up and calculate" (as the phrase goes among tough-minded natural scientists) or delete philosophy from their discourse? Because it is easier said than done. Scientists are human, after all, and the desire to know runs deeper than mere calculation can satisfy. What lies beneath the calculations is a practically irresistible line of inquiry. Scientists get into science because they want to know, and thus they, of all people, must find the urge to take the next step exceedingly strong. Feynman could not resist: "Finally, I'd like to make a little philosophical argument—this I'm not very good at, but I'd like to explain why I think theoretically science and moral questions are independent."[19] The greatest philosophized with abandon: Kepler, Galileo, Newton, Darwin, Wallace, Einstein—and Bohr. Furthermore, if science in any recognizable form is to make its appearance in public, or be capable of defending itself against attacks, or be seen as

---

[16] Hawking and Mlodinow, *Grand Design*, 47.
[17] Hawking and Mlodinow, *Grand Design*, 33–34.
[18] Hawking and Mlodinow, *Grand Design*, 34.
[19] Feynman, *The Meaning of It All*, 44.

worthy of public support, then philosophical arguments need to be invoked. Moreover, as we will see in the following section, there are yet deeper reasons why science must involve philosophy.

Mixed philosophy and the philosophy of science

If mixed philosophy is acceptable, then pure philosophy should be as well since the mixed includes portions that are pure. Even those opposed to our position on pure ontology see great value in what we call "mixed philosophy." For example, Tim Maudlin holds, "When choosing the fundamental posits of one's ontology, one must look to scientific practice rather than philosophical prejudice."[20] Nevertheless, Maudlin proceeds to work philosophically on the basis of the posits, doing superb work that includes stretches of pure philosophy. The same was true of philosophers like Reichenbach and Carnap, who fall under the heading of philosophy of science, or as Carnap preferred, "the logic of science."

It is true that Feynman scoffed, "These philosophers are always with us, struggling in the periphery to try to tell us something, but they never really understand the subtleties and depth of the problem."[21] But there is another side to the story. The cadre of extraordinarily well-informed philosophers writing today can hardly be accused of stumbling around in the dark. Some superbly trained students of physics and the history of science have voiced criticisms of the refusal to philosophize akin to that of Tim Maudlin:

> Unfortunately, physics has become infected with very low standards of clarity and precision on foundational questions, and physicists have become accustomed (and even encouraged) to just shut up and calculate, to consciously refrain from asking for a clear understanding of the ontological import of their theories. This attitude has prevailed for so long that we can easily lose sight of what a clear and precise account of physical reality even looks like.[22]

The full truth about what philosophy, particularly earlier philosophy, can contribute to the understanding of foundational issues in physics and other sciences can be established only by patient examination of a considerable range of cases. This daunting task could overwhelm the efforts of those far

---

[20] Maudlin, *The Metaphysics Within Physics*, 1.

[21] Richard P. Feynman, *The Feynman Lectures on Physics, Vol. I: Mainly Mechanics, Radiation, and Heat* (New York: Basic Books, 2010), Chapter 16, 1.

[22] Tim Maudlin, *Philosophy of Physics: Space and Time* (Princeton: Princeton University Press, 2012), xiv.

better positioned than we are for this kind of work. In the next chapter, however, we will point to a few promising ideas in the tradition and indicate how these ideas might apply. Whatever the reader thinks of the forthcoming examples, there is no obvious reason that a serious mining of the works of geniuses East and West could not illuminate aspects of modern science.

Consider how Nick Huggett's observation that "[e]ven a single quantum particle will typically fail to have a definite location or a sharp trajectory"[23] does not necessarily conflict with common sense, since "philosophers have long realized that there are many species of identity, each with their own criteria."[24] Huggett illustrates this claim by turning to John Locke.[25] He might better have referred to Aristotle, Aquinas, Scotus, Ockham, or Suarez. No matter. The point is the same: to elucidate science one needs to invoke distinctions. These can take centuries to work out. And medieval thinkers worked out enough distinctions to fill encyclopedias, lost to view for a time as Renaissance writers derided clearer thinkers for their logic chopping.

There is yet another reason to hope scientistic rejections of pure philosophy can be answered. Many like Tim Maudlin, who thinks we must take our point of departure from science, nonetheless happily proceed to do a great deal of philosophy, using sharp tools of the trade. If these tools work in the context of science, why can't they be applied to what we know just by looking around or looking within?

To take an obvious example, experimental science reasons in accordance with logical rules. It is difficult to see how the concept of testability could be applied without reasoning in accord with *modus tollens*, the rule: *If H, then O, but not O. Hence, not H.* That is, if a hypothesis H entails observable O, and O does not appear, then H is false. This rule was available to Parmenides.

Concepts used in science were also available earlier. Even when arguing that physics requires unfamiliar concepts, physicists invoke familiar concepts. Illustrating the need for new concepts with an example of high-energy collisions of particles, Bernard d'Espagnat falls back on an ancient distinction: "Now, motion is a property of objects. And so...."[26] The distinction between an object and its properties hardly escaped Aristotle, whose philosophy pivoted around the distinction.

---

[23] Nick Huggett, "Identity, Quantum Mechanics, and Common Sense," *The Monist* 80 (1997): 118.

[24] Huggett, "Identity, Quantum Mechanics, and Common Sense," 119–120.

[25] Huggett, "Identity, Quantum Mechanics, and Common Sense," 120.

[26] Bernard d'Espagnat, *On Physics and Philosophy* (Princeton, NJ: Princeton University Press, 2006), 15. For an extended discussion of the problem of properties in quantum mechanics, see R.I.G. Hughes, *The Structure and Interpretation of Quantum Mechanics* (Cambridge, MA: Harvard University Press, 1989), pt. II, Chapter 6, 155–177.

Suspicions regarding satisfaction of the necessary conditions of a successful scientistic attack on pure philosophy

The topic of the satisfaction of necessary conditions of a successful scientistic attack on philosophy has already been touched upon, and we will treat it more extensively in the next chapter. Here, however, let us at least be explicit about the matter. There are very good reasons to suspect that no convincing scientistic argument can be made against philosophy *per se*, or more particularly Thesis T. To bring this off, the argument must not put forward propositions that embed pure philosophy, presuppose philosophical propositions, use premises of any sort that are more suspect than philosophical statements, or adopt methods subject to philosophical examination. Anyone who has read much in this area senses it is impossible to meet the conditions. This is, however, a matter for fuller discussion in the next chapter.

The history of philosophy

In all likelihood, when deliberating about the prior probability of meeting scientistic objections to pure philosophy, the most significant fact for many readers is their own experience with the history of philosophy. Certainly, given the nature of philosophy, much of it will seem wrong, confusing, or even downright silly. Yet, a good deal of past pure philosophy, including ontology, strikes many as nothing less than ingenious.

The history of philosophy provides more material for ontological reflection than anyone can absorb in a dozen lifetimes. Western philosophy alone is overwhelming. Who can honestly say that he has carefully considered half the works of any of the greats of the West, to say nothing of figures in Eastern thought? Who has read with care translations—let alone the original language texts—of the six centuries of ontological writings in the corpus of the Nyāya-Vaiśeṣika or their dialectical partners, the Indian Buddhists?

Genius

This brings us to our last reason for hoping a good defense can be mounted against scientistic naysaying. Some philosophers have been eminent geniuses in other domains. Bohr's jocular gibe that all philosophers have ever written is pure drivel can be met with the question, "Do you really mean all, Professor?" Leibnitz was a coinventor, with Newton, of the calculus—the mathematics every physicist hangs on to for dear life. "Presumably, professor, you mean all the philosophers have written *when doing philosophy* is drivel." It may further be asked, "And when exactly is it that the geniuses are doing philosophy and not something else?" Was Leibniz doing mathematics or philosophy when he posited infinitesimals? Putting that aside, why should we think that a genius like Leibniz writes drivel when he stops doing mathematics? Leibnitz may or may not have been right to embrace infinitesimals, the itty-bitty mathematical entities rehabilitated in our time by Abraham Robinson. But, then, he also may or may not have been right about the principle of sufficient reason. Is anyone certain he was not? And if he was right, is anyone confident that nothing of interest follows from that principle, along with his other great principle?

Then, of course, there is Aristotle, busy cracking open chick eggs and examining them carefully, founding embryology. Is anyone certain his teachings on what life is are not only false but also beneath consideration by anyone soaked in contemporary biology? Or certain he was wrong about what a species is, when contemporary biology is at odds with itself over the concept?

Summary

The scientistic challenge to philosophy, and earlier philosophy in particular, is prevalent in our culture. There are many reasons, however, to think that scientistic arguments can be met. It is time to see what we can and should make of those arguments.

5

Scientistic Attacks on Past and Present Philosophy

The questions restated

We have set before ourselves two related questions concerned with *scientistic* objections to the value of studying *philosophical ontology*. Is it likely that pure philosophical ontology is unilluminating with respect to first-order questions about the world and our place within it? Is the study of *past pure ontology* a waste of time? Our main interest is in the more particular question about *past* ontology, but the two are intertwined and will be discussed together.

The last chapter also outlined three scientistic arguments against pure philosophic ontology, past and present. These were *The Success Argument*, *The Replacement Argument*, and *The Poverty of Means Argument*. It is now time to take a closer look at these arguments.

The argument from success

The Success Argument can be stated as follows:

(S-1)   Science has been marvelously successful.
(S-2)   By stark contrast, philosophy has not.
(S-3)   If (S-1) and (S-2) are true, then pure ontology, past and present, is worthless, and Thesis T is false.
(Con)   So, pure ontology, past and present, is worthless, and Thesis T is false.

We are not going to quibble about (S-1). Like nearly everyone else, we regard the successes of science as astonishing.

Premise (S-2) is also conceded—*but* with a crucial qualification. It is true that philosophy has not progressed, not in the way science has moved forward. Philosophy does not accumulate results and then pass them on to an ever-widening circle of satisfied recipients. Philosophy is not interpersonally, intergenerationally cumulative. In another and very significant sense, however, philosophy does indeed progress. Or more exactly, we progress in philosophy.

Here, as a reminder of what we argued in Chapter 2, is an example that should appeal to anyone with a modicum of experience with formal logic. On page one or so of just about every standard logic textbook you learn the difference between deductive and inductive arguments. Then you get a grip on the idea of a valid deductive argument *due to one or more of its forms*. This is significant progress. It took thousands of years to get to the point where we could recognize validity with respect to form. Then you learn to distinguish sound arguments from valid arguments, sound arguments moving validly from true premises. Progress once again. All this progress before finishing a few pages of a logic textbook. Years later it dawns on you that there is a distinction to be made between a sound argument and a proof. Strange, you think, that you had to recognize this point on your own. Why don't logic books move from sound argument to proof? Is it because textbook writers are not aware of the distinction and think a sound argument is as good an argument as one can have? Or is it that they are aware of the distinction, but don't quite know what to say about proof? Or what? Why the silence about proof? No matter. *You* have come to see that a sound argument can be utterly worthless. *Fermat's Last Theorem is true; therefore it is true.* The premise of this utterly trivial argument is true and the conclusion follows, and so the argument is sound. However, no one thinks that this argument advances mathematics, or that Andrew Wiles and his colleagues wasted their breath needlessly slogging through an immensely complicated proof of Fermat's Last Theorem, when all they had to do was deduce it from itself in one step. So, again, progress.

But what is a proof? That is not easy to say.[1] Does G.E. Moore's famous argument, "Here's one hand. Here's another," prove the existence of objects external to the mind? Moore thought so. Should you? This is not easily settled. You need to think more about the character of proof, read Moore and others on proof, and do more—maybe a lot more—philosophy. Still, you make personal progress. Philosophy being philosophy, calling everything into question, whatever you or anyone else decides about proof will be met with objections. No matter. You will have seen something significant and can expect to see more, the inevitable dialectic about the matter helping to open your eyes.

Here is a different example of personal progress that will perhaps be more to the liking of someone unacquainted with formal logic.

---

[1]   Some logicians obscure everything by identifying "proof" with "derivation."

As a youth you assumed your self, your very self, was hidden from all others but transparent to you. Self is open to self. But a dose of Kierkegaardian and Nietzschean irony later vaporized the illusion. Neither philosopher pounded you with Aristotelian syllogisms. Instead, Kierkegaard invited you to an evening's banquet, during which you learned much—*in vino veritas*. And at daybreak, Nietzsche's writing, with "its mock distance, its sudden intimacy, its sweeping playfulness, its jeers, sneers, jokes, and whispers—its abrupt unanticipated kills…" set you to thinking that perhaps none of your real motives have hitherto displayed themselves to you.[2] Doubts were compounded when you went on to read Freud and Marx, those other disturbing masters of suspicion. You strongly suspect there is more to your self than is recognized by your self.

About these examples, the first turning on logic, and the second on layers of the self, it might be objected that neither deals with the focus of this chapter—ontology. But that is not true. Logic does deal with ontology, though not in a clamorous voice. Ontological claims are usually implicit. Standard logical systems all presuppose the truth of the Principle of Non-Contradiction. Some nonstandard systems do not.[3] And exploring the self is an ontological exercise, since it informs us about layers within the psyche of human nature. Before launching into his memorable portrayal of a woman about to set out with a man with disturbing aspirations, Sartre rightly poses the ontological question, What must the nature of man be if he is to be capable of self-deception?[4]

Some disillusioned, anti-philosophical philosophers believe they have learned nothing from philosophy except how to see through its pretensions. Yet, professional philosophers generally believe they have made at least personal progress. They may not have succeeded in persuading their

---

[2] Søren Kierkegaard, "In Vino Veritas (The Banquet)" in *Kierkegaard's Writings XI: Stages on Life's Way*, ed. Howard V. Hong and Edna H. Hong (Princeton: Princeton University Press, 1988), 7–86. Arthur C. Danto, "Nietzsche's Daybreak," in *Reading Nietzsche*, ed. Robert C. Solomon and Kathleen Marie Higgins (Oxford: Oxford University Press, 1888), 190.

[3] For helpful brief discussion of the principle of non-contradiction and various logical systems, see Greg Restall, "Laws of Non-Contradiction, Laws of Excluded Middle, and Logics" in *The Law of Non-Contradiction: New Philosophical Essays*, ed. Graham Priest, J.C. Beall, and Bradley Armour-Garb (Oxford: Clarendon, 2006). It is worth noting that, like many logicians, Restall sees the Principle of Non-contradiction as a logical principle, overlooking its manifest ontological character.

[4] Sartre, *Being and Nothingness*, 55–56. However, we have followed Walter Kaufmann's rather than the Barne's translation at this point. For justification of our deviation from Barnes here, see Walter Kaufmann, *Existentialism from Dostoevsky to Sartre* (New York: New American Library, 1975), 280. We leave it to Sartre scholars to reconcile this with his well-known hostility to the idea that humans have natures.

colleagues that, say, their special brand of physicalism or anti-physicalism is the long-sought truth about humankind and our place in the world. Still, as they see it, they are inured to the pleadings of subtle sophistries, and they understand better the substance and shadows of their own lives. With good reason, they believe that they see what, in all likelihood, they would not have seen had they not more than once felt philosophically confused by piercing Socratic dialectic. They are not alone in making this fair surmise. Thus, premise (S-2) of *The Success Argument* needs qualification. And when the proposition is qualified, *The Success Argument* loses its smack.

This is because qualifying (S-2) affects (S-3). If (S-2) is understood to speak of success only in the way we understand success in science, then (S-2) is true, but (S-3) is false, for pure ontology could be valuable to one making progress, even though pure ontology does not progress in the same way as science. On the other hand, if (S-2) is understood more broadly to include the kind of progress suitable to philosophy, personal progress, then (S-2) is false. After the kinds of progress distinction is drawn, *The Success Argument* can be seen as specious.

The replacement argument

The Replacement Argument restated

Reduced to its main elements, *The Replacement Argument* runs:

(R-1)   Over time science has obliterated huge swaths of what once passed for philosophic wisdom.

(R-2)   So, it is likely that at sometime in the future there will be little or nothing left of this ancient practice.

(R-3)   And, if at sometime in the future there will be little or nothing left of this ancient practice, then pure ontology (past and present) is worthless, and Thesis T is false.

(Con)   So, pure ontology, and so on.

Propositions (R-1) and (R-3) are conceded. But not (R-2).

Rather than first thinking through reasons to resist (R-2), let us begin by acknowledging its appeal.

Reasons to accept (R-2)

It is often said that history is replete with examples of science replacing philosophical theorizing. The devastation of Aristotle's natural philosophy alone, it is claimed, suffices to make the point. Though it was dominant for millennia, next to nothing is left of Aristotle's ideas on the heavens, motion, space, time, causality, teleology, the hylomorphic (matter/form) composition of bodies, and of the soul as substantial form of the body. So on and on it goes. Since Kepler, Galileo, and Newton, scientists have shredded Aristotle's physical theories, while Wallace and Darwin buried his biological theories right down to the very concept of a species. Gone, all gone. Furthermore, this does not address what can be said about science trampling over the works of philosophers before and after Aristotle.

There surely is much that is true in all of this. Nonetheless, we maintain, (R-2) should be rejected. Philosophical ontology is not going to disappear.

Reasons to reject (R-2)

Overview

There are at least three reasons for doubting Premise (R-2): (1) the inductive backing of (R-1) is much weaker than it initially appears; (2) there is counter-inductive evidence; and (3) philosophy cannot be eliminated from science itself.

First reason to reject (R-2): Limits of scientistic induction

First, the inference from (R-1) to (R-2) hangs on too little inductive evidence.

For the replacement thesis to hold with respect to a topic, it is necessary that science* actually dealt with the topic.[5] Of course, sciences such as astronomy have taken up the questions posed, for example, in Aristotle's *On the Heavens*; and they have shown a great deal of its teachings to be mistaken. But there are many general questions discussed in *On the Heavens* and Aristotle's other natural works—*Physics, On Generation and Corruption, On the Soul, History of Animals*, and *On the Parts of Animals*—that science has left largely unresolved.

The most general of these works is *The Physics*. In this work, Aristotle sets out to elucidate the nature of natural substances. Immediately he confronts a number of questions: What is a substance? What is a natural substance? Are the natures of natural substances to be understood through their behavior? What is local motion? What are the properties attendant on movement and rest, place, and time? How does one unravel the paradoxes of Parmenides and Zeno? Do natural entities move toward ends? Is there such a thing as chance? Are all changes movements, or are there other kinds of change? Are all changes surface changes of enduring natural substances, or can substances be generated and corrupted? If they can, what is the underlying substratum?

---

[5] Not "science" without a *, since starless science can be indistinguishable from philosophy.

These questions certainly look legitimate. At the same time, it is not easy to find much in physics that looks like an attempt to define them, that is, to give expression to their essence. Take *motion*. Modern physics is all about motion, and dictionaries of physics often contain an entry on motion. But these entries hardly look like strict definitions of the reality. For example, *The Oxford Dictionary of Physics* tells us that motion is

> A change in the position of the body or system with respect to time, as measured by a particular observer in a particular frame of reference. Only relative motion can be measured; absolute motion is meaningless.[6]

This is pretty much what one finds in any dictionary of physics. Notice that the depiction does not distinguish motion from mere relocation, which could be effected by annihilation and recreation at a different point (by God or nature, as in the early days of quantum mechanics with its mysterious jumps from orbit to orbit within an atom.) Furthermore, the definition generates Zenonian problems about distinguishing a moving body from a resting body. If the depiction is supposed to be a definition of motion, it fails because "change" is a synonym of "motion," and the definition will be *idem per idem*.

One might respond that no one should look for a definition of motion in a physics dictionary, or for that matter, in any treatise or book on physics. Such works deal with only what is useful for formulas, predictions, and explanations that feature mathematical precision. Qualitative definitions of motion are entirely useless for these purposes. Disputing whether radian or steradian are properly basic or derived quantities can be fruitful, but not whether Aristotle's definition of motion in terms of act and potency is correct or is as basic as it can be, since his definition mentions no quantities at all and thus supports no calculations.

This response has roots in Descartes's contributions to the mechanization of the world picture and subsequent scientism. Aquinas thought no definition of motion could be better than Aristotle's. Descartes castigated Aristotle for offering a befuddling and useless definition in terms of act and potency. For the purposes of mathematical physics, perhaps Aristotle's definition *is* unimportant. But for *all* purposes? Is it a mistake to ask for an articulation of the essence of motion, one that provides a path toward the resolution of Zenonian paradoxes? It hardly seems so, and not just to philosophers smitten by Aristotle. Consider this extraordinary autobiographical remark by one of the twentieth century's major contributors to quantum mechanics, David Bohm:

> I would say that in my scientific and philosophical work, my main concern has been with understanding the nature of reality in general

---

6   *Oxford Dictionary of Physics* (Oxford: Oxford University Press, 2009), 341.

and of consciousness in particular as a coherent whole, which is never static or complete, but which is in an unending process of movement and unfoldment. Thus, when I look back, I see that even as a child I was fascinated by the puzzle, indeed the mystery, of what is the nature of movement. Whenever one *thinks* of anything, it seems to be apprehended either as static, or as a series of static images. Yet, in the actual experience of movement, one *senses* an unbroken, undivided process of flow, to which the series of static images in thought is related as a series of "still" photographs might be related to the actuality of a speeding car. This question was, of course, already raised in essence philosophically more than 2,000 years ago in Zeno's paradoxes; but as yet, it cannot be said to have a satisfactory resolution.[7]

Bohm's abiding concerns about the nature of motion should count at least as much as those of any philosopher of science renouncing questions about what it is. Like Aristotle, Bohm wants to grasp the essence of motion, and to understand motion in a way that provides a response to Zeno's captivating paradoxes. The question, "What is motion?" is perfectly legitimate, and if modern science is to advance our understanding of the nature of motion, it is nonetheless unlikely to do so by casting the definition entirely in mathematical terms.

Motion is but the first of a dozen common physical realities that Aristotle dealt with, investigating their nature, origin, and purpose. We are very far from contending either that he got all of it right or that science today has little or nothing to say about these features of the world. However, if quantum mechanics, for example, encourages us to take a fresh look at motion or chance, it does not follow that quantum mechanics has provided or can provide definitions that entirely replace the definitions of some of the better offerings of the past or future appeals to pure ontology.

Some may complain that our argument here is misleading. We found a passage in a respectable scientific source that seems to suggest that philosophers can carry on like Aristotle by asking questions of the form "What is X?" and giving penetrating answers without any reliance on advances in science. But properly understood, this passage points in an entirely different direction. Bohm is looking with guarded hope toward future science to illuminate the nature of motion. There is no suggestion here that armchair analysis could reveal the essence of motion without any regard to the advance of science.

---

[7] David Bohm, *Wholeness and the Implicate Order* (London: Routledge, 1995), ix–x. For elaboration in a more technical context, see David Bohm, *Quantum Theory* (New York: Dover, 1979), chapter 8, 144–172.

This objection receives support from a recent argument of P.D. Magnus. For him any notion of an essence independent of science is functionless. Unlike many analytic philosophers who, following Kripke and Putnam, introduce natural kinds in response to general questions about language and reference, Magnus begins with the demands of science to justify the introduction of natural kinds. Natural kinds are thus to be understood as domain specific. Essences (as distinguished from natural kinds) recede in interest, and consequently lose ontological respectability, since they do nothing to support scientific inductions or further explanations. Magnus writes:

> Conceivably…one could first (give) an independent, metaphysical account of natural kinds in terms of universals, real essences, modally robust categories. Then one could require that science be inquiry into those things. Thus, the account of natural kinds would serve as a constraint on what would count as science. This approach would be *a priori* philosophizing of the worst kind, and I do not see how it could succeed.[8]

Magnus seems to have in mind the putative essences of things, such as mallards. For Magnus, things fall into natural kinds only insofar as postulated natural kinds support induction, predictions, and explanations. But essences supposedly standing behind the natural kinds are worse than functionless, since they constrain science in hurtful ways. Given a view of essence standing behind domain-specific natural kinds, nothing will count as science unless it articulates these essences—reveals, as it were, the essence of particular essences. Philosophy, however, cannot rightly lay down the law to science in this way. Instead, philosophy must be on the receiving end of the news about fish, planets, and muffins, which are natural kinds only because they figure in inductions, predictions, and explanations in particular sciences. There are no essences independent of domains of particular sciences.

At first, Magnus's line of argument might well appear plausible, provided the focus is on things, objects, and substances; the main contention appears less attractive when account is taken of actions, properties, and relations of things. We imagine the armchair philosopher on a hot day musing on his porch about brown trout and hummingbirds, and then later informing the biologist that if biology does not eventually define the essences spirited into existence in the dark theater of the visionary's imagination, then biology has not done its job. Once it dawns on us, however, that Magnus's generalization applies as much to

---

[8]   P.D. Magnus, *Scientific Enquiry and Natural Kinds: From Planets to Mallards* (New York: Palgrave MacMillan, 2012), 8–9.

actions, properties, and relations as to the entities that possess them—objects and substances—his contentions begin to look less enthralling. Why should it be *a priori* philosophy of the worst kind to believe that movement has an essence, that science should attend to the ubiquitous phenomenon, and that, as yet, it has not yielded the insight Bohm and many others hoped would be achieved? Or again, why is it woodenheaded to attend to the nature of bad faith, self-deception, and dozens of more elevated activities and attitudes with a view to asking Sartre's question about human nature?

It is a mistake to ask of some bit of behavior, some property, or some relation X, "What is X?" without referring X to a particular domain of science only if X has no intelligible structure independent of the human mind approaching it through a scientific system. But many X's had that structure long before anyone was in a position to make such an approach. Eons before Kepler and ages before our primeval ancestors took to their stomping grounds, our earth moved around our sun. Its movement took place independent of the action or the saying-so of any human. And that movement had an intelligible structure prior to anyone being able to mathematize it or ponder the perplexities of Zeno.

If surface movements, actions, properties, and relations have science-independent structures, why shouldn't the bearers of such surface features not have intelligible structures, which the ancients called "essences"? As far as we can see, Magnus supplies no reason at all for thinking they do not, no reason at all other than unbounded deference to science, which leads generally astute writers to blurt such dubious dogmas as, "When choosing the fundamental posits of one's ontology, one must look to scientific practice rather than philosophical prejudice."[9] Why can't there be something between the two, something like common sense, ordinary experience, and *a priori* thinking?

Consider the *appearance* of goal directedness in the natural world. The appearance is there for anyone to appreciate from the farm girl to the famed geneticist she eventually becomes. The activities of birth, growth, reproduction, and survival in a competitive world require some explanation. Natural selection is half of it. Genetics provides much or all of the remainder. There could be nothing amiss in the mere quest for internal causes of variation to complement the Wallace/Darwin explanation. External behavior has internal causes. The deepest of these were called "essences." They may be called something else today, such as "constitutions" or "necessary and sufficient conditions." Nevertheless, what was sought remained identical: an answer to the question, "What must the structure of this animal be if it is to be capable of surviving and leaving offspring?"

---

[9]   Maudlin, *The Metaphysics Within Physics*, 1.

Let us recap. We are in the middle of what we called *The Replacement Argument*, an argument that sought to show that science will eventually supersede philosophical ontology, since (R-1) *Science has obliterated huge swaths of what once passed for philosophic wisdom*, which warrants (R-2) *It is likely that sometime in the future there will be little or nothing left of this ancient practice of philosophical ontology*. While acknowledging that science* has indeed taken over much philosophic turf, we maintained that the inductive evidence is far too weak for the strong conclusion that philosophy will someday go the way of astrology. There are plenty of legitimate problems for philosophy to investigate, including many with the logical form, "What is X?" Some maintain that this question has no meaning outside of particular domains of science. Complementing arguments of earlier chapters, we urged that the question certainly makes sense at the level of actions, properties, and relations, and there is no reason to think it ceases to make sense when the X in question is about the essence of such attributes.

Second reason to reject (R-2): Counter-inductive evidence

The second reason for rejecting (R-2) is the notorious difficulty contemporary science has had getting anywhere with a number of issues, including most significantly the so-called "hard problems" revolving around consciousness in its different modalities.[10] How does consciousness arise? Is consciousness entirely physical? How does consciousness impact behavior? Bookshelves and computer data banks are loaded with scientific "answers" to these questions, but even many working in the relevant scientific areas—neuroscience chief among them—have admitted being stumped. One such admission appeared in a distinguished textbook in cognitive neuroscience—an admission that disappears from a later edition. After 532 pages detailing the structure and activity of the nervous system in relationship to cognition, the authors of *Cognitive Neuroscience* lament, "Right from the start we can say that science has little to say about sentience. We are clueless on how the brain creates sentience."[11] Six hundred thirty pages into Stephen Palmer's acclaimed *Vision Science* the reader learns, "(T)o this writer's knowledge, nobody has ever suggested a theory that the scientific community regards as giving even a remotely plausible causal account of how consciousness arises or why it has

---

[10] This section develops points made in Sandra Menssen and Thomas D. Sullivan, *The Agnostic Inquirer: Revelation from a Philosophic Standpoint* (Grand Rapids, MI: Eerdmans, 2007), 242–244.

[11] Michael S. Gazzaniga, Richard B. Ivry, and George R. Mangun, *Cognitive Neuroscience: The Biology of the Mind*, 2nd ed. (New York: W.W. Norton, 2002), 659–660. A subsequent edition could find no space for this forthright acknowledgement.

the particular qualities it does."[12] How consciousness, with its strange first-person properties, is produced is one problem about which current science appears to have next to nothing to say. Of course, neuroscience provides immense detail about the activity of the nervous system. Certainly, neural activity is implicated in the production of subjective states. But, given all of the information in the world about the physics and chemistry of neural processes, you can still ask, "Yes, but why does it sound like *this*."

It is also hard to understand what subjective states are good for. In *The Quest for Consciousness: A Neurobiological Approach*,[13] a work John Searle praised as the best of its kind, Christof Koch devotes an entire chapter to his speculations about the function of consciousness. Koch feels the problem acutely, since in earlier chapters he emphasized how in a rapid and flawless manner both healthy and brain-damaged persons execute learned, stereotypical behavior. The possibility of all activity being carried out in this zombie-like fashion—Koch entitles one chapter "What You Can Do Without Being Conscious: The Zombie Within"—prompts him to raise the troubling question: "If so much processing can go on in the dark, without any feelings, why is a conscious mental life needed at all? What evolutionary advantage favored conscious brains over brains that are nothing but large bundles of zombie agents?"[14] Koch lists 17 possibilities. Consciousness might be critical for promoting access to short-term memory, and so on. Yet, as Koch proceeds to focus on one function, "executive summary," he sets the stage by reiterating a point he earlier made in a book with Francis Crick. "Our...assumption is based on the broad idea of the biological usefulness of visual awareness (or, more strictly of its neural correlate)."[15] Yes, indeed, more strictly. Because that is all we get, talk that is really about the function of the activities of the neural correlate, not consciousness itself. Contrary to Koch's intentions, his parenthetical remark undercuts the entire project of explaining the function of consciousness.[16] Crick and Koch pose a hard question about consciousness, but then sotto voce replace it with a more tractable cousin. While it is often enough proclaimed that in this millennium an answer to the hard questions will be forthcoming, as yet there has not been even a hint of what shape an answer could take.

[12] Stephen E. Palmer, *Vision Science: Photons to Phenomenology* (Cambridge, MA: MIT Press, 1999), 630.

[13] Christof Koch, *The Quest for Consciousness: A Neurobiological Approach* (Englewood, CO: Roberts, 2004).

[14] Koch, *The Quest for Consciousness*, 231.

[15] Koch, *The Quest for Consciousness*, 233, quoting F.C. Crick and C. Koch, "Are We Aware of Neural Activity in Primary Visual Context?" *Nature* 375 (1995): 121–123.

[16] In an email exchange, Koch acknowledged our claim. C. Koch, email message to author, January 20, 2006.

About such matters, philosophers and scientists are passionately divided among themselves. To some it seems clear that ever since Darwin we have made steady progress across all fronts, and we are well on our way to understanding the nature of cognition and various psychological modalities, including the subjective side of consciousness and the conscious targeting of abstract attributes.[17] Others vehemently disagree. The dissenters include prominent philosophers who believe firmly that this is the only world there is and no divine guidance is to be invoked to account for the mysteries surrounding our lives. Among noted naturalistic dissenters is Thomas Nagel, who bravely entitled his latest attack on what he takes to be an embarrassing fad, *Mind and Cosmos: Why the Materialist Neo-Darwinian Conception of Nature is Almost Certainly False*.[18] As expected, the work has provoked a scornful reaction among the true believers. Our point is not that Nagel is right and his critics wrong (though we do think Nagel is closer to the truth with respect to his position on consciousness); it is rather that there is plenty of learned resistance to the materialist dogma about the mind, and there has been ever since Alfred Wallace, the neglected coinventor of the theory of natural selection, broke with Charles Darwin over many of the same issues concerning mind and value.[19]

Third reason to reject (R-2): Science presupposes philosophy

A third reason to reject premise (R-2) is that science cannot replace all philosophy, because science* presupposes some pure ontological positions.

Science—at least science* in the tight, earlier defined sense—is tied to the idea that hypotheses must be tested. Testing entails that experiments can be repeated by multiple researchers operating at different times and sites. It further follows that there is more than one embodied consciousness manipulating devices, reading results, and comparing outcomes with others. All of these contentions are either close to or identical with everyday

---

[17] We have developed the point about conscious awareness of abstract attributes posing the most difficult challenge to physicalism in "Consciousness and the Intentional Awareness of Instantiables," in *Mind and Its Place in the World: Non-reductionist Approaches to the Ontology of Consciousness*, ed. Alexander Batthyany and Avshaloom Elitzur (Frankfurt: Ontos/Verlag, 2006).

[18] Thomas Nagel, *Mind and Cosmos: Why the Materialist Neo-Darwinian Conception of Nature is Almost Certainly False* (Oxford: Oxford University Press, 2012). Also see, Jerry Fodor and Massimo Piattelli-Palmarini, *What Darwin Got Wrong* (New York: Farrar, Straus, and Giroux, 2010); Alvin Plantinga, *Where the Conflict Really Lies: Science, Religion, and Naturalism* (Oxford: Oxford University Press, 2010).

[19] Alfred Russel Wallace, "'A Being Apart': Human Evolution," in *Infinite Tropics: An Alfred Russel Wallace Anthology*, ed. Andrew Berry (London: Verso, 2002). Fodor and Piattelli-Palmarini, *What Darwin Got Wrong*; Plantinga, *Where the Conflict Really Lies*.

ontological assumptions. If this folk ontology is somehow basically wrong—and it is exceedingly difficult to see how it could be—it is nonetheless presupposed by science. Were science* to attempt to forsake these assumptions, it would undercut itself. And the explication and defense of the ontological assumptions must be left to pure ontology.

An obvious way to reply would be to insist that unconscious robots could carry science forward. No matter how elaborately contrived, however, unconscious robots would be only physical entities, and their doings and "reports" to each other of their successes and failures would no more constitute science than would the fossil record constitute paleontology. The fossil record is the object of the study, not the study itself. Science arises only when something is aware of something. If a robot records some data or performs calculations on it, nothing is known until some conscious mind reads it.[20]

Other ontological presuppositions of science are expressed by *The Principle of Non-contradiction* (PNC) and by a number of far less frequently recognized fundamental principles. Aristotle explained the PNC in several different ways, including the following translation of a key text:

> For the same thing to hold good and not hold good simultaneously of the same thing and in the same respect is impossible . . . .[21]

The PNC is assumed in every science. No one arguing that humans descended from less complex forms of life thinks that while the conclusion of the argument holds, it may still be the case that we did not evolve. Moreover, it is an ontological principle, not a "mere" logical principle, since it pertains to entities.

It might be maintained, however, that while the PNC holds at the level governed by classical physics, it fails in the world of quantum mechanics. Rather than involve ourselves in this complex issue, however, we can sustain our general position by calling attention to a quite different, unnamed principle. Consider the proposition:

> If a proposition p is true, not-p is also true, and if the matter admits of degrees, then not-p is even more true.

For example, if it is true that snow is white, then it is also not-white, and more truly not-white than white.

---

[20] This is not to say the robot couldn't pass a Turing Test, but we stand with Searle and his Chinese room argument.

[21] Aristotle, *Metaphysics* 1005b–18–22, in *Aristotle Metaphysics Books Γ, Δ, and E*, 2nd ed., trans. Christopher Kirwan (Oxford: Oxford University Press, 2003).

Since it is sometimes said "the Devil is the Father of Lies," we might call this *The Devil's First Principle* (DFP). The falsity of the DFP is certainly presupposed by every science. The denial thus is an irreplaceable first principle of science and all other discourse. And, since the denial of the DFP covers everything, not-DFP is also an ontological claim.

The poverty of means argument

The argument restated

Reduced to its immediate premises for the conclusion, *The Poverty of Means Argument* runs:

(P-1)   Pure ontology lacks the means science has developed to explore the world.

(P-2)   If so, then pure ontology is too unreliable to produce anything of worth.

(P-3)   If pure ontology is too unreliable to produce anything of worth about ontology, then pure ontology is useless and Thesis T is false.

(Con)   Therefore, pure philosophical ontology is useless, and so on, and Thesis T is false.

As we see it, premises (P-1) and (P-3) are true, but (P-2) is false.

Though we are not going to question (P-1), it is useful to dwell a little on its appeal. Given the way we have defined science* and pure ontology, (P-1) is true in virtue of the meaning of the terms. But seeing that little carries with it none of the impact of the truth of the proposition. Proposition (P-1) carries with it an immense load of history and evidence. This is no place to dilate, but we can at least remind ourselves of how impressive the contention is when you mentally scan the history it represents, which best begins with Aristotle.

When translations of his work finally reached Western Europe thanks to the industry of Islamic scholars, the universities dominated by Christian theological teaching convulsed as they tried to assimilate a virtual encyclopedia of secular learning that dealt convincingly with an enormous range of subjects, some of it seemingly at odds with revelation. It was quite understandable that Aristotle's authority weighed heavily on thinkers through the centuries. Writing years after Aquinas wrote his treatises on Aristotle, William of Ockham, in his *Commentary on Aristotle's Physics*, could still refer to "lynx-eyed Aristotle" in a way that suggested that the master's word about reality needed to be taken seriously. While nearly everyone who has studied

Aristotle is impressed with his genius, it is obvious that a lynx's eye is no substitute for an ordinary microscope or telescope, let alone a cyclotron.

From such facts, it is tempting to infer that Aristotle knew nothing that we cannot apprehend better as a result of our wonderful instruments. You want to know about the fundamental structure of matter? You do not stare lynx-eyed. You work on a team using a particle accelerator. If you want to know about the mind, you use fMRIs to scan the brain. You do not speculate with Aristotle about the heart as the seat of thought. Aristotle stands for everyone working without the instruments of science. This is why science has been so successful and philosophy such a failure. This is why science* has replaced philosophical speculation on a thousand fronts.

Many have yielded to this enticing line of argument. It begins with an undeniable truth that carries memory back over the long history of the emergence of science from its beginnings with the Greeks. But, it is one thing to recognize the truth of (P-1) and to sense its power to persuade; it is altogether quite another to leap from (P-1) to (P-2) and infer that pure ontology is too unreliable to produce anything of worth. For it may be that pure philosophy possesses means sufficient to draw interesting conclusions about matters that elude the probing of instruments extending the human sensorium and lie beyond the territory that can be profitably explored by controlled experiment.

Maybe, you ask, but where is the evidence?

Means

Well, we have already gathered some. In earlier chapters, we depicted at some length *a priori* and other forms of intuition and reasoning, personal intuitions and experiences, the intuitions and experiences of others.[22] And in this chapter we suggested the reader recall personal experiences of philosophical progress, such as making one's way through validity to soundness to proof, and digging into the layers of one's own psyche, one's own ontology structure in response to the probings of Kierkegaard, Nietzsche, Sartre, and other "life philosophers." If any of this resonates with you, we are more than half way home. For if you know *you* made progress under the tutelage of philosophy, then you, we, and everyone else must possess adequate means. And these means manifestly are not those of science*.

But means do have something to do with science, the starless enterprise. While science* uses high-powered instruments, mathematics, experimental

---

[22] We also listed scientific and mathematical concepts and results. In the present context, however, we obviously cannot make anything of these.

techniques, and the like, science uses very much the same means available to pure ontology. Since science makes progress, so then may pure ontology, in the sense we have articulated.

Two familiar cases of progress in science calling upon only the same means as pure ontology include Galileo's *a priori* argument that heavy bodies do not fall faster than light bodies in a vacuum, and the more empirical argument by Wallace and Darwin that natural selection plays a large role in the evolution of species.

Galileo

Legend has it that Galileo smashed Aristotle's physics, finally putting an end to ungrounded Aristotelian speculation about the physical world. Aristotle guessed; Galileo performed experiments. Of course, Galileo did indeed perform fascinating experiments that, had Aristotle thought them up, would have led to a very different physical worldview than the one he assailed. In formulating the foundations of a new science of motion, Galileo also engaged in a considerable amount of pure *a priori* reasoning. What is more, he refused to let experimental results stand in the way of accepting the conclusions of his *a priori* reasoning.

In the dialogue on *Two New Sciences*, Galileo offers the following argument against the Aristotelian notion that heavier bodies fall faster than lighter bodies. It is worthwhile hearing Galileo's voice (speaking through Salviati) as he argues, in one of the great mental experiments in the history of science, that Aristotelian mechanics regarding falling bodies leads to a contradiction:

Salviati: But, even without further experiment, it is possible to prove clearly, by means of a short and conclusive argument, that a heavier body does not move more rapidly than a lighter one provided both bodies are of the same material and in short such as those mentioned by Aristotle. But tell me, Simplicio, whether you admit that each falling body acquires a definite speed fixed by nature, a velocity which cannot be increased or diminished except by the use of force (*violenza*) or resistance.

Simplicio: There can be no doubt but that one and the same body moving in a single medium has a fixed velocity which is determined by nature and which cannot be increased except by the addition of momentum (*impeto*) or diminished except by some resistance which retards it.

Salviati: If then we take two bodies whose natural speeds are different, it is clear that on uniting the two, the more rapid one will be partly retarded by the slower, and the slower will be somewhat hastened by the swifter. Do you not agree with me in this opinion?

Simplicio: You are unquestionably right.

Salviati: But if this is true, and if a large stone moves with a speed of, say, eight, while a smaller moves with a speed of four, then when they are united, the system will move with a speed less than eight; but the two stones when tied together make a stone larger than that which before moved with a speed of eight. Hence the heavier body moves with less speed than the lighter; an effect which is contrary to your supposition. Thus you see how, from your assumption that the heavier body moves more rapidly than the lighter one, I infer that the heavier body moves more slowly.[23]

Experience contradicts the result, Salviati admits. No matter, it does so less than it does Aristotle's view. A heavy stone does fall a little faster when there is air resistance. Soon after the time of Galileo, the invention of the air pump made it possible to confirm that in an evacuated glass tube a feather and a heavy coin fall at the same rate. Air resistance was responsible for the discrepancy between reasoning and fact. *A priori* reasoning, however, is what Galileo relied on. And it was perfectly all right to do so, not just because this is the style of reasoning (wrongly) imputed to Aristotle, and so fair in a dialectical context, but more importantly because the *a priori* reasoning actually explains why heavier bodies do not and cannot fall faster than lighter bodies by nature. Later experiments confirm the reasoning, but the reasoning supplies an explanation that cannot be arrived at solely by experiment.

Wallace/Darwin

Charles Darwin and Alfred Wallace are generally credited with basing their conclusions on an enormous range of empirical evidence. And they did. But while the entire case as presented was loaded with detailed observations about biological specimens, the data they gathered did not require a microscope or any other equipment that was beyond the ingenuity of the Greeks. The core

---

[23] Galileo Galilei, "First Day," in *Dialogues Concerning Two New Sciences*, trans. Henry Crew and Alfonso de Salvio (Toronto: Dover, 1954), 62–63.

ideas of the theory they advanced were justified by an argument that required nothing beyond ordinary observation of one's surroundings—and ingenious reasoning. Here is the way Wallace stated his recollection of his discovery:

> In February, 1858, I was living at Ternate, one of the Moluccas Islands and was suffering from a sharp attack of intermittent fever, which obliged me to lie down every afternoon during the cold and subsequent hot fits which lasted together two and three hours. It was during one of these fits, while I was thinking over the possible mode of origin of new species, that somehow my thought turned to the "positive checks" to increase among savages and others described in much detail in the celebrated *Essay on Population*, by Malthus, a work I had read a dozen years before. Their checks—disease, famine, accidents, wars, &c.—are what keep down the population, and it suddenly occurred to me that in the case of wild animals these checks would act with much more severity, and as the lower animals all tended to increase more rapidly than man, while their population remained on the average constant, there suddenly flashed upon me the idea of the survival of the fittest— that those individuals which every year are removed by these events causes—termed collectively the "struggle for existence"—must on the average and in the long run be inferior in some one or more ways to those which managed to survive. The more I thought of this the more certain it appeared to be; while the only alternative theory—that those who succumbed to enemies, or want of food, or disease, drought, or cold, were in every way and always as well constituted as those that survived—seemed to me impossible and unthinkable.[24]

Aristotle and hylomorphism

We have been arguing that if the means at the disposal of science (not science*, but science) suffice to establish interesting results about the way things are, then there is no reason to believe that, using the same means, pure ontology cannot do the same. In fact, as must be obvious by now, we see no deep difference between pure ontology and starless science. The only difference is that some work is generally thought to belong to the history of science, some not, and so we find two names for the same thing, differing only in connotation.

---

[24] John Langdon Brooks, *Just Before the Origin: Alfred Russell Wallace's Theory of Evolution* (New York: Columbia University Press, 1984), 181, quoting Wallace, "The Dawn of a Great Discovery: My Relations with Darwin in Reference to the Theory of Natural Selection," *Black and White* (January 17, 1903): 78–79.

This might be thought to be a slight of hand. Can we point to some work in past philosophical ontology that is not generally called science, yet is interesting in its consequences? We could gesture indiscriminately in the direction of the entire history of philosophy. But since we have made so much along the way of the limits of Aristotle's philosophy of nature, his ontology (in our terms), let us conclude with a daring proposal regarding one of his notorious teachings—the doctrine of prime matter and substantial form.

Hylomorphism (as it came to be called) is widely thought to be a paradigm of the mumble-jumble that modern science eliminated in favor of clear, testable, mathematized concepts. Yet, the generally scorned concepts of prime matter and substantial form, or something very near to them, keep coming up in the writings of the likes of Heisenberg, Bohm, Shimony, and Suppes, who have in one way or another invoked the doctrine, with the last mentioned being explicit about how Aristotle's concept of matter might be put to good use in quantum mechanics.[25] To be sure, they do not arrive at the concepts by moving down the path Aristotle marks out; rather, they find that contemporary science requires something like these ideas.

While in eclipse now, the hylomorphic doctrine has been invoked for millennia to articulate a conception of life and mind almost altogether lost amid the unsatisfying options on the table today. It is, we intend to argue, a position well worth reconsidering.

Of course, after examining it closely one might rightfully conclude that the doctrine cannot help us. But, then, we ought not scorn a theory unless we first grasp the problem to which it responds and can think of or find a better solution.

And that means thinking along with a gifted pure ontologist.

---

[25] We have in mind Patrick Suppes's proposal in an unnoticed but intriguing paper on the concept of matter. See Patrick Suppes, "Aristotle's Concept of Matter and Its Relationship to Modern Concepts of Matter," *Synthese* 28 (1974): 27–50.

6

Philosophic Attacks on Past and Present Philosophy

In Chapter 3 we distinguished two kinds of supporting arguments for a thesis: direct and indirect. Direct supporting arguments for a thesis proceed *without* detouring through arguments designed to refute the thesis. Indirect arguments for a thesis proceed *by means of* detouring through arguments intended to refute it. In Chapter 3 we also proposed direct arguments for Thesis T. In Chapters 4 and 5 we proposed indirect arguments for Thesis T, in response to scientistic objections. In this chapter we shall propose indirect arguments for Thesis T in response to a philosophical objection, one we regard as having exercised the greatest influence.

The cyclical revolutionary mandate: Inquiry into past philosophical sources for first-order philosophical purposes is pointless because philosophers must start all over again from scratch with the finally discovered correct philosophical method

The cyclical revolutionary mandate objection is based upon a call for total philosophical revolution:

> We've finally discovered the once-and-for-all correct philosophical method that renders all past philosophical efforts completely irrelevant. We must march together into the philosophical future with our new method in hand, ruthlessly cutting out by the roots everything our method deems illegitimate. Unlike Lot's daughter,[1] we must never look back. Because no past inquirers grasped the nature of our new philosophical method, their efforts were fatally misguided and consequently of no use to us.

---

[1] Genesis 19:26.

Near-contemporary revolutionaries

Revolutionary calls have been sounded in both contemporary and near-contemporary times. We begin with examples of the latter.

Wittgenstein

Although everyone believes that Wittgenstein was a philosophical revolutionary, there is a long-standing controversy over what kind of revolutionary he was. We mention just two of several possible accounts.

According to one interpretation, he invents new methods of inquiry intended to replace the faulty methods of traditional philosophy. Philosophical inquiry is a legitimate activity that deserves to continue, but only if it proceeds by using the new methods. Given the nature of philosophy, the exact nature of Wittgenstein's new methods is predictably controversial, but whatever else they involve, they involve at least the systematic practice of bringing to mind how "ordinary" people use language.

According to a second, more radical, interpretation, Wittgenstein invents new methods all right, but he does *not* intend them as a means of continuing philosophical inquiry, but rather as a means of *permanently ridding oneself altogether of the very inclination to engage in philosophical inquiry.* He longs for a world permanently cleansed of the pestilence of philosophical reflection. His methods are designed to be used as *self-therapeutic techniques*, analogous to the sense in which those undergoing psychoanalysis hope to learn self-therapeutic techniques that will eventually saw off their neurotic chains.

As usual, there is textual support for both interpretations. Support for the more radical interpretation can be found in passages like the following:

> The real discovery is the one that makes me capable of stopping doing philosophy when I want to.[2]

Again,

> What is your aim in philosophy?—To shew the fly the way out of the fly-bottle.[3]

Support for the less radical interpretation is abundant. Wittgenstein's later writings look like the products of philosophical inquiry. Granted, his writing style is unusual, but it seems that anyone with even the slightest philosophical

---

[2]   Wittgenstein, *Philosophical Investigations*, para. 133.
[3]   Wittgenstein, *Philosophical Investigations*, para. 309.

experience should recognize it as *philosophical*. He not only asserts what look like philosophical theses, for example, "Private languages are impossible," but offers what look like philosophical arguments for them, although explicating the exact structure of those arguments is difficult and controversial. On the other hand, his writings and recorded comments to friends are infused with condemnations of the philosophical impulse. So, what precisely was his attitude toward philosophical reflection?

Such a question assumes a mistake. Like everyone else, in one way or another, he is conflicted on the level of the heart. He is possessed by a deeply embedded passion to philosophize, but is also possessed by a deeply embedded passion to cleanse himself of the first passion. Not surprisingly, the second passion never triumphs. The inclination to philosophize is embedded in human nature. There is no way to escape its pull, short of unconsciousness or death.

In any case, everyone should agree that Wittgenstein believes he has discovered methods rendering all past philosophical inquiry irrelevant,[4] which follows from either interpretation of his works. Even in his *Tractarian* phase he disdained historical inquiry:

> What has history to do with me? Mine is the first and the only world! I want to report how *I* found the world. What others in the world have told me about the world is a very small and incidental part of my experience of the world. I have to judge the world, to measure things.[5]

Austin

Like Wittgenstein, Austin's revolutionary call is based upon an appeal to ordinary uses of language.[6] This appeal involves "examining *what we should say when*, and so why and what we should mean by it."[7] But why should philosophers use this method?

> our common stock of words embodies all the distinctions men have found worth drawing, and the connexions they have found worth marking, in the lifetimes of many generations: these surely are likely to

---

[4] Of course, even Wittgenstein did not adhere completely to his own prescription. Recall his interest in, for example, Kierkegaard.

[5] Wittgenstein, *Notebooks 1914–16*, trans. G.E.M. Anscombe, ed. G.H. von Wright and G.E.M. Anscombe (New York: Harper & Brothers, 1961), 82e; quoted in Gracia, *Philosophy and Its History*, 130.

[6] Although both appeal to ordinary linguistic usages, they differ in the ways in which they invoke and apply them.

[7] J.L. Austin, "A Plea for Excuses," in *Philosophical Papers*, 3rd ed., ed. J.O. Urmson and G.J. Warnock (Oxford: Oxford University Press, 1979), 175–204, at 181.

be more numerous, more sound, since they have stood up to the long test of the survival of the fittest, and more subtle, at least in all ordinary and reasonably practical matters, than any that you or I are likely to think up in our arm-chairs of an afternoon—the most favored alternative method.[8]

The sarcastic, "arm-chairs of an afternoon," expresses his attitude toward past philosophy, an attitude also expressed in this recommendation that philosophers should study "Excuses":

At the same time we should prefer a field which is not too much trodden into bogs or tracks by traditional philosophy, for in that case even "ordinary" language will often have become infected with the jargon of extinct theories, and our own prejudices too, as the upholders and imbibers of theoretical views, will be too readily, and often insensibly, engaged. Here too, Excuses form an admirable topic; we can discuss at least clumsiness, or absence of mind, or inconsiderateness, even spontaneousness, without remembering what Kant thought, and so progress by degrees even to discussing deliberation without for once remembering Aristotle, or self-control without Plato. Granted that our subject is, as already claimed for it, neighboring, analogous or germane in some way to some notorious centre of philosophical trouble, then, with these two further requirements satisfied, we should be certain of what we are after: a good site for *field work* in philosophy. Here at last we should be able to unfreeze, to loosen up and get going on agreeing about discoveries, however small, and on agreeing about how to reach agreement. How much it is to be wished that similar field work will soon be undertaken in, say, aesthetics; if only we could forget for a while about the beautiful and get down instead to the dainty and the dumpy.[9]

The sneers express his rejection of past philosophy—a hopeless mess, unworthy of consideration by serious minds. What should philosophers do instead? They should engage in "field work"—collectively and cooperatively examining the ordinary usages of words. Such field work will result in "agreeing about discoveries, however small, and on agreeing about how to reach agreement" and will thereby transform philosophy's sorry mess into an intellectually respectable and emotionally satisfying science, in perhaps something of the

[8]   Austin, "A Plea for Excuses," 182.
[9]   Austin, "A Plea for Excuses," 182–183.

way in which systematically cataloguing and distinguishing specimens of, say, deciduous trees is intellectually respectable and emotionally satisfying:

> But I owe it to the subject to say, that it has long afforded me what philosophy is so often thought, and made, barren of—the fun of discovery, the pleasures of cooperation, and the satisfaction of reaching agreement.[10]

Traditional philosophy justifiably exists solely as a clumsy and obscure prelude to the only legitimate intellectual activity—science. Consider language:

> Is it not possible that the next century may see the birth, through the joint labours of philosophers, grammarians, and numerous other students of language, of a true and comprehensive *science of language*? Then we shall have rid ourselves of one more part of philosophy (there will still be plenty left) in the only way we can ever get rid of philosophy, by kicking it upstairs.[11]

Since the only legitimate role of traditional philosophy is to be kicked upstairs, once it is kicked, there is no longer any need to climb up the stairs to look at it again. So much the worse, for past philosophy.

Quine

In contrast to Austin's appeal to ordinary language and hoped-for future incarnations of science, Quine bases his revolutionary challenge upon well-established sciences, especially physics. Although he argues that there is a sense in which philosophy is continuous with science, he does not maintain that philosophers should try to provide epistemic foundations for science:

> Unlike the old epistemologists, we seek no firmer basis for science than science itself... [12]

In asserting that

> philosophy of science is philosophy enough... ,[13]

---

[10] Austin, "A Plea for Excuses," 174.
[11] Austin, "Ifs and Cans," in *Philosophical Papers*, 205–232, at 232.
[12] W.V. Quine, *From Stimulus to Science* (Cambridge, MA: Harvard University Press, 1995), 16.
[13] W.V. Quine, "Mr. Strawson on Logical Theory," in *The Ways of Paradox and Other Essays* (Cambridge, MA: Harvard University Press, 1976), 137–151, at 151.

he apparently intends to assert that philosophy is epistemically grounded in science, rather than the reverse. Philosophy has no legitimate role independent from science:

> The fifth move, finally, brings naturalism: abandonment of the goal of a first philosophy. It sees natural science as an inquiry into reality, fallible and corrigible but not answerable to any supra-scientific tribunal, and not in need of any justification beyond observation and the hypothetical-deductive method.[14]

The implications for inquiry into past philosophical sources are obvious. In words often attributed to him, but apparently never published, there are only two classes of philosophers—those who pursue the history of philosophy and those who pursue philosophy itself. *Authentic* philosophers do not waste their creative talents burrowing into the underground caves of past philosophy. Those caves can be left to weaker minds.

Contemporary revolutionaries

Although there are many contemporary revolutionaries, we limit ourselves to three we deem representative: Tim Maudlin, James Ladyman, and John Bickle. Maudlin and Ladyman base their revolutionary calls upon physics; Bickle bases his upon neuroscience. We have already discussed them. Suffice it to say that, despite their differences, each rejects Thesis T.

Calls for philosophical revolution are not a recent development

Revolutionary rejections of past philosophy from inside the philosophical community itself are not recent events. There is a long history, which is illuminating for at least three reasons.

First, some might suppose that, even if what we have said about recent revolutionary rejections of the philosophical past is true, such rejections are only a temporary fad, destined to evaporate quickly. But that would be a mistake. Revolutionary rejections run through the entire philosophical tradition. Of course, not every past philosopher rejects the philosophical past, but revolutionary rejections are deep currents periodically surfacing in cyclical patterns. Second, an awareness of that cyclical history motivates this useful question: Is there something inherent in the activity of philosophical reflection itself that inevitably gives rise to rejections of its own past? We will

---

[14] W.V. Quine, *Theories and Things* (Cambridge, MA: Harvard University Press, 1981), 72.

return to that question shortly. Third, an awareness of the long history of revolutionary rejections of the philosophical past motivates a healthy degree of skepticism about the call-to-arms of contemporary revolutionaries—"Here we go again."

Enough motivation … let us turn to examples.

Sextus Empiricus

Sextus Empiricus is a radical Skeptic. In the course of setting out his case for skepticism, he distinguishes three classes of philosophers:[15] (1) the *Dogmatists*, who purport to assert truths about the world, for example, Aristotle; (2) the *Academics*, who deny the assertions of the Dogmatists; and (3) the *Skeptics*, who reject both the Dogmatists' affirmative claims and the Academics' negative denials.

A Skeptic realizes that every thesis can be counter-balanced by an equally persuasive denial of that thesis. There are equally persuasive arguments for each:

> The chief constitutive principle of skepticism is the claim that to every account an equal account is opposed.[16]

Sextus devotes a substantial part of his *Outlines of Skepticism* to examples[17] of the technique of countering every thesis, whether affirmative or negative, with an equally persuasive denial.

The psychological consequence of becoming aware of the possibility of countering every thesis with an equally persuasive denial is a complete suspension of judgment about all claims to truth, whether affirmations or denials:

> for it is from this, we think, that we come to hold no beliefs.[18]

In the Introduction to their translation of *Outlines of Skepticism*, Julian Annas and Jonathan Barnes describe the Skeptic's psychological transitions:

> A Sceptical argument against a Dogmatic claim is not meant to convince us that the Dogmatic claim, about time, or value, for example, is wrong, and that the Sceptical argument establishes the truth of the counter-claim.

---

[15] Sextus Empiricus, *Outlines of Scepticism*, trans. Julia Annas and Jonathan Barnes (Cambridge: Cambridge University Press, 1994), 3.

[16] Empiricus, *Outlines of Scepticism*, 6.

[17] Sextus frequently reminds readers that his treatise is intended only as an "outline" with no pretension of completeness.

[18] Empiricus, *Outlines of Scepticism*.

Rather, we are meant to feel the force of *both* claims, and to end up in suspension of judgment because we are unable to come down on one side rather than the other. For the Sceptic, a claim that one argument is decisively better than the counter-argument is a sign that we have stopped too soon, and failed to investigate the counter-argument as vigorously as we might have done.[19]

Arriving at this non-judgmental state-of-mind generates a state of *complete tranquility*, which was the Skeptic's objective from the outset. Putting this together, a successful Skeptic moves through three psychological stages: (1) coming to realize that every assertion can be exactly counter-balanced by an opposing thesis; (2) suspending judgment about all assertions, whether affirmations or denials; and (3) achieving an end-state of permanent emotional tranquility.

> Scepticism is an ability to set out oppositions among things which appear and are thought of in any way at all, an ability by which, because of the equipollence in the opposed object and accounts, we come first to suspension of judgment and afterwards to tranquillity.[20] ... Up to now we say the aim of the Sceptic is tranquillity in matters of opinion and moderation of feeling in matters forced upon us. For Sceptics began to do philosophy in order to decide among appearances and to apprehend which are true and which false, so as to become tranquil; but they came upon equipollent dispute, and being unable to decide this they suspended judgment. And when they suspended judgment, tranquillity in matters of opinion followed fortuitously.[21]

The project of a Skeptic is analogous to the therapeutic task of physicians:

> Sceptics are philanthropic and wish to cure by argument, as far as they can, the conceit and rashness of the Dogmatists. Just as doctors for bodily afflictions have remedies which differ in potency, and apply severe remedies to patients who are severely afflicted and milder remedies to those mildly afflicted, so Sceptics propound arguments which differ in strength—they employ weighty arguments, capable of vigorously rebutting the dogmatic affliction of conceit, against those who are distressed by a severe rashness, and they employ milder arguments

[19] Empiricus, *Outlines of Scepticism*, xii–xiii.
[20] Empiricus, *Outlines of Scepticism*, 4.
[21] Empiricus, *Outlines of Scepticism*, 10.

against those who are afflicted by a conceit which is superficial and easily cured and which can be rebutted by a milder degree of plausibility.[22]

What are the consequences for the philosophical past? A Skeptic who has achieved the end-state of complete tranquility comes to see that there is no reason to investigate past philosophical sources, at least for the purpose of discovering truths about the world. Of course, she might occasionally look back in order to hone her skills as a skeptical counter-balancer, but not in order to promote her own first-order inquiries, for she has none.

Sanches

In his essay on the first-order motivation for investigating works of past philosophers, John Cottingham notes that in 1581 Francisco Sanches asserted:

> To say "thus spake the Master" is unworthy of a philosopher; better to trust our own native wit.[23]

As Cottingham argues, that assertion presupposes the superiority of the speaker's own philosophical powers. Inquirers working under that presupposition have no reason to examine the works of earlier philosophers. Why should they, given their assumption that following their own "native wit" is sufficient?

Descartes

René Descartes makes a similar appeal to the complete adequacy of a sufficiently qualified inquirer's own intellectual powers:

> I would not urge anyone to read this book except those who are able and willing to meditate seriously along with me.[24]

A "sufficiently qualified" inquirer is one who follows Descartes's method of inquiry:

> Those long chains composed of very simple and easy reasonings, which geometers customarily use to arrive at their most difficult demonstrations,

---

[22] Empiricus, *Outlines of Scepticism*, 216.

[23] Discussed in John Cottingham's essay, "Why Should Analytic Philosophers Do History of Philosophy?," in *Analytic Philosophy and History of Philosophy*, ed. Tom Sorell and G.A.J. Rogers (Oxford: Clarendon, 2005), 25.

[24] Preface to *Meditations*, quoted in Cottingham, "Why Should Analytic Philosophers," 26.

had given me occasion to suppose that all the things which come within the scope of human knowledge are interconnected in the same way. And I thought that, provided we refrain from accepting anything as true which is not, and always keep to the order required for deducing one thing from another, there can be nothing too remote to be reached in the end or too well hidden to be discovered.[25]

What are the implications?

Consider first what are the things a person can learn from another; you will find that they are languages, stories, experiences, and clear and distinct demonstrations, such as those of the geometers, that bring conviction to the mind. As for the opinions and maxims of the philosophers, merely to repeat them is not to teach them. Plato says one thing, Aristotle another, Epicurus another, Telesio, Campanella, Bruno, Basso, Vanini, and all the innovators all say different things. Of all these people, who teaches me, that is, who teaches anyone who loves wisdom? No doubt it is the person who can first persuade someone with his reasons, or at least by his authority.[26]

So, although he believes that past philosophy is a disorderly mess, he also thinks that his revolutionary method provides philosophers with an unshakable foundation for starting from scratch with nothing but their own cognitive powers, permanently freed from any need to look back to the philosophical past, except perhaps on occasion to see whether some of their predecessors happened to have accidentally stumbled upon what the present qualified inquirer has already discovered on his own. But even that kind of retrospective examination should not be taken too seriously:

If a man were capable of finding the foundation of the sciences, he would be wrong to waste his life in finding scraps of knowledge hidden in the

---

[25] Descartes, *Discourse on the Method*, Part 2, in *Descartes: Selected Philosophical Writings*, trans. John Cottingham, Robert Stootfhoff, and Dugald Murdoch (Cambridge: Cambridge University Press, 1988), 25–31.

[26] Letter to Beeckman, quoted in Roger Ariew's essay, "Descartes and Scholasticism: The Intellectual Background to Descartes' Thought," in *The Cambridge Companion to Descartes*, ed. John Cottingham (Cambridge: Cambridge University Press, 1992), 80–81. Ariew describes the elaborate, but ultimately unsuccessful, efforts Descartes made to persuade the Catholic hierarchy that his philosophical methods did not conflict with the Scholastic tradition. However, it seems that Descartes's actual views are more accurately reflected in the quoted passage.

corners of libraries; and if he was no good for anything else but that, he would not be capable of choosing and ordering what he found.[27]

Bacon

Francis Bacon asserts that philosophers must begin all over:

> It is idle to expect any great advancement in science from the superinducing and engrafting of new things upon old. We must begin anew from the very foundations, unless we would revolve forever in a circle with mean and contemptible progress.[28]

They must begin all over again because all previous philosophy was based upon radical errors. There are three such hopelessly error-prone traditions: the Sophistical, the Empirical, and the Superstitious.[29]

The Sophistical tradition

> snatches from experience a variety of common instances, neither duly ascertained nor diligently examined and weighed, and leaves all the rest to meditation and agitation of wit.[30]
>
> Aristotle is the "most conspicuous" example.[31] He corrupted natural philosophy by his logic: fashioning the world out of categories; assigning to the human soul, the noblest of substances, a genus from words of the second intention; doing the business of density and rarity (which is to make bodies of greater or less dimensions, that is, occupy greater or less spaces), by the frigid distinction of act and power; asserting that single bodies have each a single and proper motion, and that if they participate in any other, then this results from an external cause; and imposing countless other arbitrary restrictions on the nature of things; being always more solicitous to provide an answer to the question and affirm something positive in words, than about the inner truth of things .... [32]

---

[27] Descartes, Letter from 1638, in *Descartes: Philosophical Letters*, ed. and trans. Anthony Kenny (Oxford: Clarendon Press, 1970), 59–60, quoted in Gracia, *Philosophy and Its History*, 110.

[28] Bacon, Aphorism XXXI, in *The New Organon*, ed. Fulton H. Anderson (Indianapolis: Bobbs-Merrill Company, 1960), 46.

[29] Aphorism LXII, Aphorism XXXI, 60.

[30] Aphorism XXXI.

[31] Aphorism LXIII, Aphorism XXXI, 60.

[32] Aphorism XXXI.

Aristotle makes the mistake of engaging in top-down analyses, beginning syllogistically from overly abstract concepts (e.g., substance, act, potentiality), which are themselves insufficiently grounded in the empirical realm, and then descending to ludicrously inadequate explanations of that realm. Even when he tries to work from the bottom up, he goes radically astray:

> Nor let any weight be given to the fact that in his books on animals and his problems, and other of his treatises, there is frequent dealing with experiments. For he had come to his conclusion before; he did not consult experience, as he should have done, for the purpose of framing his decision and axioms, but having first determined the question according to his will, he then resorts to experience, and bending her into conformity with his placets, leads her about like a captive in a procession. So that even on this count he is more guilty than his modern followers, the schoolmen, who have abandoned experience altogether.[33]

The Empirical tradition is just as hopeless:

> There is also another class of philosophers who, having bestowed much diligent and careful labor on a few experiments, have thence made bold to educe and construct systems, wresting all other facts in a strange fashion to conformity therewith.[34]

The Empirical tradition

> gives birth to dogmas more deformed and monstrous than the Sophistical … school. For it has its foundations not in the light of common notions (which though it be a faint and superficial light, is yet in a manner universal, and has reference to many things), but in the narrowness and darkness of a few experiments. To those therefore who are daily busied with these experiments and have infected their imagination with them, such a philosophy seems probable and all but certain; to all men else incredible and vain.[35]

As for the Superstitious tradition,

> And there is yet a third class, consisting of those who out of faith and veneration mix their philosophy with theology and traditions; among

---

[33] Aphorism XXXI, 61.
[34] Aphorism LXII, Aphorism XXXI, 60.
[35] Aphorism LXIV, Aphorism XXXI, 61.

whom the vanity of some has gone so far aside as to seek the origin of sciences among spirits and genii.[36]

Of all three fatally flawed traditions, this one is the most "widely spread" and causes the "greatest harm."[37] It "misleads" human understanding by "flattery" because

> there is in man an ambition of the understanding, no less than of the will, especially in high and lofty spirits.[38]

Here are examples:

> some of the moderns have with extreme levity indulged so far as to attempt to found a system of natural philosophy on the first chapter of Genesis, on the book of Job, and other parts of the sacred writings, seeking for the dead among the living; which also makes the inhibition and repression of it the more important, because from this unwholesome mixture of things human and divine there arises not only a fantastic philosophy but also a heretical religion. Very meet it is therefore that we be sober-minded, and give to faith that only which is faith's.[39]

Thus, Bacon excludes from genuine philosophical inquiry even the attempt to synthesize philosophical concepts and beliefs with their theological counterparts. Having torched all past philosophy, what is left? His answer is engaging in genuine scientific inquiry:

> So much concerning the several classes of Idols and their equipage; all of which must be renounced and put away with a fixed and solemn determination, and the understanding thoroughly cleansed; the entrance into the kingdom of man, founded on the sciences, being not much other than the entrance into the kingdom of heaven, whereinto none may enter except as a little child.[40]

We must all renounce the past chaos of philosophical misdeeds and march into the brave new world of scientific discovery, as children who have been cleansed from the stains of past epistemic sin. That world will be guided by a

---

[36] Aphorism LXII, Aphorism XXXI, 60.
[37] Aphorism LXV, Aphorism XXXI, 62.
[38] Aphorism XXXI.
[39] Aphorism XXXI.
[40] Aphorism LXVIII, Aphorism XXXI, 66.

new method of systematic experimentation, synthesized with a new method of inductive inference.[41] How will that work? Suppose that our objective is identifying the cause of P. Here are Bacon's instructions. Experimentally identify all the positive instances in which, given condition C, P temporally follows. Then experimentally identify all the negative instances in which, C being absent, P does not follow temporally. Finally, experimentally identify all the instances in which P varies in proportion to the degree in which C varies. Combining the results of these three procedures will identify the cause of P.[42]

So, Bacon sees absolutely no point in looking back for first-order purposes.

Hume

In his characteristic rhetorical fashion, David Hume urges an imaginative revolutionary method:

> When we run over libraries, persuaded of these principles, what havoc must we make? If we take in our hand any volume; of divinity or school metaphysics, for instance; let us ask, *Does it contain any abstract reasoning concerning quantity of number?* No. *Does it contain any experimental reasoning concerning matter of fact and existence?* No. Commit it then to the flames: for it can contain nothing but sophistry and illusion.[43]

So much for the philosophical past.

Kant

According to Immanuel Kant, traditional metaphysics is a hopeless mess:

> If metaphysics is a science, why is it that it cannot, like other sciences, attain universal and lasting acclaim? If it is not, how does it happen that, under the pretense of a science it incessantly shows off, and strings along the human understanding with hopes that never dim but are never fulfilled... It seems almost laughable that, while every other science

---

[41]   For Bacon's detailed account of this new method of induction, see ibid., Book 2, 121–268. We make no attempt to present his method in anything close to its complete detail.

[42]   Obviously, Bacon's inductive method anticipates later inductive methodologies, such as John Stuart Mill's. See, for example, Mill, *A System of Logic* (London: Longmans, Green, 1961).

[43]   David Hume, "An Enquiry Concerning Human Understanding," in *Enquiries: Concerning Human Understanding and Concerning the Principles of Morals*, 3rd ed., ed. A. Selby-Bigge and P.H. Nidditch (Oxford: Oxford University Press, 1975), 165.

makes continuous progress, metaphysics, which desires to be wisdom itself, and which everyone consults as an oracle, perpetually turns round on the same spot without coming a step further.[44]

Kant urges all philosophers

to suspend their work for the present, to consider all that has happened until now as if it had not happened, and before all else to pose the question: "whether such a thing as metaphysics is even possible at all."[45]

In the absence of a rigorous demonstration of the possibility of traditional metaphysics "there is as yet no metaphysics at all."[46]

Responding to his own question, Kant asserts that traditional metaphysics is *not* possible. What exactly is it that is not possible? A necessary condition for understanding a denial is first understanding exactly what is being denied. What exactly is Kant's conception of traditional metaphysics?

Answering that question requires an account of two of his famous distinctions. First, he distinguishes between *a posteriori* and *a priori* knowledge. *A posteriori* knowledge is epistemically based upon sensory inputs, for example, sight, hearing. *A priori* knowledge is not.[47] But that is just a negative account. According to Kant's positive account, *a priori knowledge* is expressible by propositions that are both necessarily and universally true.[48] In contrast, *a posteriori* knowledge is expressible only by propositions that are neither necessarily nor universally true.

Second, he distinguishes between *analytic* and *synthetic* knowledge. Focusing (as it happens, regretfully) upon affirmative subject–predicate propositions, he defines *analytic* knowledge as knowledge expressible by propositions whose truth is solely a function of the "concept" semantically expressed by the proposition's subject term. Thus, a proposition of the form "S is P" is an analytic truth if and only if P predicates of S an attribute that is an element of the concept customarily associated with the subject

---

[44] Kant, "Prolegomena to Any Future Metaphysics that will be Able to Come forward as Science," in *The Cambridge Edition of the Works of Immanuel Kant: Theoretical Philosophy After 1781*, ed. Henry Allison and Peter Heath, trans. Gary Hatfield (Cambridge: Cambridge University Press, 2002), 53.

[45] Kant, "Prolegomena," 53.

[46] Kant, "Prolegomena," 54.

[47] Kant, "Introduction (as in the second edition)," in *The Cambridge Edition of the Works of Immanuel Kant: Critique of Pure Reason*, trans. and ed. Paul Guyer and Allen W. Wood (Cambridge: Cambridge University Press, 1998), 136–137.

[48] Kant, "Introduction (as in the second edition)," 137.

term "S."[49] Putting the matter in contemporary terms, analytic truths are true solely in virtue of the conventional meanings of the words used in their propositional expressions. Kant offers as an example the proposition, "All bodies are extended," where he assumes that the attribute *being extended* is a constituent of the concept semantically tied to the term "body."[50] In contrast, *synthetic* knowledge is expressible by propositions whose predicates add to the attributes customarily associated with their corresponding subject terms. In short, the predicates of true synthetic propositions

> add to the concept of the subject a predicate that was not thought in it at all, and could not have been extracted from it through any analysis.[51]

Kant offers as an example the proposition, "All bodies are heavy," on the basis of his assumption that the property *being heavy* is not a constituent of the concept customarily tied to the subject term "bodies."[52]

When combined in a matrix format, these two distinctions generate four *prima facie* categories of knowledge: (1) synthetic *a posteriori*, (2) synthetic *a priori*, (3) analytic *a priori*, and (4) analytic *a posteriori*. But Kant rejects the fourth combination as impossible.[53]

With these distinctions in hand, we can take up Kant's conception of the traditional metaphysical enterprise. The enterprise possesses two essential characteristics. First, it purports to demonstrate the truth of certain synthetic *a priori* propositions. Examples are the propositions that the world had a beginning,[54] that God exists, that humans have freedom of will, and that they have immortal souls.[55] What ties all such propositions together is that each presupposes the human capacity to ascertain the truth about things that transcend all possibility of sensory experience. Thus, they purport to

> expand the domain of our judgments beyond all bounds of experience through concepts to which no corresponding object at all can be given in experience.[56]

---

[49] For convenience, we ignore use-mention distinctions here and elsewhere.
[50] Kant, *Critique of Pure Reason*, 141.
[51] Kant, *Critique of Pure Reason*.
[52] Kant, *Critique of Pure Reason*.
[53] Kant, *Critique of Pure Reason*, 142.
[54] Kant, *Critique of Pure Reason*, 146.
[55] For the latter three, see Kant, *Critique of Pure Reason*, 139.
[56] Kant, *Critique of Pure Reason*.

Second, it "dogmatically" purports to transcend human sensory experience without first performing

> an antecedent examination of the capacity or incapacity of reason for such a great undertaking.[57]

In his *Critique of Pure Reason*, Kant challenges this "dogmatic" approach by undertaking just such an "antecedent examination" of reason's power to transcend sensory experience.[58] He first focuses upon mathematics and physics, maintaining that both contain synthetic *a priori* truths, such as, "7 + 5 = 12": "In all alterations of the corporeal world the quantity of matter remains unaltered"[59]; "that substance remains and persists ... "[60]; and "everything that happens always previously is determined by a cause according to constant laws ... "[61]

Kant goes on to ask *how it is* that mathematics and physics are capable of achieving such cognitive success. He answers that they do it in virtue of the fact that a complex *a priori* structure, including both *a priori* concepts and synthetic *a priori* judgments, is built into the human mind, a structure that incorporates both powers of sensation and judgment. Human minds are structured in such a way that they cannot avoid perceiving and judging in certain pre-established patterns. For example, with respect to sense perception, the human mind necessarily perceives events as occurring in space and time. That necessity does not result from any mind-independent attribute of nature, but rather from the structure of the mind itself. The mind cannot help but perceive things and events *as if* they occur in space and time, but that is not because space and time are attributes of events considered independently of human perception. A possible analogy is having a hearing disability that causes a constant ringing in the ears. Everything is heard against the background of this constant ringing sound, but not because the sound emanates from an outside source. The ring is "built in." Similarly, with respect to judgments, the mind cannot help but judge that everything that happens has a sufficient cause, not because events have sufficient causes in any mind-independent sense, but rather because the causal principle is built into the *a priori* structure of the mind itself.

---

[57] Kant, *Critique of Pure Reason*, 139.
[58] In the following paragraphs, we offer just a brief sketch of Kant's argument, a sketch that passes over much of the labyrinthine complexity of the *Critique*.
[59] Kant, *Critique of Pure Reason*, 144–145.
[60] Kant, *Prolegomena*, 90.
[61] Kant, *Prolegomena*.

Thus, the only necessary and universal truths we can know are propositions we believe solely because they are built into the structure of our own minds. We believe them, not because reality conforms to them, but rather because the structure of our own minds compels us to believe them:

> *the understanding does not draw its (a priori) laws from nature, but prescribes them to it ...* [62]

Kant expresses the point in terms of Copernicus's revolutionary theory in physics:

> Up to now it has been assumed that all our cognition must conform to the objects; but all attempts to find out something about them *a priori* through concepts that would extend our cognition have, on this presupposition, come to nothing. Hence let us once try whether we do not get farther with the problems of metaphysics by assuming that the objects must conform to our cognition, which would agree better with the requested possibility of an *a priori* cognition of them, which is to establish something about objects before they are given to us. This would be just like the first thoughts of Copernicus, who, when he did not make good progress in the explanation of the celestial motions if he assumed that the entire celestial host revolves around the observer, tried to see if he might not have greater success if he made the observer revolve and left the stars at rest. [63]

In short,

> we can cognize of things *a priori* only what we ourselves have put into them. [64]

Underlying Kant's thesis is the assumption of a fundamental distinction between the realm of *things-in-themselves* and the realm of *appearances*. The realm of things-in-themselves consists of the world as it exists independently of human experience, whereas the realm of appearances consists of the ways in which that independent world of things-in-themselves is subjectively experienced by humans. The *a priori* structure of the human mind applies only to the realm of appearances, not to things-in-themselves. [65]

---

[62] Kant, *Prolegomena*, 112.
[63] Kant, *Critique of Pure Reason*, 110.
[64] Kant, *Critique of Pure Reason*, 111.
[65] Kant, *Prolegomena*, 104, 106.

The argument can be expressed in terms of the concept of *sense-data.* The realm of things-in-themselves presents itself to human consciousness through sensory inputs such as sights, sounds, and tastes. Once ingested by the mind's sensory apparatus, those inputs are filtered through the mind's *a priori* structures. The output of that process consists, in part, of synthetic *a posteriori* judgments, synthetic *a priori* judgments, and analytic *a priori* judgments. Knowledge is produced by a synthesis of incoming sense-data and a built-in *a priori* mental structure. However, the built-in *a priori* structure does not apply to anything other than incoming sense-data. It does not apply to things-in-themselves.

Given this background, Kant's position about the epistemic status of traditional metaphysics can be expressed with this simple argument:

[1] If traditional metaphysics is possible, then it is possible for human reason to discover synthetic *a priori* truths about things transcending all possible human sensory experience.

[2] It is not possible for human reason to discover synthetic *a priori* truths about things transcending all possible human sensory experience.

[3] Hence, traditional metaphysics is not possible.

Since traditional metaphysics is not even possible, there is no point in looking back to historical examples of traditional metaphysics. So, Thesis T is false.

However, although Kant believes that he has demonstrated that traditional metaphysics is a waste of time, he nevertheless believes that there is hope for the philosophical future in the form of a radically new form of metaphysics—the scientific investigation of the *a priori* structure of the human mind that was initiated, but not completed, in the *Critique.* The *Critique* established the *core* of this new metaphysics by identifying the boundaries of reason's synthetic *a priori* powers, thereby extinguishing traditional metaphysics once-and-for-all. But much work remains[66]—work consisting of creating an *organon* of pure reason that "would be a sum total of all those principles in accordance with which all pure *a priori* cognitions can be acquired and actually brought about."[67] Such an organon would be a *transcendental philosophy*, which would "contain an exhaustive analysis of all human cognition *a priori*."[68] This transcendental philosophy would be a genuine science.[69]

---

[66] Kant, *Critique of Pure Reason*, 149.
[67] Kant, *Critique of Pure Reason*.
[68] Kant, *Critique of Pure Reason*, 150.
[69] Kant, *Critique of Pure Reason*.

Even the "propaedeutic"[70] to this future science, set forth in the *Critique*, is itself a genuine science that "stands to the ordinary school metaphysics precisely as *chemistry* stands to *alchemy*, or *astronomy* to the fortune-teller's *astrology*."[71] The reason that the preliminary path established by the *Critique* is a genuinely scientific path is that

> here reason has the sources of its cognition not in objects and their intuition (through which reason cannot be taught one thing more), but in itself, and, if reason has presented the fundamental laws of its faculty fully and determinately (against all misinterpretation), nothing else remains that pure reason could cognize *a priori*, or even about which it could have cause to ask.[72]

Traditional metaphysics' attempt to investigate the realm of things-in-themselves was fruitless, unscientific, and ultimately incoherent. However, by turning away from hopeless attempts to apprehend cognitively the realm of things-in-themselves, and focusing instead upon the *a priori* structure of the human mind itself, this revolutionary new metaphysics has discovered the yellow-brick road to genuine science.[73]

Husserl

Inflamed with the exhilaration of discovering the method of transcendental phenomenology, Edmund Husserl proclaims that he has transformed

---

70 Kant, *Critique of Pure Reason*, 149.
71 Kant, *Prolegomena*, 154.
72 Kant, *Prolegomena*, 155.
73 We will not take up Kant's attempt to soften the blow of his *Critique of Pure Reason* in his later *Critique of Practical Reason*, in which he argues that "God, freedom, and immortality" can be justified, after all, by means of "practical" reason, as opposed to "pure" reason. Kant, "Critique of Practical Reason," in *The Cambridge Edition of the Works of Immanuel Kant: Practical Philosophy*, ed. Mary J. Gregor (Cambridge: Cambridge University Press, 1996). This attempt has been enormously controversial. J.L. Austin says about philosophers in general, "There's the bit where you say it and the bit where you take it back." Austin, *Sense and Sensibilia*, ed. G.J. Warnock (Oxford: Oxford University Press, 1962), 2. The interpretive controversy about Kant's apparent attempt to soften his attack upon traditional metaphysics raises the question, "Exactly how much of a bit did Kant take back?" On one view, he did not take back much, if anything. Can't his *Critique of Practical Reason* be read as a precursor to later positivist noncognitive accounts of normative reasoning? On another view, he took back a great deal. Can't his *Critique of Practical Reason* be read as maintaining that, in the end, "practical" reason governs "pure" reason, where "practical" reason is understood as being capable of ascertaining objective truth in a more fundamental way? Think about, for example, Kierkegaard and William James. In

philosophy into a rigorous science. He dismisses all past philosophical inquiry because it "is incapable of assuming the form of rigorous science."[74] In contrast to rigorous science, it is "utterly incapable of teaching in an objectively valid manner."[75] Husserl writes:

> One cannot learn philosophy, because here there are no such insights objectively grasped and grounded, or to put it another way, because here the problems, methods, and theories have not been clearly defined conceptually, their sense has not been fully clarified.[76]

Rigorous science is radically different:

> No reasonable person will doubt the objective truth or the objectively grounded probability of the wonderful theories of mathematics and the natural sciences. Here there is, by and large, no room for private "opinions," "notions," or "points of view."[77]

In depressing contrast

> The imperfection of philosophy is of an entirely different sort from that of the other sciences just described. It does not have at its disposal a merely incomplete and, in particular instances, imperfect doctrinal system; it simply has none whatever. Each and every question is herein controverted, every position is a matter of individual conviction, of the interpretation given by a school, of a "point of view."[78]

Husserl concedes that there might be some marginal value in studying earlier philosophy insofar as it might here or there contain phenomenological

---

any case, as important as these issues may be, we choose to focus upon Kant's "bit where you say it," rather than upon his "bit where you take it back," because we think it important to focus upon his generally acknowledged status as a philosophical revolutionary who claimed to have converted philosophy into a science. If he took this bit back, he would not be so regarded. Keep in mind that neither Kierkegaard nor James claimed that their reliance upon practical reason served to transform philosophy into a science.

[74] Edmund Husserl, "Philosophy as a Rigorous Science," in *Husserl: Shorter Works*, ed. Peter McCormick and Frederick Elliston, trans. Quentin Lauer (Notre Dame: University of Notre Dame Press, 1981), 166.

[75] Husserl, "Philosophy as a Rigorous Science."

[76] Husserl, "Philosophy as a Rigorous Science," 167.

[77] Husserl, "Philosophy as a Rigorous Science."

[78] Husserl, "Philosophy as a Rigorous Science."

insights that can be definitively confirmed by Husserl's method. Nevertheless, historical studies are not essential to the new phenomenological science:

> But it is not through philosophies that we become philosophers. Remaining immersed in the historical, forcing oneself to work therein in historico-critical activity, and wanting to attain philosophical science by means of eclectic elaboration or anachronistic renaissance—all that leads to nothing but hopeless efforts. The impulse to research must proceed not from philosophies but from things and from the problems connected to them.[79]

Husserl's new method provides an absolutely secure foundation for all future philosophical inquiry, a foundation that does not depend upon earlier philosophy in any essential way. From now on, philosophers need never look back.

Schlick

Moritz Schlick begins his revolutionary manifesto with a deeply pessimistic view of past philosophy:

> But it is just the ablest thinkers who most rarely have believed that the results of earlier philosophizing, including that of the classical models, remain unshakable. This is shown by the fact that basically every new system starts again from the beginning, that every thinker seeks his own foundation and does not wish to stand on the shoulders of his predecessors. Descartes (not without reason) felt himself to be making a wholly new beginning; Spinoza believed that in introducing the (to be sure quite adventitious) mathematical form he had found the ultimate philosophical method; and Kant was convinced that on the basis of the way taken by him philosophy would at last adopt the sure path of a science. Further examples are superfluous, for practically all great thinkers have sought for a radical reform of philosophy and consider it essential.
> ...
> This peculiar fate of philosophy has been so often described and bemoaned that it is indeed pointless to discuss it at all. Silent scepticism and resignation seem to be the only appropriate attitudes. Two thousand years of experience seems to teach that efforts to put an end to the chaos of systems and to change the fate of philosophy can no longer be taken seriously.[80]

---

[79] Husserl, "Philosophy as a Rigorous Science," 196.
[80] Moritz Schlick, "The Turning Point in Philosophy," in *Logical Positivism*, ed. A.J. Ayer (New York: Free Press of Glencoe, 1959), 53–54.

However, despite his skepticism about the past philosophical "chaos," Schlick announces that he has discovered a new philosophical method that will provide a secure foundation for all future philosophy:

> For I am convinced that we now find ourselves at an altogether decisive turning point in philosophy, and that we are objectively justified in considering that an end has come to the fruitless conflict of systems. We are already at the present time, in my opinion, in possession of methods which make every such conflict in principle unnecessary. What is now required is their resolute application.[81]

So, what are these revolutionary new methods? Putting aside details unnecessary for our purposes, suffice it to say that the crucial insight was proposed by Wittgenstein in his *Tractatus Logico-Philosophicus*:

> So, all knowledge is such only by virtue of its form. It is through its form that it represents the fact known. But the form cannot itself in turn be represented.[82]

With historical hindsight, some readers may find Schlick's revolutionary enthusiasm about Wittgenstein's famously obscure statements about logical form an embarrassing example of philosophically naive hubris. In any case, Schlick argues that Wittgenstein's conception of logical form once-and-for-all shows that all past philosophers made the fundamental mistake of assuming that philosophy's proper function is formulating true statements about the world. In contrast, philosophy's only legitimate role is clarifying "meanings," a role that is just an "activity," rather than a "system of statements."[83]

> The great contemporary turning point is characterized by the fact that we see in philosophy not a system of cognitions, but a system of *acts*; philosophy is that activity through which the meanings of statements is revealed or determined. By means of philosophy statements are explained, by means of science they are verified. The latter is concerned with the truth of statements, the former with what they actually mean.[84]

---

[81] Schlick, "The Turning Point in Philosophy," 54.
[82] Schlick, "The Turning Point in Philosophy," 55.
[83] Schlick, "The Turning Point in Philosophy," 55–59.
[84] Schlick, "The Turning Point in Philosophy," 56.

Thus, Wittgenstein's revolutionary discovery shows that all past philosophy was grounded in a vain pursuit of "pseudo-questions," and should therefore be abandoned:

> Certainly there will still be many a rear-guard action. Certainly many will for centuries continue to wander further along the traditional paths. Philosophical writers will long continue to discuss the old pseudo-questions. But in the end they will no longer be listened to; they will come to resemble actors who continue to play for some time before noticing that the audience has slowly departed. Then it will no longer be necessary to speak of "philosophical problems" for one will speak philosophically concerning all problems, that is: clearly and meaningfully.[85]

Reichenbach

Hans Reichenbach distinguishes "speculative" philosophy from "scientific" philosophy,[86] and characterizes the former in this way:

> Speculative philosophy sought to acquire a knowledge of generalities, of the most general principles that govern the universe. It was thus led to the construction of philosophic systems including chapters that we must regard today as naive attempts at a comprehensive physics, a physics in which the function of scientific explanation was assumed by simple analogies with experiences of everyday life. It attempted to account for the method of knowledge by a similar use of analogies; questions of the theory of knowledge were answered in terms of picture language rather than by logical analysis.[87]

So, speculative philosophy was hopelessly misguided from the start and must be abandoned. But the philosophical millennium is at hand, provided that philosophers adopt a scientific philosophy:

> Scientific philosophy, in contrast, leaves the explanation of the universe entirely to the scientist; it constructs the theory of knowledge by the analysis of the results of science and is aware of the fact that neither the physics of the universe nor that of the atom can be understood in terms of concepts derived from everyday life.[88]

---

[85] Schlick, "The Turning Point in Philosophy," 59.
[86] Reichenbach, *Rise of Scientific Philosophy*, 303.
[87] Reichenbach, *Rise of Scientific Philosophy*, 303.
[88] Reichenbach, *Rise of Scientific Philosophy*, 303.

The consequences for past philosophy are dramatic:

> Philosophy is regarded by many as inseparable from speculation. They believe that the philosopher cannot use methods which establish knowledge, be it knowledge of facts or of logical relations; that he must speak a language which is not accessible to verification—in short, that philosophy is not a science. The present book is intended to establish the contrary thesis. It maintains that philosophic speculation is a passing stage, occurring when philosophic problems are raised at a time which does not possess the logical means to solve them. It claims that there is, and always has been, a scientific approach to philosophy. And it wishes to show that from this ground has sprung a scientific philosophy which, in the science of our time, has found the tools to solve those problems that in earlier times have been the subject of guesswork only. To put it briefly, this book is written with the intention of showing that philosophy has proceeded from speculation to science.[89]

In addition,

> The comparison between the old and the new philosophy is a matter for the historian and will be of interest to all those who were brought up in the old philosophy and wish to understand the new one. Those who work in the new philosophy do not look back; their work would not profit from historical considerations. They are as unhistorical as Plato was, or Kant, because like those masters of a past period of philosophy they are only interested in the subject they are working on, not in its relations to previous times. I do not wish to belittle the history of philosophy; but one should always remember that it is history, and not philosophy. Like all historical research, it should be done with scientific methods and psychological and sociological explanations. But the history of philosophy must not be presented as a collection of truths. There is more error than truth in traditional philosophy; therefore, only the critically minded can be competent historians. The glorification of the philosophies of the past, the presentation of the various systems as so many versions of wisdom, each in its own right, has undermined the philosophic potency of the present generation. It has induced the student to adopt a philosophic relativism, to believe that there are only philosophical opinions, but that there is no philosophical truth.[90]

---

[89] Reichenbach, *Rise of Scientific Philosophy*, vii.
[90] Reichenbach, *Rise of Scientific Philosophy*, 325.

Scientific philosophy should proceed in strict accordance with the most recent theories of physical science. One of the consequences of that agenda is eliminating traditional philosophy's normative concern with formulating guiding principles for living:

> Scientific philosophy has abandoned completely the plan of advancing moral rules. It regards moral aims as products of acts of volition, not of cognition; only the relations between aims, or between aims and means, are accessible to cognitive knowledge. The fundamental ethical rules are not justifiable through knowledge, but are adhered to merely because human beings want these rules and want other persons to follow the same rules. Volition is not derivable from cognition. Human will is its own progenitor and its own judge.[91]

Similarly,

> A scientific philosophy cannot supply moral guidance; that is one of its results, and cannot be held against it. You want the truth, and nothing but the truth? Then do not ask the philosopher for moral directives. Those philosophers who are willing to derive moral directives from their philosophies can only offer you a sham proof. There is no use in asking the impossible.[92]

Progress at last.

Generalizations

Generalizations can be drawn from this sample of the long history of revolutionary rejections of using past philosophy for one's own first-order philosophical purposes.

Philosophical revolutionaries assume that past philosophy is a hopeless chaos of conflicting views

Revolutionary calls are based on the assumption that past philosophy can produce nothing but a chaotic series of conflicting views. A makes assertions. B rejects A's assertions and makes her own. C rejects the assertions of both A and B, and makes his own. D rejects the assertions of A, B, and C, and makes her own, and so on.

---

[91] Reichenbach, *Rise of Scientific Philosophy*, 304.
[92] Reichenbach, *Rise of Scientific Philosophy*, 323.

Philosophical revolutionaries deem this history of conflict disastrous

Philosophical revolutionaries are disillusioned and frustrated by the chaotic history of conflicting views, regarding it as disastrously harmful. There are at least two classes of revolutionary attitudes.

In the first case, some believe that the past chaos is harmful because they believe that philosophical inquiry, *as such*, is harmful, both to the inquirers themselves and to those they influence. Philosophical reflection should be avoided—period. Sextus Empiricus and the "radical" Wittgenstein are examples, where by "radical" we mean the interpretation of Wittgenstein proposed by the more radical of the two interpretations we distinguished. We will refer to members of this class as *anti-philosophy* revolutionaries.

In the second case, there are revolutionaries who, while agreeing that the past philosophy has been disastrously harmful, maintain that it has been harmful simply because it was pursued in the wrong way—not because philosophical inquiry *per se* is harmful. Philosophy is a legitimate, and even important, activity, but only when pursued with the revolutionaries' newly discovered methods. We shall refer to members of this class as *methodological* revolutionaries.

Two clarifications are in order. First, according to some usages, methods are algorithmic, or at least quasi-algorithmic, procedures, for example, the method of computing long-division problems or the method of planting corn. Our usage is much broader. In our sense, Kant's systematic focus on the structure of the human mind constitutes a method, even though it is obviously not algorithmic.

Second, we assume that methodological revolutionaries do not propose that their methods replace *all* traditional philosophical methods. No methodological revolutionary would advocate doing away with arguments. However, they do maintain that their newly discovered methods should shape, limit, and control other methods. For example, Husserl would presumably say that arguments are legitimate so long as they rely upon his phenomenological method. Similarly, Reichenbach would presumably say that arguments are legitimate so long as they do not contradict or go beyond his method of systematically conforming to the latest findings of science.

Philosophical revolutionaries assume that there is a fundamental explanation for this past chaos of philosophical conflict

Although revolutionaries agree that there is a fundamental explanation for the chaotic history of philosophy, they disagree about the content of that explanation. For anti-philosophy revolutionaries, the explanation inheres in the nature of philosophical reflection itself. Being intrinsically and destructively incoherent itself, it could not possibly have produced written products that were not also destructively incoherent.

In contrast, for methodological revolutionaries, the explanation is that past philosophers simply failed to use the correct methods.

Philosophical revolutionaries do not believe that the past chaos is certain to persist indefinitely

Again, we must distinguish the two classes. Anti-philosophy revolutionaries do not believe that the past chaos is certain to persist indefinitely because they think not only that philosophy should be abandoned altogether but also that it is possible for philosophers to do so. The self-destructive passion to philosophize is similar to the self-destructive passion of drug addiction. Just as drug addicts can choose to cast off their addictions, so can those addicted to the narcotic of philosophical reflection. The cure for cleansing oneself of philosophical addiction is self-therapeutic methods. Predictably, the substance of those methods varies across revolutionaries. Note the differences between the methods of Sextus Empiricus and those of the "radical" Wittgenstein. However, despite such differences, the ultimate aim is always the same—a self-transformation that permanently roots out the passion to philosophize from both the head and the heart.

In contrast, methodological philosophical revolutionaries maintain that the past philosophical chaos can be cured by adherence to the new methods.

Both classes agree on the need for a philosophical revolution, but differ over its nature

For anti-philosophy revolutionaries, the needed revolution consists in rejecting philosophy itself. Once having extricated themselves from philosophy's narcotic spell, inquirers will no longer suffer cravings for any new methods to replace the old ones. "New" philosophical methods are still philosophical methods, the very thing that must be discarded.

For methodological revolutionaries, the needed revolution consists in adopting the new methods. Don't abandon philosophy. Transform and redeem it with the once-and-for-all correct methods.

Both classes differ over the question whether philosophy should be transformed into a science

Again, it is easy to predict the contrast. Anti-philosophy revolutionaries urge abandoning philosophy altogether. Of course, they would concede that philosophers could justifiably turn to pursuing genuine science, for example, physics, but they would reject pursuing philosophy itself in any guise, including the guise of "science."

Methodological revolutionaries answer the question affirmatively. Past philosophy is a tangle of conflicting views that can be cleared away only by reliance on new methods, which will transform philosophy into a genuine science in its own right, alongside the established sciences of mathematics and physics.

The proposition that philosophy should be transformed into a science presupposes that it should proceed cumulatively, in two senses

The methodological revolutionaries' proposal to transform philosophy into a science presupposes that, like the already-established sciences, philosophy should proceed *cumulatively*, in two senses. First, its results should be *interpersonally cumulative*. Results achieved by inquirers who have correctly applied the new methods should be accepted by all contemporary inquirers. Second, results achieved by means of the new methods should be *intergenerationally cumulative*. Results achieved by inquirers who have correctly applied the new methods should be accepted by all later generations of philosophers.

This twofold conception of scientific philosophy as inherently *cumulative* is based upon two underlying assumptions. First, the methods of science provide the only reliable source of knowledge. Science has achieved its justifiably lofty degree of epistemic status by using methods whose results are cumulative in both senses. It is only by using such methods that science has made collective progress toward the ultimate objective of understanding reality.

Second, it follows that, if philosophy is to achieve the same degree of epistemic status, it must also transform itself into a science whose results are interpersonally and intergenerationally cumulative. Of course, presumably, few methodological revolutionaries believe that their new methods will involve controlled-and-repeatable empirical experiments of the kind conducted in physics. However, they do believe that philosophy should use methods that will yield cumulative results, even though such methods may differ to some extent from those of physics.

Where does contemporary analytic philosophy fit into this analysis?

It is obvious that contemporary analytic philosophers do not urge an anti-philosophy revolution. They publish thousands of books and articles at an ever-increasing rate, which would be unintelligible if they had resolved to abandon philosophy.

Some might try explaining this ever-mounting flood of publications by positing a collective missionary passion to persuade others to abandon philosophy. Such an explanation is doubtful, however, given that none of those publications advocates getting rid of philosophy.[93] Rather, it seems that most analytic philosophers adhere to the two underlying assumptions just described.

As to the first assumption, that the methods of science provide the only reliable source of knowledge, an overwhelming majority agree. Notice the widely shared assumption that the "obvious" truths of physicalism and determinism have been "proved" by science. Nothing more need be argued.

The same holds for the second assumption, that philosophy should transform itself into a science by using methods whose results are interpersonally and intergenerationally cumulative. Witness the widely shared assumption that the only legitimate way to philosophize is to *specialize, specialize*, and then *specialize* again. Burrow down into as many deep and narrow tunnels as reviewers and publishers will tolerate. The best explanation for this collective drive for specialization is the shared assumption that doing so is necessary for producing cumulative results. Splitting the log of philosophy into a growing pile of ever-thinner splinters will generate genuine consensus. By imitating the division-of-labor pattern of the established sciences, philosophers will finally create the conditions for genuine collective philosophical progress, after all these thousands of years of fruitless stumbling around.

These two underlying assumptions are expressed in analytic philosophy in four ways. First, there is the increasing frequency with which candidates for faculty positions respond to "big" questions, such as, whether there is libertarian free will, or whether there are nonphysical entities, by responding, "Sorry, but my area of research is ... [e.g., a proper subset of the responses to Etchemendy's analysis of Tarski's analysis of logical consequence] ... , and that area does not include your issue."[94] The assumption is that, like physics or mathematics, philosophy is appropriately divisible into an ever-increasing number of specialties. Just as it would be unfair to ask a mathematics candidate whose area of specialization is, for example, degrees of recursive unsolvability to respond to difficult questions in the foundations of analysis, similarly it would be unfair to ask a philosophy candidate who specializes in, for example, the Intuitionist account of the existential quantifier to respond to questions about the metaphysical basis for consciousness.

---

[93] Readers might wonder why we are discussing the entire class of contemporary analytic academic philosophers. Surely, the vast majority of those thousands will never make it on to anyone's list of world-historical revolutionaries. However, those casts of thousands participate as disciples in revolutions sparked by authentic revolutionaries.

[94] See John Etchemendy, *The Concept of Logical Consequence* (Cambridge, MA: Harvard University Press, 1990).

Second, there is the widespread use of the language of "results." Physicists refer to, for example, the Stern-Gerlach results or Bell's results. Analytic philosophers refer to, for example, Quine's or Davidson's results: "Quine 'showed' this"; "Davidson 'showed' that." The assumption is that some philosophical theses stand on their own for all time and for everyone, in the way that results in physics or in mathematics do.

Third, there are the widely invoked maxims that no worthwhile purpose can be served by reading any philosophical publication more than ___ years old, where the blank is filled in by some small number, five, or perhaps even ten. The presupposition is that anything worth saving in the process of philosophical inquiry will be automatically retained and restated with ever-greater precision every ___ years, and, as such, anything not worth preserving will be filtered out. The presupposed paradigm of physics and mathematics is at work once again. Scientists and mathematicians justifiably talk in this way because both science and mathematics do proceed cumulatively. The assumption that philosophy could ever proceed cumulatively, however, is mistaken. Believing in an Invisible Philosophical Hand unerringly filtering out The False and passing on and reformulating The True with ever-increasing clarity is an unfounded act of faith.

Fourth, there is the widely shared assumption that the primary objective of publishing is persuading others that one's claims are correct, and that failure to do so constitutes philosophical failure. Read book reviews on the *Notre Dame Philosophical Reviews* website for a few weeks. Reviewer after reviewer asserts that the book reviewed fails because it will not succeed in persuading those who disagree with its claims. The underlying assumption is analogous to the shared assumption in the established sciences that scientists who fail to persuade other qualified scientists have failed, *qua* scientists. In the latter case, the assumption is justifiable because scientific disciplines proceed in a cumulative fashion,[95] unlike philosophy.

Both classes of revolutionaries agree, or at least should agree, that investigating past philosophical sources in order to further one's own first-order philosophical inquiries is pointless

Despite the fact that the two classes of revolutionaries differ over the nature of the needed revolution, both reject, or at least should reject, the thesis that the investigation of past philosophical sources is an excellent means of

---

[95] Of course, we do not deny the obvious historical fact of scientific revolutions, for example, the Einsteinian revolution, or the quantum mechanics revolution. The difference between revolutions in physics and revolutions in philosophy is that, in the former case

promoting one's own first-order inquiries. Anti-philosophy revolutionaries should reject it because they believe that philosophy *per se* is a dead-end mess. Their revolution calls for permanently ridding oneself of the vice of philosophical inquiry altogether, a prescription that, *a fortiori*, includes all past philosophical inquiry.[96] In contrast, methodological revolutionaries reject the thesis, not because they believe that first-order philosophical inquiry is inherently pointless, but rather because past first-order philosophy was pursued with inadequate methods. The discovery of new methods renders irrelevant all past first-order inquiry because no past inquirers had the benefit of the new methods.

We inserted the qualifying phrase, "or at least should agree," in the heading of this section because at least some revolutionaries did investigate past sources. Wittgenstein read Augustine. Kant read Hume. Descartes read some of the late Scholastics. Husserl read Kant. We offer two comments. First, backward looks by revolutionaries typically involve either strengthening their own resolve for carrying through their revolutions, for example, Kant on Hume, Husserl on Kant, or reconfirming for themselves the truth of their claim that past philosophy is a hopeless mess, for example, Wittgenstein on Augustine. Typically, revolutionaries' backward looks do not involve looking to the past in order to assist their own first-order inquiries. Second, even if some do occasionally stumble and rely upon a past philosophical source for their own first-order inquiries, for example, Kant on Rousseau, our (qualified) thesis would not be falsified. Such cases can be understood as examples of revolutionaries failing to consistently pursue their own agendas.

---

all qualified physicists eventually accept the revolution and go on to do mid-level science within the conceptual framework of that revolution, whereas nothing like that occurs in philosophy. It's not the case that all philosophers invariably accept philosophical revolutions, because it's not the case that all philosophers move on to working within the conceptual framework of any particular philosophical revolution.

[96] An interesting exception to this generalization is the Harvard philosopher, Burton Dreben, who frequently asserted that first-order philosophical inquiry is a complete waste of time. However, he also spent his academic life investigating the history of mathematical logic and the philosophy of logic. W.D. Hart, a former student of Dreben's, elegantly captures the conjunction of these two aspects of Dreben's thought: "Dreben described himself as a logical positivist, but he was really a philosophical nihilist. He once said in lecture, 'Rubbish is rubbish, but the history of rubbish is scholarship.'" W.D. Hart, *The Evolution of Logic* (Cambridge: Cambridge University Press, 2010), ix. One way of understanding this is to interpret Dreben as a conflicted anti-philosophy revolutionary. His public position was that first-order philosophical inquiry is rubbish. However, as many of his former students would acknowledge, he nevertheless injected a powerful element of his own first-order philosophical interests into his supposedly philosophically neutral presentations of past philosophy. Perhaps he was an anti-philosophy revolutionary who was unable to let go of his own first-order philosophical impulses.

The short list of revolutionaries we have offered may be puzzling, in light of their great historical impact

Our list of revolutionaries might induce some readers to wonder how such a small number (12) could have had the extraordinary impact upon the overall current of philosophy that they had. How could just 12, out of the thousands who have engaged in philosophical inquiry over the centuries, have had any significant impact? Granted, 12 is a small number, but even if we extended the list, the resulting number would still be minute in comparison to the total number of philosophers, past and present. But small numbers are not decisive. Every *successful* revolutionary creates a flotilla of disciples, sometimes extending for generations.[97] This was true even for Greek philosophy, with its Platonic, Aristotelian, Skeptic, and Stoic traditions.

It is even truer for societies in which philosophy has become almost exclusively a professional activity. You will not see many following the amateur path taken by Descartes, Locke, Hume, Leibniz, Spinoza, Kierkegaard, Nietzsche, and Marx. The vast majority of current philosophical publications are written by academics. Consequently, there is a predictable motivation to follow the patterns established by the currently accepted generals: "There are thousands of us, each struggling to promote our own professional status. It is therefore prudent for each of us to follow the path cleared by our leaders. We'll all benefit from the shield of large numbers."

For every (successful) revolutionary, there are disciples ready to follow. That is a necessary truth. No disciples—no successful revolutionary. Perhaps most of them will not have reflected seriously on the philosophical merits of discipleship. Their motivation is more likely to be a concern for their own professional standing and advancement. Nonetheless, the fact that many disciples follow with mundane motivations is possible only because the revolutionaries they follow were driven by more authentic motivations. Wakes of ships do not form by themselves.

Evaluation of the revolutionary agenda

Is past philosophy a chaos of conflicting views?

We agree with revolutionaries that past philosophy is a chaotic tangle of conflict. Even a cursory examination of philosophical history should suffice for that.

---

[97] We have already anticipated at least part of this general point in an earlier subsection.

But is that history harmful?

All revolutionaries presuppose that this history has been harmful, but we disagree. The essential purpose for pursuing philosophy is working through issues *for oneself*, not in order to reach a *communal consensus*. Why did you choose a life of philosophical inquiry in the first place? Was it to pursue and resolve *for yourself* the fundamental issues that initially drew you to philosophical reflection? Or, was it to join a cast of thousands in marching toward a consensus-based philosophical account of reality? We think that many were initially motivated in the first way. It is only when they discover that the train they boarded is headed in a very different direction that they begin to regard their original motivations as naïve.

Assuming that the essential purpose of pursuing philosophy is working through fundamental questions for oneself, what is the best means to that end? Put yourself in situations in which you are continually confronted with a chaos of conflicting views of the very kind revolutionaries decry. Fruitful philosophical inquiry requires *continual dialectical reflection*, which is best achieved by being immersed in a context of intense and sustained interpersonal disagreement about philosophical issues.

Some might argue that *actual* conflicts about philosophical issues are not necessary because *hypothetical* conflicts, which are *imagined* by inquirers, are a sufficient means for fully engaging in dialectical reflection. However, although the sustained activity of imagining hypothetical conflicts is a necessary means for achieving full dialectical reflection, it cannot by itself duplicate the enormous benefit of daily confronting the motley flood of *actual* conflicts, both present and past. Any individual inquirer's own dialectical imagination has its limits.

Is there an explanation for the past chaos of conflict?

We have argued that, although both classes of revolutionaries propose explanations for the past philosophical chaos, those explanations differ. The explanation of the anti-philosophy revolutionaries is that philosophical inquiry *per se* is harmful. The explanation of the methodological revolutionaries is that past philosophers failed to apply the correct methods. We agree that there is an explanation for the history of chaos, but our explanation differs from both of those. The chaotic history of philosophy can be explained in terms of two factors: the nature of philosophical inquiry, and the human nature of the inquirers themselves.

As to the first factor, philosophy focuses upon issues that are neither amenable to the consensus-based *empirical* methods of physics nor to the consensus-based *a priori* methods of mathematics. Consider, for example, the question, "Is there a personal Ground of Being?" As to physics, there is no hope of resolving that question by controlled and repeatable empirical experiments. As to mathematics, any axioms that might be invoked to deductively derive either an affirmative or a negative answer to the question would inevitably fail to garner a consensus even about their meanings, much less their truth values.

The second factor is the human nature shared by the inquirers. Given that philosophical issues are neither amenable to the methods of empirical science nor those of mathematics, there is ample room for individual inquirers to resolve philosophical issues in radically differing ways. The fundamental need to work through issues for oneself can't be repressed altogether. When working inside the subject matter and methodological constraints of physics and mathematics, the need to think for oneself can express itself in ways that do not conflict with the possibility of a communal consensus. However, in the absence of such built-in constraints, as in philosophical inquiry, this individualizing passion to see for oneself does conflict with the possibility of a communal consensus. Free from such intrinsic constraints, the passion is free to roam where it will, resulting in the controversy and conflict pervading the history of philosophy.

But why is conflict the inevitable result? Why don't liberated individualizing passions to understand result in a consensus? Putting aside for a moment the *why* question, the *fact* of the matter is certain. Put 100 randomly selected philosophers in a room for a day and ask them to discuss and resolve a single fundamental philosophical question. The predictable result will be radical disagreement about the meaning of the question, the appropriate methods for resolving it, how those appropriate methods should be applied in this case, the question's resolution, and, given a resolution, its ideal formulation. One hundred is a relatively small number, but the same result would be generated by just two or three randomly selected philosophers.

Some might respond,

> Sure, but that's because it's only people with hugely aggressive and egocentric personalities who are drawn to philosophy in the first place. They're bound to squabble, no matter what the issue. Philosophy provides an ideal Coliseum for people like that to wield their aggression upon each other. One can't draw justifiable generalizations about everyone from a sample of untamed neurotics.

We disagree. Put 100 randomly selected mathematicians or physicists in a room for a day and ask them to discuss and resolve a fundamental philosophical question, without first translating it into their professional terms and equations. Freed from the subject matter and methodological constraints of their specialized occupations, the result would be the same.

So, the *fact* of the matter is unquestionable. But *why* is that the fact of the matter? The answer involves at least three factors: (1) humans have a significant measure of freedom in choosing how to use their powers of imagination, memory, observation, analysis, and reasoning; (2) they have significantly varying degrees of those powers; and (3) they have significantly varying personal histories, resulting in a bewildering diversity of deeply embedded attitudes, emotions, and assumptions. These three factors, working together, guarantee conflict.

Will philosophical chaos persist indefinitely?

We have argued that neither revolutionary camp believes that the past chaos will inevitably persist, although for different reasons. Setting aside their reasons, we disagree with their shared conclusion. The chaos will inevitably persist for the reasons just mentioned. The chaos is a causal function of two factors: the nature of philosophical inquiry and the human nature of the inquirers. Neither factor will change. So, philosophy will inevitably continue as a process of conflict.

Should philosophy become a science in its own right?

We have argued that the two classes of revolutionaries differ over whether philosophy should become a science. Anti-philosophy revolutionaries answer "No" because they maintain that philosophical reflection should be abandoned altogether. Methodological revolutionaries answer "Yes" because they believe that, by adopting their new methods, philosophy will be transformed into a cumulative activity.

We agree with the anti-philosophy group that philosophers should not try to transform philosophy into a cumulative science, but for a different reason. We have argued that although sciences, such as physics and mathematics, are appropriate sources for philosophical inquiry, their methods are significantly different. Physics, the paradigmatic empirical science, proceeds primarily by means of controlled and repeatable empirical experiments. Given the nature of the issues it pursues, philosophical inquiry could not proceed in that way. Mathematics, the paradigmatic *a priori* science, proceeds primarily by means of deduction from posited axioms. Given the nature of the ultimate issues it pursues, philosophy could not proceed exclusively in that way either. It is true that philosophical reflection requires deductive inference, but it requires other activities as well, for example, inductive inference, empirical observation, and first-person reflection.

Moreover, as we have argued, the primary objective of engaging in philosophy is pursuing issues that are personal to each inquirer. Because a necessary condition for flourishing as a philosopher is working in situations that encourage dialectical reflections, the most fruitful context for such individualizing inquiry is a constant context of conflicting arguments and views, both actual and imagined. Such contexts could not survive the transformation of philosophy into a cumulative science.

What form does the methodological revolutionary approach take in contemporary analytic philosophy?

We have argued that the explanation for analytic philosophy's ever-increasing emphasis upon specialization is its presupposition that specialization is a necessary condition for transforming philosophy into a cumulative science. However, even a brief examination of the publications of contemporary analytic philosophers shows that specialization has failed to generate anything even approximating a cumulative science. Given the pretensions, the display of unending conflict is astounding. There is nothing remotely similar to the kind of cumulative consensus inherent in physics and mathematics. Instead, there is the same old refrain, sung again and again, "A, B, and C are hopelessly mistaken about Issue X. So, we must start again from scratch on Issue X, and here's my proposal for doing just that." You will not find that in genuine science.

Sure, you will find philosophical agreement of sorts, for example, "We're all physicalists now." But look closer and you will see deep conflicts popping up all over. "Granted, we're all physicalists now, but the relevant question is, 'Which of these eleven alternative formulations of physicalism is the *right* one?' I say it's #5. You say it's #9. Either you're acting in bad faith or you're completely confused, and here's why...."[98]

Why is there such a chasm between the methodological revolutionaries' ideal of transforming philosophy into a cumulative science and the reality of endless hand-to-hand intellectual combat? As before, the explanation lies in the nature of philosophical inquiry itself, together with the human nature of the inquirers. The issues that philosophy essentially focuses upon are not

---

[98] For helpful discussions of some of the various alternative senses of "physicalism," see Daniel Stoljar, *Physicalism* (New York: Taylor and Francis, 2010); Stoljar, "Physicalism," *The Stanford Encyclopedia of Philosophy*, fall 2009, ed. Edward N. Zalta, http://plato.stanford,edu/archives/fall2009/entries/physicalism/>.

amenable to the consensus-based methods of either physics or mathematics. The fact that even those working in the most narrowly specialized trenches of philosophy can't stop disagreeing is evidence that the train of specialization they have boarded will not carry them to the promised land of scientific philosophy. Why not? They are working with two distinct motivations and those motivations are incompatible. On the one hand, they want to participate in a mode of inquiry that will generate cumulative results. They want to be scientists in their own right, *qua* philosophers. That desire expresses itself in the drive for specialization, with its tall fences separating tiny garden plots of inquiry. On the other hand, given their human nature, they also want to pursue philosophical issues for themselves, *qua* individuals. Given the inevitable lack of consensus about philosophical issues, of which most analytical philosophers are probably aware, on some level of consciousness, that desire naturally expresses itself in conflict and disputation. Even in the current lockstep of analytical philosophy, it is nevertheless *not good form* to agree completely with any other philosopher, no matter the issue. Part of this is just pride and juvenile competitiveness ("Sorry, but I'm just a lot quicker and smarter than the rest of you"), but another part is an authentic urge to think things for oneself. These motivations conflict and the second inevitably triumphs because it is stronger, given the unbalanced situation. The fact that chaotic disagreement invariably surfaces, even in the face of a sustained collective effort to transform philosophy into a science, is evidence that it's just not possible.

Is cumulative progress possible in philosophy?

We reject the underlying assumption of methodological revolutionaries that cumulative progress in philosophy is possible. As we have argued, progress is possible only in the particular investigations of individual inquirers. The dream that philosophical inquiry could achieve the kind of cumulative progress exhibited in physics or mathematics is groundless.

Why so? Make your own list of methodological revolutionaries. Ask yourself whether any of them ever succeeded in transforming philosophy into a cumulative science. What you will witness is an ever-expanding series of methodological revolutionaries, each predictably announcing the revolutionary dawn of a scientific philosophy, and each just as predictably failing to produce one. Their ultimate philosophical impact is always the same—more of the same old disputation and conflict.

Why? First, there are the inevitable disputes over what exactly the Master held. Think about the endless controversies over what, for example, Kant, Husserl, Quine, Wittgenstein, or Davidson *really held*. Those disputes, in turn, generate diverse interpretive traditions, each pledging allegiance to the Master, and each rejecting other interpretations.

Second, there are always at least a few stubbornly independent inquirers who reject the views of the Master. For every Bacon, a Descartes. For every Descartes, a Locke. For every Locke, a Hume. For every Hume, a Reid. For every Reid, a Kant. For every Kant, a Hegel. For every Hegel, a Kierkegaard. For every Husserl, a Heidegger. For every Heidegger, a Carnap. For every Carnap, a Quine. For every Quine, a Chisholm. For every Bradley, a Russell. For every Russell, a Wittgenstein. For every Wittgenstein, an Austin. Thus, the writings of methodological revolutionaries invariably generate fundamental conflicts not only among their disciples, but also between the revolutionaries' views and the views of those contrarians who reject them.

Some might question our claim that there is a sense in which individual inquirers can make philosophical progress, *qua* individuals. What could that mean? Here we enter a Socratic or Kierkegaardian realm. The question whether an individual inquirer has made philosophical progress is a question ultimately directed to, and answerable by, the inquirer himself. Of course, some observers are certain to disagree with such self-appraisals, but individual inquirers might modify their self-appraisals in the light of third-party criticisms. Nevertheless, an inquirer must live at each moment with his own self-evaluation, whatever it happens to be at any given time. Philosophical reflection is an inherently individualizing activity. The fundamental issues must ultimately be responded to by each inquirer standing alone, separated from all the cheering, or jeering, crowds. The primary question is always the same, "What do *you* believe?" The relevant question is never, "What do *you and they* believe?"

What an inquirer must avoid is permitting the question, "Have I made philosophical progress?" to slide into the question, "Do others think I have made progress?" That would be fatal to the authenticity of an inquirer's inquiry. Imagine an inquirer asking herself, just after writing each sentence, "But what would Professor X think about what I just wrote?" She might as well give up philosophical reflection altogether. X's views are already published, and X is responsible for them. Of course, it would be justifiable to ultimately agree with X's views, after the inquirer worked through the issues for herself. Antecedently shaping her views in order to clone X's views, however, is a waste of the inquirer's own time and that of anyone who pays attention to what she has to say.

Our thesis that an individual inquirer's self-appraisal is ultimate is subject to an important qualification. Any inquirer must answer to his philosophical conscience: "It seems to me that I've just formulated a better resolution of issue Y than ever before. However, I must always remind myself that I might eventually work out an even-better resolution, as I continue to reflect upon my own experiences and others' dialectical responses to my thoughts."

In emphasizing the individualizing nature of philosophical inquiry and the ultimate responsibility of individual inquirers to make their own self-evaluations, we are not suggesting that philosophical progress is just a relativistic affair of subjective self-appraisals and that there is no truth-of-the-matter to be discovered. There is a single world with a single nature, and the views of individual inquirers approximate that nature to varying degrees, some better than others. So, the ultimate criterion for individual philosophical success is conformance to the nature of reality. Of course, the epistemic problem is recognizing the extent to which one's own views conform to that nature. The absolute truth about reality is the ultimate standard for evaluating philosophical views, but it seems impossible to achieve demonstrative certainty about the application of that standard in any particular case.

Religion can play an important role in this regard, although demonstrative certainty about religion is also beyond human grasp. However, there are modes of religious inquiry that, although falling short of Aristotelian demonstrability, can provide inquirers with the possibility of finding evidence that becomes available only after first venturing beyond the boundaries of certainty in acts of faith.[99] In addition, such modes of inquiry can raise questions for inquirers that they otherwise would not have thought about.

Some might question our pessimism about the prospects for cumulative progress in philosophy. Haven't there been at least piecemeal advances in particular areas? What about the advancements in logic, from Boole, Peano, Frege, Russell, to Hilbert, Skolem, Gödel, Tarski, Turing, Gentzen, Kleene, and Kripke? Of course, there have been significant advancements in logic. Nevertheless, we dispute the assertion that piecemeal advancements in logic have produced a cumulative advance in philosophical inquiry as a whole. The advancements in logic have not generated anything even close to uncontroversial results accepted by the philosophical community as a whole. On the contrary, the increasing sophistication of logic has generated increased controversy about the nature of logic itself.

On the deductive side, there are the proliferating developments of nonstandard logics—intensional logics, relevance logics, paraconsistent logics, quantum logics, fuzzy logics, conditional logics, modal logics, temporal

---

[99] See Pascal's *Pensées* for an insightful discussion of evidence that is discoverable only by first stepping beyond the evidence presently at hand through an act of faith. Pascal's focus is upon religious belief, but his analysis can be generalized to many other kinds of belief.

logics, and epistemic logics. Indeed, the increasing sophistication of logic has expanded the areas of potential conflict among philosophers, rather than building any cumulative consensus.

On the inductive side, the situation is even more disorderly. Radically differing accounts of inductive inference proliferate—competing systems of Bayesian inference, frequency inference, and *a priori* inference as well as denials of the very possibility of formulating any systematic theory of inductive inference.

Putting aside the proliferation of conflicts about the nature of logic itself, there is a proliferation of conflicts about logic's application. Even those who accept the truth-functional and extensional principles of classical first-order logic, nevertheless differ over the applications of those principles in particular contexts. The situation becomes even more chaotic when those focusing upon particular contexts disagree about which of the many competing systems of logic apply. In general, the increasing sophistication of logic has resulted in a dramatic expansion of the potential areas for conflict, rather than in the promotion of a cumulative overall progress of the kind inherent in physics and mathematics. Giving inquirers more sophisticated conceptual tools has only created the conditions for increasing conflict.[100]

The same analysis applies to the claim that philosophy has progressed in virtue of advancements in the philosophy of language, which have made it possible to formulate issues and propose resolutions in more precise terms than was possible for earlier inquirers.[101] Granted, there are tools for increased clarity, but we disagree with the inference that philosophy as a whole has thereby been cumulatively advanced in any significant way. The better inference is the opposite. Increased clarity in the formulation of issues and their attempted resolutions has increased the potential for conflict, rather than lessened it. As with advances in logic, giving philosophers new linguistic tools of intellectual combat just creates the conditions for more combat. Nothing like this exists in the genuine sciences. The invention of calculus contributed to the advancement of cumulative results in physics. The metamathematical methods discovered by Gödel contributed to the advancement of cumulative results in mathematics. Nothing like this is true for the new linguistic tools in the hands of philosophers.

---

[100] Another instructive example is the sophisticated development of possible-worlds interpretations of systems of modal logic. Not only have these developments generated a host of disagreements about which interpretations are better than others, but also disagreements about the ontological status of possible worlds themselves and whether their invocation helps or hinders philosophical inquiry.

[101] See Gracia, *Philosophy and Its History*, 318.

Indeed, the same tools that yield cumulative advances in the sciences fail to yield corresponding cumulative advances in philosophy. Again, consider calculus. As just noted, its adoption by physicists contributed to cumulative advances in physics. The fact that many philosophers have studied calculus has failed to contribute to cumulative advances in philosophy as a whole. The very subject matter of calculus raises deep philosophical questions, to say nothing about applications of calculus purporting to resolve philosophical issues such as Zeno's paradoxes. Dismissing his paradoxes with the casual remark that Zeno failed to anticipate the mathematical concept of the limit of a real-number sequence does not carry much philosophical weight. Philosophers will be quick to point out that invoking the concept of limits in order to dissolve Zeno's paradoxes begs the question. Does not the concept of a limit presuppose the conception of the real-number line as an ordered series of dimensionless points, and does not that conception itself incorporate all the materials needed to generate Zeno's paradoxes? Further, there is the assumption that, at any given time during its movement, a moving object is "at" a point, contrary to Aristotle's thesis.

Similarly, whereas the adoption of Gödel's metamathematical methods by mathematicians contributed to cumulative advances in mathematics, those same methods, when applied to philosophical issues, have failed to contribute to collective advances in philosophy. Read any recent philosophical discussion of Gödel's incompleteness theorems. You will find that, although Gödel's methods are accepted in the cumulative activity of mathematics, they are nothing but fodder for continuing dispute in philosophy.

Is the study of past philosophy for the purpose of assisting one's own first-order philosophical inquiries pointless?

In this book we have devoted most of our efforts to arguing for Thesis T—that investigating past philosophical sources is an excellent means of assisting one's own first-order philosophical inquiries. Reiterating all of our arguments would be redundant. We think it helpful, however, to summarize our responses to the two arguments against Thesis T that we've been discussing in this chapter: (1) the argument of anti–philosophy revolutionaries, and (2) the argument of methodological revolutionaries.

We reject the argument of anti-philosophy revolutionaries because we reject their claim that first-order philosophical inquiry is a waste of time. First-order philosophical inquiry is an essential constituent of the human nature itself and, as such, could not possibly be a waste of time. Even the most determined anti-philosophy revolutionaries, for example, Sextus Empiricus and Wittgenstein, left behind works that are obvious examples of first-order philosophical inquiry—strong evidence for our conclusion that it is not humanly possible to abandon first-order philosophical inquiry.

We also reject the anti-history argument of methodological revolutionaries. The idea that new philosophical methods could bring the dawn of a genuinely cumulative philosophy is a fantasy. There are no such methods. The essential human drive to engage in first-order philosophical inquiry expresses itself in the fundamental methods of engaging in that inquiry, several of which we discussed in Chapter 2. As both present and past philosophy has shown, those traditional methods are not sufficient to generate a collective philosophical consensus, and there are no methods that could. That is part of our human condition, for better or worse. We might as well learn to live with it.

7

Philosophy, Time, and Eternity

Introduction

We have worked through a long argument supporting the thesis that earlier philosophy is an excellent means to enhance understanding of the world and ourselves. After making a direct case largely resting on an account of the dialectical nature of philosophy, we considered a number of objections, some based on advances in science and others prompted by developments within philosophy itself, especially voicings of the ever-present temptation to begin anew. Even if all we have urged in reply is accepted, two important questions remain.

First, is the pursuit of philosophy via earlier writers an efficient means of throwing light on living issues? All gold is valuable, but some is locked into surroundings that make recovery extremely expensive. However beautiful the gifts given to us by earlier thinkers, however reasonable the arguments bidding us to care for such gifts, however intriguing the particular illustrations, it may still seem unwise to plunge into the works of genius composed before the present. All choices involve trade-offs. There are opportunity costs to spending appreciable stretches of irrecoverable time to look back. Does it simply take too long to attend to past philosophy with any degree of seriousness?

Second, much has been made of the indispensability of dialectic and the personal nature of philosophic progress. Doesn't this suggest philosophy is perpetually incomplete and unsettled? Is not such a process inconsistent with the attainment of the highest end of human existence—eudemonia?

Philosophy and time

Let us begin with a particular case. You are interested in getting some light on epistemological and ontological problems. You chance on the writing of the neo-Kantian philosopher Ivan Ivanovich Lapshin, and you suspect there might be much in Lapshin that can help. Fortunately, you know a little late-nineteenth-century Russian—that is part of Lapshin's allure. However, you remember the admonition of countless commentators on literature and philosophy: you cannot really profit from a work unless you understand what the author intends to communicate. E.D. Hirsch put it this way: "Understanding of an author's intended meaning is logically and psychologically prior to consideration of significance," where " 'significance' results from the reader's judgment about the text's relationship to his or her world ...."[1] "Well, then," you wonder, "how shall I come to understand Lapshin's intended meaning? Can I just pick up his books and read as if I were going through the sports section of today's paper?" That would be very bold—too bold, even though I know some Russian. I understand the sports section because I understand our culture and know the teams, players, rules, and the general setting in which it all happens. But Russian philosophy and cultural milieu? That is an altogether different matter. It is so different that some world-renowned intellectual historians talk as if what past philosophers thought is locked into a temporal frame that all but precludes our grasping, even its essential teachings. Even if that extreme theoretical historicism is to be rejected, you might reason, it must be acknowledged that getting into Lapshin's head would take considerable work. You worry: I would have to read his Russian contemporaries and his predecessors, most notably among the latter, Kant. But to understand Kant, I would also need to know what Kant's contemporary interlocutors, disciples, and students had to say. Then, backing up, I will need to delve deep into Hume and Leibniz. That means knitting my brow for months over what exactly Hume meant by "object" and Leibniz by "monads." Backing up further, I will need to plow through the endlessly ambiguous Locke, along with his contemporaries and predecessors, to say nothing of recent commentary. And so on, and so on, and on and on. I begin by wanting to satisfy my epistemological and metaphysical cravings, only to find myself locked in a dark and forbidding Kierkegaardian Infinite Parenthesis. I cannot understand *this* until I understand *that*, with no end of the series in sight. Forget Lapshin. I will pick up *Philosophical Review* and see what is happening now.

Clearly, there is much in this line of reasoning, enough to have locked many in a Kierkegaardian Infinite Parenthesis. Yet, for all that, the line of reasoning is not without its severe limitations and should not paralyze us.

Consider the premise of the worry leading to the Kierkegaardian Infinite Parenthesis: "To understand a text, I must first understand what the author was attempting to communicate." Abraham Lincoln's biographer, David Herbert Donald, reports that

---

[1] This is the summary judgment of the article on Hirsch in *The Encyclopedia of Contemporary Literary Theory: Approaches, Scholars, Terms*, ed. Irena R. Makaryk (Toronto: University of Toronto Press, 1993), 360.

the three sections of Lincoln's house-divided speech had the inevitability of a syllogism: The tendency to nationalize slavery had to be defeated. Steven A. Douglas powerfully contributed to that tendency. Therefore, Steven A. Douglas had to be defeated.[2]

Lincoln's law partner, William Herndon, and other advisers censured him for taking such a strong position on slavery. Lincoln distanced himself from what everyone took to be his point. "Whether the clause used by me will bear such construction or not, I never so intended it," he told John Locke Scripps. "I did not say I was in favor of anything.... I made a prediction only—it may have been a foolish one perhaps."[3] Lincoln rightly distinguished between what an author intends to communicate and the construction a clause will bear. Furthermore, in the course of distancing himself from one interpretation of his speech, Lincoln implicitly acknowledged that he had no more right than any other competent user of the language to determine the construction a clause will bear. Anyone listening to Lincoln could read his remarks as conveying the message that one ought not to vote for Douglas. Every adult user of English knows that statements with the syntactic form of prediction often function as implied normative assertions. Lincoln: "If you keep whipping the horse it will die." You: "Abe, are you telling me how to handle my horse, or are you merely making a prediction?" Lincoln: "You are free to take it any way you'd like." And so you are. So too were the nation's citizens when they took Lincoln to be making a normative claim about the need to defeat Douglas. Of course, it would have mattered at the time (and perhaps matters now for us) that Lincoln tried to glissade out of a tight political corner. But there was more to be judged than Honest Abe's honesty. There was the country's future to worry about. Lincoln's argument certainly could have been read as supporting the conclusion that Douglas had to be blocked, even if in his heart Lincoln was "only making a prediction." And that message was something to ponder.

The upshot for philosophy? We can legitimately put to one side a philosopher's intentions. It would be nice to know what was going on in a philosopher's mind, but it is often hard to know that. Moreover, the philosopher's internal ruminations are inessential for using the text to advance philosophy. All that needs to be known is what constructions the clauses may bear, be they several or one.

However, a second objection can be made without reliance on the premise that the author's intentions have to be grasped.

---

[2]   David Herbert Donald, *Lincoln* (New York: Touchstone, 1995), 209.
[3]   Donald, *Lincoln*. Donald does not give a reference for this statement by Lincoln.

> Very well, have it your own way about the author's intentions. There is still an obstacle in our way. What about the cultural milieu and intellectual debts? Even if we put to one side authorial intentions to focus on the language of the text, the language itself requires interpretation. If we want to know what Lapshin's writing means, we are still off and running from Lapshin to Kant to Leibniz to Hume to Locke, endlessly. Bypassing intentions changes none of this.

It certainly helps with the text itself to grasp relevant cultural facts and debts. But the help is not generally indispensable, and there is a limit to what one must understand about the milieu. That limit is not so far out of reach as to immobilize us completely. Suppose Lapshin sets out to express Kantian points in language far more rigorous and perspicuous than Kant's. (He wouldn't be the first.) Why would anyone need to consult Kant's works if Lapshin should succeed? Of course, it would be necessary if the aim were to understand Lapshin's contributions to the history of thought. If, however, the aim is to do first-order philosophy, then one need no more retreat to Kant than to penetrate gnomic Heraclitian fragments to understand Aristotle or to grasp the nuances of Hilbert's Program to understand Gödel's proofs on the incompleteness of arithmetic. It is good to know that it was the talented Princess Elizabeth of Bohemia who first raised the problem of mental causation with Descartes, but this background is not essential for doing first-order philosophy. Were it always essential to grasp predecessor of X's thought to grasp the thought of X, shall we then call everything to a halt with respect to the problem of mental causation if we know nothing of the Princess's ideas other than what we know from her exchanges with Descartes? Do we need to know who influenced her? Is nobody to be understood in her own terms?

> "Her own terms, indeed," an objector might reply. "Understanding a text composed ages ago is fraught with peril. It can take years to get anything like a good grip on the meaning of a text. And it is not just the language barrier that is a major problem. Sensible handling of a text requires immersing oneself in the corpus of writings. In the case of a major author, this also is a formidable task."

Take that favorite of anthologies in the philosophy of religion, Aquinas's Five Ways. The standard English translation causes serious trouble from the very first line of the "Response," the part of the *Summa Theologiae* representing Aquinas's position on God's existence. "The first and more manifest way is the argument from motion. It is certain and evident to our senses, that in the world some things are in motion. Now whatever is in motion is put in motion by another . . . ."[4] So translated, as it often is, the argument for God's existence is over with its first breath. The assumption that what is in motion requires a mover conflicts with the Newtonian inertial principle. The Latin of the passage, however, reads: "Respondeo dicendum quod Deum esse quinque viis probari potest. Prima autem et manifestior via est, quae sumitur ex parte motus. Certum est enim, et sensu constat, aliqua moveri in hoc mundo. Omne autem quod movetur, ab alio movetur."[5] The word "*moveri*" is in the passive. The sense of the passage is that we see that some things *are moved* and *whatever is moved is moved by another*. On this reading, there is no conflict with Newtonian science.

Yet, the situation is more complicated than just made out. *Movetur* also functioned as a deponent verb, that is, passive in form but active in meaning. If that was how Aquinas was using the expression, the argument is again wrecked by modern physics. Which is the right meaning? Professor Michael Weiss, a specialist in the history of Latin, argues that the correct sense of "*movetur*" is the passive "is moved."[6] His argument trades, in part, on what he believes Aquinas would have been willing to risk by using a fancy deponent in this context. However, even if it is allowable to set aside an author's intention, as we argued a few paragraphs ago, and focus on the Latin text, it will take some doing to figure out the sense of the passage. That means either becoming an expert in Latin or finding an expert in the Latin of the period to help at every stage of work on Aquinas.

Understanding the language is just part of the problem. Within a dozen sentences or so, Aquinas's text presents us with another interpretive problem. In the third argument for God's existence based on possibility and necessity, the so-called Third Way, Aquinas offers the following bit of reasoning on his way to the conclusion that there must be a necessary being (a God): "It is impossible for things that can be always to exist, for that which is possible not

---

[4] Thomas Aquinas, *Summa Theologiae* I. Q. 2. A.3, trans. Fathers of the English Dominican Province (New York: Benzinger Bros., 1948), 13.

[5] Thomas Aquinas, *Summa Theologiae* I. Q. 2. A.3. "Corpus Thomisticum: S. Thomae de Aquino Opera Omnia," accessed August 7, 2013, http://www.corpusthomisticum.org/iopera.html.

[6] It is true that in the later Latin period what linguists call hypercorrect deponent forms do occur. This is because in the popular language, deponents were dying out and hence deponency was taken as a sign of literary style. Hence, traditional active verbs are found here and there with deponent endings. However, this phenomenon is mainly seen in the pre-Carolingian period, which was a period of rather low standards in Latin education. By Aquinas's day, it was pretty unlikely that an educated author would permit any hypercorrect deponents. Furthermore, it seems unlikely that a philosopher like Aquinas would take the risk of being misunderstood by using an innovative deponent form of a verb, which he must use as a normal transitive many times, precisely at such a key point in the argument.

to be at some time is not." Where in the world does the latter proposition come from? It just seemingly drops out of the blue. As it happens, Aquinas actually argues for the claim, not in the vicinity of these remarks in the *Summa*, but in his *Commentary on Aristotle's On the Heavens*, which he doesn't even cite. So, it is impossible to evaluate Aquinas's Third Way unless the reader knows an enormous amount of Aquinas's mammoth corpus. It seems hopeless in the case of Aquinas.

These problems of translation and context within the author's corpus of writings plague every student of past philosophy. Kant's German is a challenge even to Germans. In the case of Kant, it is dangerous to say that Kant held P, since elsewhere in his writings P may look just like what Kant is denying. Some distinguished commentators have despaired of getting even his single work straight. Norman Kemp Smith maintained that Kant "flatly contradicts himself in almost every chapter" of the *Critique of Pure Reason* in such an obvious way that "every commentator has felt constrained to offer some 'explanation' of the inconsistencies."[7] In the more recent *Oxford Companion to Kant*, Karl Ameriks says, "If one looks closely at the *Critique of Pure Reason*, it is not easy to show precisely how even on its own terms it has definitely undermined all claims of traditional metaphysics; indeed, from the *Critique* alone it is difficult to find out what all those claims are."[8] Evidently, the reader must look outside the *Critique of Pure Reason* to other challenging works in the Kantian corpus even to figure out what his most famous arguments mean. Why would a first-order philosopher want to devote half a lifetime to join Smith and Ameriks in their puzzlement?

While sensible up to a point, this disquiet about rightly construing earlier thought should not discourage the first-order philosopher.

First of all, to gain something of importance from earlier philosophy it is scarcely necessary to "spend half a life-time" at it. Professional historians of philosophy might do just that. But the objective of the first-order philosopher need not be to become a world-class authority on Plato, Augustine, Kant, or even just one work, such as *Critique of Pure Reason*. The first-order philosopher can aim to get help from earlier philosophy without an exorbitant expenditure of time. And *some* help is surely not hard to get. This is because help comes in many forms. Ideally, it yields knock-down proofs and compelling explanations regarding important phenomena. It might do far less and still be helpful, enormously so. As probable arguments abound

---

[7] Norman Kemp Smith, *A Commentary to Kant's Critique of Pure Reason*, 2nd ed. (Atlantic Highlands, NJ: Humanities Press International, 1992), xx.

[8] Karl Ameriks, "The Critique of Metaphysics: Kant and Traditional Ontology," in *Cambridge Companion to Kant*, ed. Paul Guyer (Cambridge: Cambridge University Press, 1992), 258.

in contemporary philosophy, where incessant appeal is made to "intuitions," so do arguments and explanations in past philosophy. In his *Topics*, Aristotle insisted that dialectic was the road to the foundations of all sciences. Moreover, he spells out several ways of gathering materials to philosophize that fall short of plucking arguments out of the libraries of predecessors. Philosophers who provide us with important plausible propositions note similarities between very different objects and properties, or see differences between objects and properties that appear very much the same, or distinguish the senses of terms in an argumentative context—all of which can be significantly helpful. Moreover, beyond full arguments, explanations, and the elements Aristotle lists that make them up, there is the great advantage of suggestions about the whole, about how all things hand together and what is behind it all, as when Plato paints his picture of the cave in the *Republic*. Even mere attitude can be helpful: the reverence of the philosophical Hindus for the Vedas, Jews and Christians for the old and new testaments, Muslims for the Koran, and Chinese for the founding works on Confucianism, Mohism, Legalism, and Daoism. All inspire us with a desire to give shape to a personal but whole philosophy.

Second, for ferreting out an earlier writer's meaning, help is readily available. Many commentaries on particular figures are available in a form that lays out the chief arguments of the more difficult works, as the commentator understands them. This care with the logical structure of systems and arguments is largely due to the influence of analytic philosophy. Of course, analytic philosophers often disagree about what an author means to say and on what grounds, but the very disagreements can be useful. The disagreements draw attention to the text, which one can then re-examine with the disagreements in mind. Commentators may fail to provide the final word about a text—indeed, there may be no such thing— but they state alternatives and explain what meanings the clauses can bear, to use Lincoln's happy phrase. The display of alternatives helps first-order philosophers take what they can get and make use of every line of argument that appears to offer access to reality. For *again*, the aim is not to learn just what a philosopher was thinking or to ascertain *the only* meaning the philosopher's words could signify, but to provide materials for doing first-order philosophy. Such secondary sources can be useful even if they offer only creative misreadings.

Third, as argued earlier, profit can be had even if we cannot settle on what an author intended or the best reading of a text independent of the authorial intention. Lincoln could be read as offering an argument against Douglas or as merely making a prediction. We are free to choose what serves our purpose in order to learn the truth about the way things are.

Fourth, not all earlier texts are extremely demanding. All kinds of help can be had by reading reasonably accessible texts. Suppose, for example, you believe there is something to the idea that virtuous conduct lies in attaining a mean of some sort. You are persuaded that affability is inconsistent with maintaining a perpetually gloomy exterior and playing the role of a high school class clown. It is not so easy, however, to find the mean in one's own case across the whole spectrum of virtues. What general guidelines come to mind? If none occurs readily, what significant loss would be incurred by consulting Aristotle's *Nichomachean Ethics*, Bk. II, c. 9? Whatever complications the Greek text may pose, the basic message is one we can easily grasp and absorb to great profit. A number of distinguished philosophers in the past century have found much to admire and write about with respect to Greek ethics and politics, and beyond that to the reflections on those topics offered by the likes of Locke, Hobbes, Rousseau, and Kant. Much of what the earlier writers and their commentators have had to say is not all that far from common understanding. It has been said of Aristotle, for example, that much of his writing is common sense touched by genius. Even philosophers who generally make for arduous reading offer reflections that any educated adult can understand, for example, as Kant did in his *Lecturers on Ethics* and his marvelous little book *Observations on the Feeling of the Sublime and the Beautiful*. Heidegger, whose *Being and Time* perplexes endlessly with what appear to be linguistic butcheries, sometimes writes in a quite lucid way. The sympathetic A.W. Moore suggests that despite the peculiar scholarly focus of *Being and Time*, this early and unfinished work is not typical of Heidegger's writings. His *History of the Concept of Time* is almost a model of unadulterated plain speech.[9]

Fifth, the concern about understanding a philosopher in the context of the entire corpus of writings, illustrated by earlier remarks on Aquinas and Kant, is largely based on a commendable desire to apply the principle of charity. We want to put the best construction on a philosopher's thought, and that is best done by taking into account the entire corpus of writings. Defects in the third argument for God's existence in the *Summa Theologiae* can be partially patched by consulting Aquinas's *Commentary on Aristotle's On the Heavens*. And if, as Ameriks warns about Kant, "it is not easy to show precisely how even on its own terms it [*The Critique of Pure Reason*] has definitely undermined all claims of traditional metaphysics; indeed, from the *Critique* alone it is difficult to find out what all those claims are,"[10] the

---

[9]   A.W. Moore, *The Evolution of Modern Metaphysics: Making Sense of Things* (Cambridge: Cambridge University Press, 2012), 459–460.
[10]   Ameriks, "The Critique of Metaphysics," 258.

principle of charity requires close scrutiny of much else in his demanding and enormous body of work. All this is true enough. Yet we can get much that is useful even if we cannot meet an ideal, especially if we are willing to receive the aid of commentators on Aquinas and Kant. Yes, we may not see clearly what their arguments, reconstructed according to the principle of charity, would be. The same can be said of the thinking of our friends and of even ourselves. Still, even a variety of incomplete interpretations can bring to our notice neglected problems, solutions, and overarching conceptions of the world and thinkers like us. Moreover, while as arduous in its own way as swimming in deep waters, philosophizing is a joyful activity, as much because discovery itself is pleasant as because the objects discovered are delightful. Among the discoveries we can make is just what philosophers, who are our acquaintances, yield up to their best friends.

Sixth, although there is no getting around the fact that exploring earlier philosophy presents serious challenges, the same can be said of reading those who are still with us. It is not obvious that reading past philosophy with care is substantially more time consuming than digging into the nooks and crannies of leading figures today. Of course, we do not have the same problems about language—at least our common ordinary language. Nevertheless, contemporary philosophy is replete with technical expressions that have a multitude of meanings. And some of the more careful writers, who would have fit in well with the most ardent logic choppers of the late medieval period, develop what amounts to an idiolect, a nearly impenetrable private language. Take, for example, writings by Richard Montague, described by John Passmore as "exceptionally difficult to summarize." Montague believes the only way to do philosophy is formally, and consequently he heaps freshly coined symbolism on top of a presupposed background of set theory. Yet, for all the rigor, Montague's positions on even fundamental points keep running away from him as he changes his mind from article to article. Passmore repeats the story told about the five seminars Montague devoted to the exposition of two pages in one of his essays. "That," Montague announced, "is the rate at which I ought to be read."[11]

Montague represents an extreme, but an extreme not all that far from a considerably more appealing and influential philosopher, Roderick Chisholm. While Chisholm eschewed forbidding notation, his later work is replete with interlocking idiosyncratic definitions, rendering impenetrable the work of a philosopher who, on many earlier occasions, gave analytic philosophers models of simplicity and clarity. Again, it may be felt that these are extreme extremes, and, in general, contemporary philosophy, particularly

---

[11] John Passmore, *Recent Philosophers* (LaSalle, IL: Open Court, 1985), 41–42.

analytic philosophy, is far from obscure. Though there is considerable truth in that rejoinder, contemporary analytic philosophy often poses challenges as difficult as offered by great writers of the past. Moreover, intense study of even the most lucid writers can leave one wondering whether the time has been profitably spent.

Imagine, for example, that you intend to come to grips with the nuances of the mind–body problem. Knowing that contemporary expositions of this problem make use of the concept of supervenience, you resolve to retrace the recent history of that concept in the works of one of its most articulate expositors, Jaegwon Kim. Taking in hand his collection of articles on the topic entitled *Supervenience and Mind*, you find that nearly every page falls within the grasp of anyone with a philosophic background. Still, the collection as a whole raises serious questions about how much time to give to mastering the sequence of views put forward over a period of about 20 years when Kim himself alerts the reader in the preface that he not only has changed his mind about a number of matters and expects to keep on changing his mind, but that he has also come to think that the ontological apparatus he struggled to secure is largely optional:

> Concerning such questions as whether there "really are" events ... Along with *many other* similar questions about facts, properties, continuants, time slices, and so forth, it just seems wrongheaded to think that there are "true" answers, answers that are true because they correctly depict some pre-existing metaphysical order of the world.[12]

Why it is wrongheaded to think so, Kim does not say. Given a choice of reading someone confident in our ability to say true things about the way things are and someone who has given up on the project, it hardly seems foolish to prefer the former, especially if the more hopeful philosopher has held a position of eminence for centuries. In any event, the question of how to spend our time in working up materials to philosophize cannot be settled by appealing to the supposed greater clarity in the writings of contemporary philosophers, who keep changing their minds about substantive issues and exhibit little confidence in what they have to offer. This is by no means to say that thinkers like Kim are not worth reading. Far from it, we find him immensely illuminating on some points, and his work is indispensable to those working on the mind–body problem. The question is not whether first-order philosophy today requires reading our contemporaries. It is evident

---

[12] Jaegwon Kim, *Supervenience and Mind: Selected Philosophical Essays* (Cambridge: Cambridge University Press, 1993), ix.

that it does. Rather, the question is whether current philosophy is so superior to past philosophy that we need not spend any precious time pondering messages from those who have gone before us.

Considered in isolation, construing past philosophy appears daunting. Yet, viewed in relation to construing contemporary philosophy, the difficulties shrink, not to nothing but to something manageable. Or, if not something manageable, then something no more unmanageable than current philosophy. "Fine things are hard," Plato reminded those who wish to understand the really real. We can take pride and pleasure in understanding, to whatever degree we can manage, both the achievements of the present and the brilliant gifts of the best of those who have gone before us.

Dialectic and eternity

The results of our study, we hope, are encouraging. Philosophy is a wonderful enterprise. Past philosophy can be enormously helpful; it should not all be scrapped in favor of new beginnings. It must be acknowledged that the results of centuries of work may not be as uplifting as one might reasonably desire. Still, at its best, philosophy enlightens us on a wide spectrum of issues in a way nothing else does, unless the something else is conjoined to philosophy. It opens worlds to us and takes us out of ourselves, particularly if we attend to the contributions of past thinkers. Nonetheless, at no point have we dared to say that this enterprise leads to incontestable results. Given the nature of the human mind, we will never fully satisfy the craving for insight from which philosophy springs. Some philosophers have taken the view that it is all or nothing: proof or worthless jabber. We have taken a different tack, following Plato and Aristotle. There can be no deep inquiry into any problem of life without taking the dialectical path. "For dialectic is the process of criticism wherein lies the path to the principles of all inquiries."[13] The *more geometrico* method of Spinoza and Fichte and the absolute science of Husserl are beyond our reach or disappointing in their results. Wholly in line with the lessons taught by the history of philosophy, we must assume that to get anywhere we must carefully listen to what is said both for and against the positions that initially attract, and we cannot claim to have fully established any philosophical proposition unless we have defended it against the most plausible objections.

This position largely coincides with Aristotle's view that no proposition is properly described as literally "incontestable." For Aristotle, it is the business

[13]   Aristotle, *Topics* Bk I, c.2., *The Complete Works of Aristotle*, 168.

of the first philosopher to take on denials of propositions that are taken for granted, including the principle of noncontradiction and allied propositions extensively dealt with in Book 4 of his *Metaphysics*.

Yet, as we draw this study to a close, we know it is difficult these days to share Aristotle's confidence in the possibility of achieving demonstrations that, if properly understood, can meet all assaults. Moreover, it seems impossible to share his view that philosophy can constitute the core of genuine human bliss. This is not something newly recognized. It has always been evident that humans desire a bliss that is complete and secure. Your understanding of the world is incomplete in the extreme, with slight prospects of ever reaching the bottom of things and what stands behind it all. Endless dialectic is an intrinsic part of philosophy. If so, the philosophic core of bliss remains unstable to the extent that whatever genuine understanding we achieve, it nonetheless leaves us baffled by objections. Bliss is also unstable due to the unavoidable tribulations of life and the eventuality of death. Aristotle seems to say that while human beings cannot achieve perfect bliss, they can imitate it and for that reason be called blissful, so that human bliss does not have to last forever without fluctuation in the ordinary sense. Though in general an Aristotelian, Aquinas remarks that on this matter the master was mistaken:

> For all agree that happiness or bliss is a good of rational or intellectual natures and so wherever such natures truly exist, not by imitation, we should find true bliss and not just an imitation of it. Now human beings don't simply echo understanding … but are truly rational and intellectual; so we must believe that they can sometime attain true bliss and not simply an imitation of it; for otherwise a natural desire of their intellectual nature will have no function.[14]

Aquinas believed that a revelation from God faithfully promised a world after this in which our rational desires would be more than satisfied, since a vision of God was a reward for those who responded to his graces. Such a claim, of course, takes us beyond the realm of philosophy. Yet, whether such a claim is coherent, defensible, and adequately warranted is something human beings can judge for themselves without *assuming* some revelation is true. And it is at this point that philosophy today and yesterday remain most pertinent.

---

[14] Thomas Aquinas, *Commentary on the Sentences*, in *Aquinas: Selected Philosophical Writings*, ed. Timothy McDermott (Oxford: Oxford University Press, 1993), 325.

Bibliography

Ameriks, Karl, "The Critique of Metaphysics: Kant and Traditional Ontology." In *Cambridge Companion to Kant*. Edited by Paul Guyer, 249–279. Cambridge: Cambridge University Press, 1992

Aquinas, Thomas, *Summa Theologiae*. Translated by Fathers of the English Dominican Province. New York: Benzinger Bros, 1948

———, "Commentary on the Sentences." In *Aquinas: Selected Philosophical Writings*. Edited by Timothy McDermott. Oxford: Oxford University Press, 1993

———, *Summa Theologiae*. "Corpus Thomisticum: S. Thomae de Aquino Opera Omnia." Fundación Tomás de Aquino. Accessed August 7, 2013, http://www.corpusthomisticum.org/iopera.html.

Ariew, Roger, "Descartes and Scholasticism: The Intellectual Background to Descartes' Thought." In *The Cambridge Companion to Descartes*. Edited by John Cottingham, 59–80. Cambridge: Cambridge University Press, 1992

Aristotle, "Metaphysics." In *Aristotle, The Basic Works of Aristotle*. Edited by Richard McKeon. Translated by G. R. G. Mure, 681–926. New York: Random House, 1941

———, "Posterior Analytics." In *The Basic Works of Aristotle*. Edited by Richard McKeon. Translated by G. R. G. Mure, 106–186. New York: Random House, 1941

———, "Sophistical Refutations." In *The Complete Works of Aristotle*. Vol. 1. Edited by Jonathan Barnes. Translated by W. A. Pickard-Cambridge, 278–314. Princeton: Princeton University Press, 1984

———, "Topics." In *The Complete Works of Aristotle*. Vol. 1. Edited by Jonathan Barnes. Translated by W. A. Pickard-Cambridge, 167–277. Princeton: Princeton University Press, 1984

———, "Metaphysics." In *Aristotle Metaphysics Books Γ, Δ, and E*. 2nd ed. Translated by Christopher Kirwan. Oxford: Oxford University Press, 2003

Armstrong, D. M., *A World of States of Affairs*. Cambridge: Cambridge University Press, 1997

Atkins, Peter, "Science as Truth." *History of the Human Sciences* 8 1995: 97–102

Audi, Robert, *Practical Reasoning and Ethical Decision*. London: Routledge-Taylor and Francis, 2006

Austin, J. L., *Sense and Sensibilia*. Edited by G. J. Warnock. Oxford: Oxford University Press, 1962

———, *Philosophical Papers*. 3rd ed. Edited by J. O. Urmson and G. J. Warnock. Oxford: Oxford University Press, 1979

Bacon, Francis, *The New Organon*. Edited by Fulton H. Anderson. Indianapolis: Bobbs-Merrill Company, 1960

Bickle, John, *Philosophy and Neuroscience: A Ruthlessly Reductive Account.* Dordrecht: Kluwer Academic, 2003

Bobik, Joseph, *Aquinas on Being and Essence: A Translation and Interpretation.* Notre Dame: University of Notre Dame Press, 1965

Bohm, David, *Quantum Theory.* New York: Dover, 1979

———, *Wholeness and the Implicate Order.* London: Routledge, 1995

Bonjour, Laurence, *In Defense of Pure Reason.* Cambridge: Cambridge University Press, 1998

———, *Epistemology: Classic Problems and Contemporary Responses.* Lanham, MD: Littlefield, 2002

Bratman, Michael E., *Intentions, Plans, and Practical Reason.* Cambridge, MA: Harvard University Press, 1987

Breuer, Joseph, *Introduction to the Theory of Sets.* Mineola, NY: Dover, 2006

Brooks, John Langdon, *Just Before the Origin: Alfred Russell Wallace's Theory of Evolution.* New York: Columbia University Press, 1984

Burge, Tyler, *Foundations of Mind: Philosophical Essays, Vol. 2.* Oxford: Clarendon, 2007

Castaneda, Hector-Neri, *The Structure of Morality.* Springfield, IL: Charles C. Thomas, 1974

Chisholm, Roderrick M., *Theory of Knowledge.* 2nd ed. Englewood Cliffs, NJ: Prentice-Hall, 1977

———, *On Metaphysics.* Minneapolis: University of Minnesota Press, 1989

Cottingham, John. "Why Should Analytic Philosophers Do History of Philosophy?." In *Analytic Philosophy and History of Philosophy.* Edited by Tom Sorell and G. A. J. Rogers, 25–41. Oxford: Clarendon, 2005

Courant, Richard and Herbert Robbins, *What is Mathematics?.* 2nd ed. Revised by Ian Stewart. Oxford: Oxford University Press, 1996

Crick, F. C. and C. Koch, "Are We Aware of Neural Activity in Primary Visual Context?." *Nature* 375 1995: 121–123

Cullity, Garrett, and Berys Gaut, eds, *Ethics and Practical Reason.* Oxford: Clarendon, 1997

Danto, Arthur C., "Nietzsche's Daybreak." In *Reading Nietzsche.* Edited by Robert C. Solomon and Kathleen Marie Higgins, 186–191. Oxford: Oxford University Press, 1988

David, Velleman J., *The Possibility of Practical Reason.* Oxford: Clarendon, 2000

Dennett, Daniel C., *The Intentional Stance.* Cambridge, MA: MIT Press, 1987

Descartes, René, *Descartes: Philosophical Letters.* Edited and translated by Anthony Kenny. Oxford: Clarendon Press, 1970

———, *Descartes: Selected Philosophical Writings.* Translated by John Cottingham, Robert Stootfhoff, and Dugald Murdoch. Cambridge: Cambridge University Press, 1988

———, *Meditations on First Philosophy: With Selections from the Objections and Replies.* Edited and translated by John Cottingham. Cambridge: Cambridge University Press, 1996

d'Espagnat, Bernard, *On Physics and Philosophy*. Princeton: Princeton
 University Press, 2006
Donald, David Herbert, *Lincoln*. New York: Touchstone, 1995
Dostoevsky, Fyodor, *Notes from Underground*. Translated by Richard Pevear and
 Larissa Volokhonsky. New York: Vintage, 1993
Einstein, Albert, *Albert Einstein: Philosopher-Scientist Volume 1*. Edited by Paul
 Arthur Schilpp. New York: Harper Torch, 1951
Empiricus, Sextus, *Outlines of Scepticism*. Translated by Julia Annas and
 Jonathan Barnes. Cambridge: Cambridge University Press, 1994
Etchemendy, John, *The Concept of Logical Consequence*. Cambridge, MA:
 Harvard University Press, 1990
Feynman, Richard P., *The Meaning of It All: Thoughts of a Citizen-Scientist*.
 Reading, MA: Perseus, 1998
——, *The Feynman Lectures on Physics, Vol. I: Mainly Mechanics, Radiation,
 and Heat*. New York: Basic Books, 2010
Fodor, Jerry and Massimo Piattelli-Palmarini, *What Darwin Got Wrong*. New
 York: Farrar, Straus, and Giroux, 2010
Fraenkel, Abraham, *Abstract Set Theory*. 3rd ed. Amsterdam: North-Holland,
 1968
Galilei, Galileo, *Dialogues Concerning Two New Sciences*. Translated by Henry
 Crew and Alfonso de Salvio, 1–108. Toronto: Dover, 1954
Gazzaniga, Michael S., Richard B. Ivry, and George R. Mangun, *Cognitive
 Neuroscience: The Biology of the Mind*. 2nd ed. New York: W.W. Norton, 2002
Gracia, Jorge J. E., *Philosophy and Its History: Issues in Philosophical
 Historiography*. New York: State University of New York Press, 1992
——, *A Theory of Textuality: The Logic and Epistemology*. New York: State
 University of New York Press, 1995
——, *Metaphysics and its Tasks: The Search for the Categorial Foundation of
 Knowledge*. Albany, NY: State University of New York Press, 1999
Hahn, Alexander J., *Basic Calculus: From Archimedes to Newton to Its Role in
 Science*. New York: Springer-Verlag, 1998
Halmos, Paul, *Naive Set Theory*. New York: Springer-Verlag, 1974
Hannay, Alastair, ed, and trans. *Søren Kierkegaard: Papers and Journals: A
 Selection*. London: Penguin, 1996
Hare, Peter H. ed, *Doing Philosophy Historically*. Amherst, NY: Prometheus
 Books, 1988
Hare, R. M., *Practical Inferences*. London: Macmillan, 1971
Harré, Rom, *The Principles of Scientific Thinking*. Chicago: University of Chicago
 Press, 1970
Hart, W. D., *The Evolution of Logic*. Cambridge: Cambridge University Press, 2010
Hawking, Steven and Leonard Mlodinow, *The Grand Design*. New York:
 Bantam, 2010
Heisenberg, Werner, *Physics and Philosophy: The Revolution of Modern Science*.
 New York: Harper Torch, 1958

Hocking, William Ernest, *Types of Philosophy*. New York: Charles Scribner's Sons, 1929

Holton, Gerald, *The Advancement of Science and Its Burdens*. Cambridge, MA: Harvard University Press, 1998

Huggett, Nick, "Identity, Quantum Mechanics, and Common Sense." *The Monist* 80 1997: 118–130

Hughes, R. I. G., *The Structure and Interpretation of Quantum Mechanics*. Cambridge, MA: Harvard University Press, 1989

Hume, David, *Enquiries: Concerning Human Understanding and Concerning the Principles of Morals*. 3rd ed. Edited by A. Selby-Bigge and P. H. Nidditch. Oxford: Oxford University Press, 1975

Husserl, Edmund. "Philosophy as a Rigorous Science." In *Husserl: Shorter Works*. Edited by Peter McCormick and Frederick Elliston. Translated by Quentin Lauer, 166–197. Notre Dame: University of Notre Dame Press, 1981

James, William, *The Will to Believe and Other Essays in Popular Philosophy and Human Immortality: Two Supposed Objections to the Doctrine*. New York: Dover, 1956

Kant, Immanuel, "Critique of Practical Reason." In *The Cambridge Edition of the Works of Immanuel Kant: Practical Philosophy*. Edited by Mary J. Gregor, 133–272. Cambridge: Cambridge University Press, 1996

———, *The Cambridge Edition of the Works of Immanuel Kant: Critique of Pure Reason*. Translated and edited by Paul Guyer and Allen W. Wood. Cambridge: Cambridge University Press, 1998

———, "Prolegomena to Any Future Metaphysics that will be Able to Come Forward as Science." In *The Cambridge Edition of the Works of Immanuel Kant: Theoretical Philosophy After 1781*. Edited by Henry Allison and Peter Heath. Translated by Gary Hatfield, 29–196. Cambridge: Cambridge University Press, 2002

Kaufmann, Walter, *Existentialism from Dostoevsky to Sartre*. New York: New American Library, 1975

Kierkegaard, Søren, *The Sickness Unto Death: A Christian Psychological Exposition for Upbuilding and Awakening*. Edited and translated by Howard V. Hong and Edna H. Hong. Princeton: Princeton University Press, 1980

———, "In Vino Veritas (The Banquet)." In *Kierkegaard's Writings XI: Stages on Life's Way*. Edited by Howard V. Hong and Edna H. Hong, 7–86. Princeton: Princeton University Press, 1988

———, *Concluding Unscientific Postscript to Philosophical Fragments*. Edited and translated by Howard V. Hong and Edna H. Hong. Princeton: Princeton University Press, 1992

Kim, Jaegwon, *Supervenience and Mind: Selected Philosophical Essays*. Cambridge: Cambridge University Press, 1993

Kline, Morris, *Calculus: An Intuitive and Physical Approach*. 2nd ed. Mineola, NY: Dover, 1977

Koch, Christof, *The Quest for Consciousness: A Neurobiological Approach*. Englewood, CO: Roberts, 2004

Ladyman, James and Don Ross, with David Spurrett and John Collier, *Everything Must Go: Metaphysics Naturalized*. Oxford: Oxford University Press, 2007

Lang, Serge, *Basic Mathematics*. New York: Springer-Verlag, 1988

Lear, Jonathan, *Aristotle: The Desire to Understand*. Cambridge: Cambridge University Press, 1988

Loux, Michael J., *Primary Ousia*. Ithaca, NY: Cornell University Press, 1991

Lowe, E. J., "Form Without Matter." In *Form and Matter: Themes in Contemporary Metaphysics*. Edited by David S. Oderberg, 1–21. Oxford: Blackwell, 1999

——, *The Four-Category Ontology*. Oxford: Oxford University Press, 2006

Magnus, P. D., *Scientific Enquiry and Natural Kinds: From Planets to Mallards*. New York: Palgrave MacMillan, 2012

Makaryk, Irena R. ed, *The Encyclopedia of Contemporary Literary Theory: Approaches, Scholars, Terms*. Toronto: University of Toronto Press, 1993

Maudlin, Tim, *The Metaphysics Within Physics*. Oxford: Oxford University Press, 2007

——, *Philosophy of Physics: Space and Time*. Princeton: Princeton University Press, 2012

McDowell, John, *Mind and World*. Cambridge, MA: Harvard University Press, 1994

Menssen, Sandra and Thomas D. Sullivan, *The Agnostic Inquirer: Revelation from a Philosophic Standpoint*. Grand Rapids, MI: Eerdmans, 2007

Mill, John Stuart, *A System of Logic*. London: Longmans, Green, 1961

Millgram, Elijah, *Practical Induction*. Cambridge, MA: Harvard University Press, 1997

Moore, A. W., *The Evolution of Modern Metaphysics: Making Sense of Things*. Cambridge: Cambridge University Press, 2012

Nagel, Thomas. "*What is it Like to be a Bat?*." In *Mortal Questions*. Edited by Nagel, 165–180. Cambridge: Cambridge University Press, 1979

——, *Mind and Cosmos: Why the Materialist Neo-Darwinian Conception of Nature is Almost Certainly False*. Oxford: Oxford University Press, 2012

Nola, Robert, and Howard Shankey, eds, *Theories of Scientific Method*. Montreal: McGill-Queen's University Press, 2007

Oderberg, David S., *Real Essentialism*. New York: Routledge, 2008

Olafson, Frederick, *Naturalism and the Human Condition: Against Scientism*. London: Routledge, 2001

Olson, Richard D., *Science and Scientism in Nineteenth-Century Europe*. Urbana, IL: University of Illinois Press, 2008

Oxford Dictionary of Physics. Oxford: Oxford University Press, 2009

Pais, Abraham, *Niels Bohr's Times in Physics, Philosophy, and Polity*. Oxford: Clarendon, 1991

Palmer, Stephen E., *Vision Science: Photons to Phenomenology*. Cambridge, MA: MIT Press, 1999

Pannier, Russell and Thomas D. Sullivan, "Mindful Logic: How to Resolve Some Paradoxes of Identity." *Notre Dame Journal of Formal Logic* 29 1988: 246–266

———, "Consciousness and the Intentional Awareness of Instantiables." In *Mind and Its Place in the World: Non-reductionist Approaches to the Ontology of Consciousness*. Edited by Alexander Betthyany and Avshaloom Elitzur, 77–100. Frankfurt: Ontos/Verlag, 2006

Pascal, Blaise, *Pensées and Other Writings*. Translated by Honor Levi. Oxford: Oxford University Press, 1995

Passmore, John, *Recent Philosophers*. LaSalle, IL: Open Court, 1985

Patterson, Richard, *Aristotle's Modal Logic: Essence and Entailment in the Organon*. Cambridge: Cambridge University Press, 1995

Peterson, Aage, *Quantum Physics and the Philosophic Tradition*. Cambridge, MA: MIT Press, 1969

Peterson, Martin, *An Introduction to Decision Theory*. Cambridge: Cambridge University Press, 2009

Plantinga, Alvin, *The Nature of Necessity*. Oxford: Clarendon, 1974

———, *Where the Conflict Really Lies: Science, Religion, and Naturalism*. Oxford: Oxford University Press, 2010

Poincare, Henri, *The Value of Science: Essential Writings of Henri Poincare*. Edited by Stephen Jay Gould. New York: Modern Library, 2001

Polanyi, Michael, *Personal Knowledge: Towards a Post-Critical Philosophy*. Chicago: University of Chicago Press, 1962

Polya, G., *How to Solve It: A New Aspect of Mathematical Method*. 2nd ed. Princeton: Princeton University Press, 1973

Quine, W. V., *The Ways of Paradox and Other Essays*. Cambridge, MA: Harvard University Press, 1976

———, *Theories and Things*. Cambridge, MA: Harvard University Press, 1981

———, *From Stimulus to Science*. Cambridge, MA: Harvard University Press, 1995

Raz, Joseph. ed., *Practical Reasoning*. Oxford: Oxford University Press, 1978

———, *Practical Reason and Norms*. Princeton: Princeton University Press, 1990

Reichenbach, Hans, *The Rise of Scientific Philosophy*. Berkeley: University of California Press, 1951

Rescher, Nicholas, *Pascal's Wager: A Study of Practical Reasoning in Philosophical Theology*. Notre Dame: University of Notre Dame Press, 1985

Restall, Greg, "Laws of Non-Contradiction, Laws of Excluded Middle, and Logics." In *The Law of Non-Contradiction: New Philosophical Essays*. Edited by Graham Priest, J. C. Beall, and Bradley Armour-Garb, 73–84. Oxford: Clarendon, 2006

Richardson, Henry S., *Practical Reasoning About Final Ends*. Cambridge: Cambridge University Press, 1994

Russell, Bertrand, *Principles of Mathematics*. 2nd ed. New York: W.W. Norton, 1938

———, *The Analysis of Mind*. Introduction by Thomas Baldwin. London: Routledge, 1995

Sartre, Jean-Paul, *Being and Nothingness: An Essay on Phenomenological Ontology*. Translated by Hazel E. Barnes. New York: Philosophical Library, 1956

Schlick, Moritz, "The Turning Point in Philosophy." In *Logical Positivism*. Edited by A. J. Ayer, 53–59. New York: Free Press of Glencoe, 1959

Smart, H. R., *Philosophy and Its History*. La Salle, IL: Open Court, 1962

Smith, Norman Kemp, *A Commentary to Kant's Critique of Pure Reason*. 2nd ed. Atlantic Highlands, NJ: Humanities Press International, 1992

Sorell, Tom, *Scientism: Philosophy and the Infatuation with Science*. London: Routledge, 1991

Sorell, Tom and G. A. J. Rogers, eds., Rogers *Analytic Philosophy and History of Philosophy*. Oxford: Clarendon, 2005

Stillwell, John, *Roads to Infinity: The Mathematics of Truth and Proof*. Natick, MA: A.K. Peters, 2012

Stoljar, Daniel, "Physicalism." *The Stanford Encyclopedia of Philosophy*. Fall 2009. Edited by Edward N. Zalta. <http://plato.stanford,edu/archives/fall2009/entries/physicalism/>.

———, *Physicalism*. New York: Taylor and Francis, 2010

Styer, Daniel F., *The Strange World of Quantum Mechanics*. Cambridge: Cambridge University Press, 2000

Suppes, Patrick, "Aristotle's Concept of Matter and Its Relationship to Modern Concepts of Matter." Synthese 28 1974: 27–50

Von Wright, Georg Henrik, *Practical Reason*. Ithaca, NY: Cornell University Press, 1983

Wallace, Alfred Russel, "The Dawn of a Great Discovery: My Relations with Darwin in Reference to the Theory of Natural Selection." *Black and White* (17 January 1903): 78–79

———, "'A Being Apart': Human Evolution." In *Infinite Tropics: An Alfred Russel Wallace Anthology*. Edited by Andrew Berry, 175–211. London: Verso, 2002

Wallace, William A., *The Remodeling of Nature*. Washington, DC: Catholic University of America Press, 1996

Weinberg, Steven, *Dreams of a Final Theory: The Scientist's Search for the Ultimate Laws of Nature*. New York: Vintage, 1994

Williamson, Timothy, *The Philosophy of Philosophy*. Oxford: Blackwell, 2007

Wittgenstein, Ludwig, *Philosophical Investigations*. 3rd ed. Translated by G. E. M. Anscombe. New York: Macmillan, 1958

———, *Notebooks 1914–1916*. Translated by G. E. M. Anscombe. Edited by G. H. von Wright and G. E. M. Anscombe. New York: Harper & Brothers, 1961

———, *Recollections of Wittgenstein*. Edited by Rush Rhees. Oxford: Oxford University Press, 1984

Index